ELYSIAN KITCHENS

ELYSIAN KITCHENS

JODY EDDY

Recipes Inspired by the Traditions
and Tastes of the World's Sacred Spaces

PHOTOGRAPHY BY
KRISTIN TEIG

W. W. NORTON & COMPANY
Independent Publishers Since 1923

For information about permission to reproduce selections from this book, write to
Permissions, W. W. Norton & Company, Inc., 500 Fifth Avenue, New York, NY 10110

For information about special discounts for bulk purchases, please contact
W. W. Norton Special Sales at specialsales@wwnorton.com or 800-233-4830

Manufacturing by Imago
Book design by Clare Skeats
Art director: Allison Chi
Production manager: Julia Druskin

Library of Congress Cataloging-in-Publication Data Available

ISBN 978-0-393-65173-7

W. W. Norton & Company, Inc.
500 Fifth Avenue, New York, N.Y. 10110
www.wwnorton.com

W. W. Norton & Company Ltd.
15 Carlisle Street, London W1D 3BS

1 2 3 4 5 6 7 8 9 0

For my mother, Mary Ann Eddy, and
my grandmother, Evelyn Bragelman

Contents

Introduction

Monasteries, temples, mosques, and synagogues have long safeguarded our culinary traditions, not only ensuring that a region's gastronomic heritage endures but, in many instances, defining it and facilitating its evolution. Religious leaders from all denominations forged some of our earliest trade routes, carrying with them as they traveled seeds, ingredients, tools, techniques, and kitchen wisdom gleaned over centuries. The information exchanged was instrumental in the establishment of ancient foodways and continues to play a vital role in safeguarding and protecting these culinary legacies for future generations.

Much as monastic cooking is steeped in history and tradition, religious practitioners around the world take immense pride in work that pays homage to their forebears while simultaneously charging ahead into a dynamic future. They relish their role as modern cooks, farmers, and food and beverage producers. The gastronomic and agrarian activities of monasteries today reflect the do-it-yourself trend and commitment to self-sufficiency that has been embraced in home kitchens and backyard gardens around the globe by people seeking a more enriching and empowering way of life. From canning, pickling, brewing, and cheese and charcuterie making to foraging, gardening, distilling, beekeeping, winemaking, and bread baking, monks and nuns celebrate the future potential and past traditions of the region surrounding them with the same enthusiasm as professional and home cooks.

I began this book project after visiting the Tibetan Buddhist monastery Thikse in the Indian Himalayan region of Ladakh. I was looking for comfort following the unexpected death of my mother a few months before my trip to India. I spent a few days with the monks, who so generously invited me to participate in all of their rituals—lighting the kitchen fire and making yak butter tea at sunrise, participating in drumming ceremonies after breakfast and at sunset, and preparing food all day long. Food preparation and consumption anchored every aspect of their day, connected the monks to their past, and seemed to be the thing that made them feel optimistic about their future; if the barley harvest was successful in the fall and the apricot and walnut trees flourished in the summer, there was no need to worry about anything. Everything was going to be OK.

After my visit to Thikse, I reflected upon the culinary traditions of the monks at Saint John's University in my hometown in Minnesota. There was nothing better during my childhood than the monks' freshly baked rye and whole wheat Johnnie bread that families throughout the region stocked up on after Sunday church service. I also considered a recent conversation with a food writer in Morocco who talked about how the poetry of Rumi was stitched into the culinary traditions of the Sufis in Fes. I recalled a group of chefs at a food conference in Copenhagen enthusiastically sharing the culinary traditions they learned about during their recent visits to monasteries in Korea, Brazil, and Ethiopia.

I saw signposts everywhere guiding me to write this book. My intention is to celebrate the culinary traditions embraced by the world's religious peoples. The way they grow, harvest, prepare, and share their food is fundamental to who they are as a community. It is a daily reminder of the struggles and triumphs of the past and a hopeful promise of a more encouraging future.

There are many different religions represented in this book; many have been marred by conflict and have endeavored impressively to survive. I do not want this to be a divisive or polarizing book, as religion can often be. My goal is to showcase the universal truth of food: the way it can enrich our communities, offer us hope during times of hardship, be used to celebrate milestones, and continuously breathe life into our most ancient traditions.

I finished traveling for this book right before the Covid-19 pandemic began. I moved home to Minnesota in between trips to help care for my grandmother, who was suffering from Lewy body dementia. Every time I returned to Minnesota, I felt stronger and wiser, fortified by the wisdom I learned from the spiritual people I met on the road. I hope you will find the same comfort and inspiration that I discovered in the process of making this book. I hope that the recipes offer reassurance that the culinary traditions we safeguard throughout times of struggle and uncertainty will carry us through the tumult, reminding the next generation of our hardships and our triumphs, encouraging them to keep going, one recipe, one shared meal at a time.

I visited Buddhist, Jewish, Muslim, Sikh, Sufi, Maronite Catholic, and Roman Catholic kitchens in the United States, Canada, Ireland, France, Spain, Morocco, Lebanon, India, and Japan to research their culinary traditions and learn about their contemporary cooking practices. Along the way I discovered, much to my surprise and delight, that spiritual practitioners are on the cutting edge of food technology and that they take their work very seriously. They infuse their culinary pursuits with the same kind of energy as food lovers everywhere, experiencing abiding joy in producing a notable cheese or baking an exquisite loaf of bread.

The stereotype of a religious leader as an older man whose youth is nothing but a memory is also a cliche my visits have dispelled. The ages, genders, incomes, backgrounds, hobbies, educational levels, and work history of the spiritual practitioners I visited vary wildly, resulting in a rich and dynamic tapestry of fascinating individuals who generously offered me their time, wisdom, and kitchen know-how. Many candidly shared intimate details of the lives they lead, the challenges they face, their struggle with remaining relevant in their communities, their connections to the past, and their hopes for the future. They opened up to me about the ways in which they foster solidarity and support one another and the people of their region through philanthropic pursuits and how they fortify themselves and their commitment to their vocation and to their community.

Above all, from a culinary perspective, monasteries are places of sublime ingredients and beloved, time-tested recipes. Food—and the rituals surrounding them—aids religious practitioners in their spiritual practices by fortifying their bodies and minds, fostering fellowship with one another, and reinforcing their appreciation for nature and the higher power they believe created it. I hope this cookbook will show you these religious spaces for what they really are: dynamic epicenters of modern, ever-evolving spiritual and culinary wisdom.

A Note on Religion

Religious strife is nearly as old as humanity's existence on Earth, and while organized religion is historically the origin of conflict, food traditions and communal dining are a universal way to bring people together. Where necessary, I explain and introduce the religion of the location visited in the chapter. Many of the culinary rituals, traditions, and recipes are directly tied to the religious belief itself. As a result of researching and writing this book—during conversations with the spiritual leaders who guided me through their religious traditions, while enjoying their recipes, and after turning to their guidance and strength long after I had tested the final recipe—I believe more than ever that there is wisdom and truth at the heart of every religion.

Many of the spiritual leaders I met while writing this book have become dear friends of mine. Most were very curious about the other locations I visited, and some asked to be put in touch with one another, regardless of their religious beliefs. The WhatsApp groups that were formed as a result of this book are made up of wise men and women throughout the world who are keenly interested in one another and enjoy sharing knowledge, swapping recipes, offering support to one another, and identifying and celebrating the passions of cooking, community, learning, and meal sharing that we all have in common.

A Note on the Recipes

The recipes you'll find in these pages were selected for various reasons. Several are traditional dishes beloved by the spiritual communities I profile, whose members have enjoyed sharing these mainstays with one another for decades, sometimes centuries. Others are inspired by ingredients or cooking techniques my guides told me were integral to the region or their spiritual practices. Still others are modern twists on favorite classics or contemporary recipes born of dietary requirements or today's health trends. The common thread is their ability to transport the home cook to the farthest reaches of the world to capture the elusive beauty of each location and bring it home to their own community of friends and family gathered around the table.

I've replaced more elusive ingredients with items that are more widely available in a typical supermarket whenever possible. I swapped out instructions that require special equipment or complex preparation techniques for methods that are feasible for home cooks.

I hope you enjoy making these dishes at home and sharing them with the people who make you feel like a valued member of the community.

BELOW
The dining hall at the Abbey of Saint-Wandrille in Normandy, France

10 kilo orgu ✓
12 kilo poivre rouge ✓
10 Kilo magues ✓

8 1/4 + 8 litre huile

8 kilo sucre + 2 kilo
14 '' tomate

3 x 2 kilo mais

8 1/4

1,25 g sel + 250 g ✓

pêche
ananas

5 + 12 lit vinaigre + 4 + 3 litre + 2 lit.
6 gramme de clou de girofle + 4 grame ✓
6 grame de cavelle + 6 grame ✓
90 grame de poivre
25 grame de estragou ✓
500 '' de gingembre ✓
500 gramme de Basilique ✓

List of Recipes

Monastery of Saint Anthony of Qozhaya

MARONITE CATHOLIC
QADISHA VALLEY, LEBANON

"We are the ones who sought refuge in caves during the era
of injustice and darkness for hundreds of years so that
faith in God and worship of God would be delivered to us on
our way in these mountains and on these beaches, and we
would have the freedom that if we do not have then we will
have no life."
—*Former Maronite Patriarch Nasrallah Boutros Sfeir*

The Maronite priest Father Jad Kossaify meets me at a pastry shop in Byblos, on the Lebanese Mediterranean coast. The storied city, one of the oldest continuously inhabited places in the world, was founded by the Phoenicians, legendary merchants, traders, and explorers. The ancient Greeks first referred to the town as Byblos, which means "the book." Indeed, Byblos is the root of the word *bible*, a fact that the enthusiastic priest proudly shares with me while we wait for our order of manakish, a wood-fired flatbread with thyme and olive oil, to tide us over during the hour-long journey to the monastery.

We ascend Mount Lebanon through an ancient cedar forest from which King Solomon purportedly sourced the trees for his temple. The area is referred to as the Forest of the Cedars of God. The Latin name for this specific endangered cedar variety is *Cedrus libani*. The firm, unyielding wood was highly prized during biblical times and is mentioned 103 times in the bible. So beloved is the cedar that it is the national symbol of Lebanon and decorates its flag.

The dense, aromatic forests eventually give way to the Qadisha Valley. *Qadisha* means "holy" in the biblical language of Aramaic, and this ethereal land, its ancient history stretching as far back as the written word, its deep ravine carved out over millennia by the Holy River of Qadisha, flourishes with ancient pine and oak forests, olive groves, and orchards fed by natural springs. The region has long been a sacred space for Christians who have journeyed here seeking peace and meditation and, in times of conflict, safe refuge.

The Maronite monastery we are visiting, Saint Anthony of Qozhaya, rests at the foot of Mount al Makmal, yet still hovers 2,700 feet above the sea, appearing from afar to be precariously attached to the cliffside. *Qozhaya* translates to "treasure of life, an abundance of water endowing an evergreen nature."

The cavernous grotto located near the entrance to the monastery was established as a place of worship by Saint Hilarion in the fourth century and served for centuries as a spiritual refuge for Christians fleeing persecution. It was used exclusively until the tenth century, when a church was carved into the cliffside of soft pink stones joined with lead instead of mortar. The church entrance is flanked by imposing pink pillars resting atop massive copper foundations. The labyrinthine monastery comprises fifty rooms, including a library. The library houses thousands of ancient books and manuscripts, among them a copy of the oldest surviving book printed on the east coast of the Mediterranean Sea, *The Book of Psalms*. The original version is now protected in the library of the Holy Spirit University of Kaslik, north of Beirut. Printed in 1610 on the oldest printing press in the Near East (also in the monastery), it is written in Garshuni and Syro-Aramaic, the language of Jesus.

The Maronites are Catholics aligned with Roman Catholicism but also follow their own spiritual traditions. In the seventh century, the Maronites arrived in the Qadisha Valley seeking solace from the persecution they were experiencing in other regions of the Levant. The acclaimed Lebanese poet and philosopher Kahlil Gibran was a Maronite from the region, and one has to think that he was referring to the Maronites who have suffered countless injustices throughout centuries of turmoil when he wrote in his book *The Broken Wings*: "Out of suffering have emerged the strongest souls; the most massive characters are seared with scars."

In the centuries-old greeting room at Saint Anthony, a monk named Father Fadi Imad greets Father Jad with a warm embrace and offers us

" Appreciation for the rituals that make
up the course of a day are essential
when living a life separate from others.
It is also important to have gratitude,
for your life, for nature, for the miracle
of things."

cooling glasses of rose water spiked with mint leaves. Father Fadi, a man in his mid-forties with a hearty black beard, is dressed in a traditional black Maronite hooded habit with a thick black leather belt tied around his waist. "Roses are a symbol of resiliency in Lebanon. May you carry this resiliency with you wherever you go," he says with a smile.

The monks and I spend the cool, sunny day exploring the sprawling grounds of the monastery. We pass by massive copper pot stills used to produce arak, a distilled, anise-flavored Levantine spirit. There is winemaking equipment in one cavernous room and in another, a vast pantry where baskets of the region's bounty are stored. I see large vats of olive oil, pressed at the monastery from the olive groves that flourish on the grounds, and glass jars filled with pomegranate molasses and other juices and syrups that the monks produce for themselves and sell in the monastic gift shop.

Our mezze-style lunch is arranged on one side of a banquet table stretching from one end of the millennia-old vaulted stone dining hall to the other. There's labneh bi toum, a thick, tangy whipped yogurt drizzled with olive oil and sprinkled with sumac; hummus; baba ghanouj; plates piled high with charred pita bread; triangles of kibbeh; olives; tahini; fatayers, flaky dumplings stuffed with spinach and onions; foul moudammas, a fortifying dish of warm fava beans; and zaatar manakish. Served in drinking glasses, or sometimes in translucent drinking vessels similar to the Spanish porrón, is red and white wine produced at the monastery.

We settle into a noisy meal where it seems every monk is talking at once, animatedly telling stories and laughing at the punchlines in between generous forkfuls of mezze. Father Jad, in his late thirties with short black hair and a buoyant nature, explains to me that he is only visiting for the summer from Rome, where he lives and conducts research in the Vatican archives. He speaks Italian, English, French, and Arabic and reads and writes Latin and Syro-Aramaic. He tells me about the history of the Maronites in the region and we discuss the seemingly endless regional conflicts, including the

OPPOSITE
Qadisha Valley

RIGHT
Dehydrated corn silk used to make tea

devastating civil war that raged between 1975 and 1990.

"We don't like to focus on this now. We try to look forward into a more positive and optimistic future, and we try to learn from the lessons of the past. For example, the Maronite monks who live at Saint Anthony's monastery and in the other monasteries located in the valley have long supported the villagers who live alongside them in this region, regardless of their religious affiliation. After World War I, when a devastating famine encroached upon the people of Mount Lebanon, killing one-third of the population, the monks sold much of their land in an effort to feed their fellow citizens, Muslim and Christian alike."

Father Fadi chimes in: "After centuries of living alongside one another in this valley and in this nation, we have learned that in order to attain peace and harmony, we must support one another through our collective hardships and celebrate with one another when there is joy. We invite Muslims here to enjoy our Christian feast days and they reciprocate. In the greeting hall today, there were both Muslim and Christian visitors because our message is that all are welcome here. This is the true heart of religion and is what we Maronites try to hold firm to even during times of strife."

Just after the monks finish their first course and move on to the second, an elderly monk with a flowing silver beard emerges in the doorway. The other monks stand to greet him, bowing their heads in reverent respect. One of the monks pulls the chair out for him at the head of the table and helps him settle in, filling a plate with portions of each dish on the table and pouring him a glass of water. The monk squints his eyes and smiles softly in silent gratitude. Father Jad whispers, "That is Father Youhanna Khawand. There are still hermits living at the monastery as they have lived for over a thousand years. He lived in isolation in the mountains for over twenty years. His fellow monks would bring him food and water each day, but he did not leave his hermitage for over two decades. He returned to the communal life only a few months ago. The monks who live here told me it was a surprise as they did not know he desired to return to live within the community."

"Can I ask him a few questions?" I ask Father Jad. "Of course," he says. "The first is if he has any advice on how to live a contented solitary life?" Father Jad translates and, after several moments of silence Father Youhanna replies, "Routine is very important when you live alone. Appreciation for the rituals that make up the course of a day are essential when living a life separate from others. It is also important to have gratitude, for your life, for nature, for the miracle of things." "Why did you decide to rejoin your community?" I ask Father Youhanna. He closes his eyes for several moments of contemplation. He opens them slowly and replies, "Because I missed laughter. I missed the community. I missed sharing a meal with my friends."

ABOVE
Manakish

RIGHT
Za'atar with olive oil

Manakish

SERVES: 4
PREPARATION TIME: 1½ hours

1 cup whole wheat flour
⅓ cup all-purpose flour, plus more
    for dusting
1 tablespoon kosher salt
½ teaspoon baking powder
1 cup plain whole-milk yogurt
    (not Greek-style)
1 tablespoon dried thyme
1 tablespoon dried mint
2 teaspoons ground sumac
1 teaspoon ground cumin

Manakish is a flatbread, traditionally served with finely chopped thyme combined with olive oil until a thick paste is formed. At Saint Anthony, the monks harvest their thyme in the summertime and sun-dry it on the rooftop of the monastery. It's then ground in a stone mill until it's very fine before adding aromatics such as sumac and cumin. Manakish is essentially a whole wheat pizza dough made with whole-milk yogurt, which infuses it with tanginess and pluck. The monks also enjoy variations that include ground lamb (lahem baajin) or cheese such as feta (mankoushet jibné) baked until it's bubbling and slightly golden. It's enjoyed mainly for breakfast, folded in half or sliced into triangles, but could also be served for lunch and dinner.

SIFT THE WHOLE wheat flour, all-purpose flour, salt, and baking powder into a medium bowl. Stir in the yogurt, thyme, mint, sumac, and cumin. Transfer the dough to a clean work surface and knead until it's smooth, about 2 minutes. Dust the surface with a bit of flour if the dough is sticking to it. The dough should be smooth and moist but not too moist and not too shaggy. Divide the dough into 4 pieces, shape into balls, and wrap them individually in plastic. (At this point the dough can be stored in a covered container in the refrigerator for up to 1 month.) Let rest at room temperature for 15 minutes.

WORKING ONE AT a time, roll out each ball of dough on a lightly floured surface, sprinkling the dough with flour as needed to prevent sticking, until it's about ⅛ inch thick.

HEAT A MEDIUM cast-iron or other heavy-bottomed skillet over medium-high heat until very hot. Cook one flatbread until the underside is golden brown and puffy with a few charred spots, about 2 minutes. Turn with tongs and cook on the other side until golden brown, about 1 minute. Transfer to a plate, then repeat with the remaining flatbreads. Leftover manakish will keep in a covered container in the refrigerator for up to 3 days.

Fattoush Salad

SERVES: 4
PREPARATION TIME: 20 minutes

FOR THE DRESSING:
2 tablespoons ground sumac
2 teaspoons warm water
Juice of 1 lemon
⅓ cup pomegranate molasses
1 tablespoon white wine vinegar
4 garlic cloves, finely chopped
1 tablespoon dried mint
1½ cups extra-virgin olive oil
Salt and freshly ground black pepper
    to taste

FOR THE SALAD:
4 pitas, toasted in a 350°F oven until golden
    brown, cooled to room temperature, and
    torn into bite-size pieces
½ cup extra-virgin olive oil
Salt and ground sumac to taste
5 ripe Roma tomatoes, chopped
2 cucumbers, halved lengthwise and thinly
    sliced crosswise
8 scallions, thinly sliced
4 heads Little Gem or baby romaine lettuce
    or 1 large head romaine lettuce, trimmed
    and cut into bite-size pieces
2 cups loosely packed fresh flat-leaf parsley
    leaves
2 cups fresh purslane leaves
1 cup loosely packed fresh mint leaves

Fattoush salad loosely translates as "mixed salad," and in northern Lebanon where Saint Anthony's monastery is located, the cooks of the region are so obsessed with day-old pita scraps that they have a name, khubz. Pomegranate molasses is available at any Middle Eastern or Indian market or can be ordered online. It's a must for countless Lebanese dishes; its bright tanginess and vibrant red hue make it worth sourcing. It's also fantastic stirred into a vodka spritzer or a pitcher of seltzer water garnished with lime slices. The dried mint is easily sourced in Middle Eastern grocery stores and should be used if possible instead of fresh mint because it is more potent. This salad reflects the monk's philosophy that nothing should be wasted, and during the hot summer months when tomatoes, lettuce, and cucumbers are at their peak, fattoush salad graces the monastic table at least once a week. Toss with shredded leftover chicken, slices of freshly cooked albacore tuna, or a few poached eggs for a heartier meal.

TO MAKE THE DRESSING: put the sumac in a medium bowl and add the water. Set aside to soak for 15 minutes, then add the lemon juice, pomegranate molasses, vinegar, garlic, and dried mint. Gradually add the oil, whisking constantly, until well blended. Season with salt and pepper; add more lemon juice, pomegranate molasses, and vinegar to taste, if desired.

TO MAKE THE SALAD: put the pita pieces in a large bowl; drizzle the oil over them, and toss to coat. Season with salt. In a second bowl, combine the tomatoes, cucumbers, scallions, lettuce, parsley, purslane, and mint. Add half of the dressing and toss to coat, adding more dressing by the tablespoonful until the salad is glistening. Season with salt. Add the pita pieces just before serving (to prevent them from getting soggy) and toss once. Sprinkle with sumac and serve immediately. Leftover salad will keep in a covered container in the refrigerator for up to 3 days, although the pita will not stay crisp.

Mezze

Mezze is a wonder enjoyed throughout the Middle East. It's essentially an assortment of flavorful small appetizers that are typically served together on a large board or platter. In Lebanon, where the cuisine has a more delicate quality than in other parts of the region, mezze is an artful, complex dance of colors, textures, flavors, and aromas. At Saint Anthony, where there are many monks and frequent visitors to feed, the mezze is served up in small bowls and plates that adorn the long dining table in the thousand-year-old dining hall. It's not something that the monks enjoy every day, but it's a frequent and welcome commencement to the meal, often accompanied on Sundays and on feast days by a glass of crisp white Obaideh wine or, more traditionally, with a glass of arak (see page 29). It's a celebratory meal best enjoyed in the company of others, signaling the communal spirit that the monks of Saint Anthony hold so dear.

Here are some ideas for your next mezze party:

- Tabouleh (page 22)
- Hummus (page 21)
- Baba Ghanouj (page 20)
- Olives
- Assorted nuts: almonds, pistachios, walnuts, pine nuts
- Cherry tomatoes, halved
- Thinly sliced cucumbers, red onions, bell peppers, radishes
- Dolmades (stuffed grape leaves)
- Labneh with Olive Oil, Pistachios, and Sea Salt (page 16)
- Muhammara
- Extra-virgin olive oil (the monks leave a bottle on the table to use as needed)
- Manakish (page 13)
- Pita bread (preferably warm)
- Figs, halved
- Fresh dates
- Feta
- Torn fresh mint, basil, and flat-leaf parsley leaves
- Marinated artichokes
- Lemon wedges
- Baby carrots
- Khyar bi Laban (page 18)
- Seasonal berries
- Thinly sliced pears or apples
- Crunchy sea salt, such as Maldon
- Ground sumac

Labneh with Olive Oil, Toasted Pistachios, and Sea Salt

MAKES: about 2 cups
PREPARATION TIME: 24 to 48 hours

4 cups whole-milk yogurt
1¼ teaspoons kosher salt
Extra-virgin olive oil, for serving
Torn fresh mint leaves, for garnish
Toasted pistachios, for garnish
Crunchy sea salt, such as Maldon,
     for garnish

No Lebanese mezze (see page 15) is complete without a bowl of labneh, a thick strained yogurt. The monks at Saint Anthony enjoy it for breakfast and at dinner as a savory accompaniment to the main meal. The savory version in this recipe is drizzled with olive oil, garnished with torn mint leaves and toasted pistachios, and sprinkled with black pepper and crunchy sea salt. Sometimes mashed garlic is added to labneh, and this version is served during the mezze or with lunch or dinner. Other ideas for mix-ins include chili powder, zaatar, toasted sesame seeds, pumpkin or sunflower seeds, other toasted nuts (such as walnuts, hazelnuts, or pine nuts), smoked salmon, fig slices, or chopped dates. Serve the labneh with a side of raw vegetables such as carrot sticks, cucumber spears, and bell pepper slices for dipping, use it as a sandwich base, or just eat it the way Father Fadi prefers it, by the spoonful.

When I asked Father Charbel Kayrouz, the monk in charge of the cooking at Saint Anthony, what his secret was for perfect labneh, he replied, "Like most things in life, patience." Father Charbel strains his labneh in the traditional way, wrapped in a cotton kitchen towel tied up and hung from a sink faucet above a large bowl. This version calls for a strainer over a bowl and a double layer of cheesecloth. Depending upon your texture preference, strain it for about 24 hours for a dense, creamy dip or up to 48 hours for a thick, cheese-like consistency. Don't discard the residual whey. At Saint Anthony, Father Charbel serves this tangy, flavorful, probiotic-rich beverage in a pitcher at breakfast time. He also marinates meat in it since whey is a natural tenderizer and infuses the protein with a vibrant flavor.

LINE A COLANDER or large strainer with a double layer of cheesecloth and set it over a large bowl that enables the colander to rest at least 3 inches from the bottom of the bowl. In another bowl, stir together the yogurt and kosher salt until incorporated. Transfer the mixture to the cheesecloth-lined colander and wrap the cheesecloth around the yogurt, tying it up to create a ball. Place a plate on top of the ball to weigh it down. Refrigerate for 24 to 48 hours.

SPOON A DOLLOP of the labneh onto a plate and spread out to the edges using a wooden spoon or spatula. Drizzle it with olive oil, garnish with mint leaves and pistachios, and sprinkle with crunchy sea salt. Labneh can be refrigerated in an airtight container for up to 1 week.

Khyar bi Laban

Similar to Greek tzatziki, this thick and tangy yogurt dip is served at virtually every meal in Lebanon. It's enjoyed as a flatbread spread, tucked between delicacies on a mezze table, as a vegetable dip, or on its own as a creamy, cooling salad. It's traditionally made from whole-milk yogurt, which results in a rich flavor and thick consistency. Salting the cucumbers to enable them to release their liquid is key to avoiding a watery texture.

TOSS TOGETHER THE cucumbers and salt in a colander and set it over a large bowl. Allow the cucumbers to drain for 45 minutes.

IN A MEDIUM bowl, stir together the yogurt, mint, lemon juice, and garlic. Gently stir in the cucumbers. Store leftovers in a covered container in the refrigerator for up to 4 days.

MAKES: 4 cups
PREPARATION TIME: 50 minutes

2 large cucumbers, peeled, quartered
    lengthwise, and thinly sliced crosswise
2 tablespoons kosher salt
3 cups whole-milk Greek-style yogurt
Leaves from 2 mint sprigs, thinly sliced
1 tablespoon freshly squeezed lemon juice
1 garlic clove, minced

Baba Ghanouj

SERVES: 6
PREPARATION TIME: 1 hour

6 (8-ounce) eggplants, halved lengthwise
Extra-virgin olive oil, as needed
4 garlic cloves, finely chopped
2 tablespoons tahini
2 teaspoons ground cumin
1 teaspoon chili powder
Freshly squeezed lemon juice to taste
Salt and freshly ground black pepper
    to taste
Pita bread, warmed, for serving

Baba ghanouj originated in Lebanon during what food historians approximate were the Middle Ages and is now beloved throughout the Middle East. The name in Arabic translates as "pampered father," and it's unknown whether this refers to a folkloric take in which a dutiful daughter mashed up food to make it more palatable for her ill father or if it refers to a coddled sultan. Even people who claim to not like eggplant typically have a soft spot for this smoky dip. At Saint Anthony, the cook Father Charbel uses fresh juice from lemons he harvests from the lemon trees each morning along with a robust, deep green olive oil that is pressed at the monastery—but even if you don't have these luxuries, as long as you let the eggplant bake long enough, you're on your way to becoming pampered, too.

PREHEAT THE OVEN to 350°F. Line two rimmed baking sheets with parchment paper.

SCORE THE CUT sides of the eggplant halves in a crisscross pattern with a sharp paring knife, making sure you don't cut through the skins. Drizzle the flesh with olive oil, then rub the skins with additional oil. Arrange the eggplants, cut-side up, on the prepared baking sheets and bake until the skin is charred and dark brown along the edges and the flesh is very tender, about 45 minutes. Set aside to cool, then remove and discard the skin.

TRANSFER THE EGGPLANT flesh to the bowl of a food processor, then add the garlic, tahini, cumin, chili powder, and 2 tablespoons olive oil. Blend on medium speed until completely incorporated but still a bit chunky. Season with lemon juice, salt, and pepper. Serve with a basket of warm bread. Baba ghanouj will keep in a covered container in the refrigerator for up to 5 days.

Hummus

SERVES: 4 to 6
PREPARATION TIME: 2 hours, plus overnight to soak the chickpeas

2 cups dried chickpeas
1½ teaspoons baking soda
3 tablespoons tahini
Juice of 2 lemons
4 garlic cloves, coarsely chopped
2 tablespoons ice water
Salt and freshly ground black pepper to taste
Extra-virgin olive oil, for serving
Coarsely chopped flat-leaf parsley, for garnish
Pita bread, warmed, for serving

It is extraordinary that such a humble dish could be so divisive throughout the Middle East, but it's a testament to how adored hummus is that virtually every nation in the Levantine region tries to stake its claim on its origin. Regardless of which nation actually invented hummus, one thing is certain: no proper mezze board or family table would be complete without a plate of creamy hummus drizzled with olive oil.

At Saint Anthony, hummus is prepared by first soaking the chickpeas overnight, then simmering them with baking soda until tender. The baking soda raises the pH level of the water, which encourages the chickpeas to break down more easily so they blend into a creamier consistency, and it also helps them shake off their husks. Feel free to omit the baking soda for a chunkier hummus, but for an ultra-creamy texture, removing the husks is the way to go. A can of chickpeas, drained, will also work, but they won't achieve the creamy texture or the fresh flavor of their dried counterparts. The monks like to keep their hummus simple by drizzling it with olive oil and garnishing it with parsley. Other add-ins could include ground sumac, toasted ground cumin, chili powder, torn fresh basil leaves, freshly ground black pepper, or toasted sesame seeds. Hummus also makes a plucky sandwich spread or dip for grilled skewers of vegetables and chicken. For a more robust option, top with shredded lamb.

PUT THE CHICKPEAS in a large bowl, then pour in enough water to cover by 3 inches. Let soak overnight at room temperature.

DRAIN THE CHICKPEAS, transfer to a colander, and rinse for a few minutes under cold running water to remove any debris. Transfer to a large pot and cover with 3 inches fresh water. Bring to a boil over high heat. Reduce the heat to medium, add the baking soda, and simmer until very tender, 1½ to 2 hours. Drain and, once they are cool enough to handle, use your fingers to remove and discard as many of the husks as possible. They should slip off very easily, and many will already have completely separated.

TRANSFER THE CHICKPEAS to the bowl of a food processor, add the tahini, juice of 1 lemon, garlic, and ice water, and pulse until incorporated. If the hummus is too thick, add a bit more ice water to loosen it up. Adjust the flavor with the remaining lemon juice and season with salt and pepper. Spoon onto a serving plate and smooth into a thick layer using a spatula or large spoon. Drizzle with olive oil and garnish with parsley. Serve with warm pita wedges. Hummus will keep in a covered container in the refrigerator for up to 5 days.

Tabouleh

SERVES: 6
PREPARATION TIME: 30 minutes

1 cup fine bulgur
6 tablespoons extra-virgin olive oil
2 cups boiling water
4 cups finely chopped fresh flat-leaf parsley
    (about 3 bunches)
1 cup finely chopped fresh mint
4 Roma tomatoes, cut into ¼-inch pieces
1 large cucumber, peeled, cored, and cut
    into ¼-inch pieces
6 tablespoons freshly squeezed lemon juice
Salt and freshly ground black pepper
    to taste

It would be easy to make the argument that tabouleh is the national dish of Lebanon, a necessity on every mezze platter at family gatherings and feast day celebrations. It originated during the Middle Ages in the mountains of Lebanon, where it is prized not only for its vibrant flavor and brilliant colors that are reflected in the colors of the Lebanese flag, but also for its health benefits. The bulgur (burghul in Arabic) gives it heft, and the parsley and mint balanced by the tomatoes and cucumber brightened by a generous amount of lemon juice come together for a salad that the monks at Saint Anthony could not live without. This version is inspired by their recipe, which has been passed down for decades from one chef to the next.

STIR TOGETHER THE bulgur and 2 tablespoons oil in a medium heatproof bowl. Pour in the boiling water, then cover the bowl tightly with plastic wrap and let stand at room temperature for 15 minutes.

DRAIN THE BULGUR in a fine-mesh strainer, pressing on the bulgur to remove any excess liquid. Transfer the bulgur to a large bowl and toss with the remaining ¼ cup oil, parsley, mint, tomatoes, cucumber, and lemon juice until well combined. Season with salt and pepper. Chill until ready to serve. Tabouleh will keep in a covered container in the refrigerator for up to 3 days.

Kibbeh Laktin

MAKES: about 36 kibbeh; serves 6 to 8
PREPARATION TIME: 1 hour, plus 1 hour
to chill

FOR THE KIBBEH LAKTIN:
2 medium yellow onions, finely chopped
2 teaspoons minced garlic
2 (15-ounce) cans pumpkin puree
2 ½ cups fine bulgur
1 tablespoon dried mint
2 teaspoons ground allspice
1 teaspoon salt
1 cup whole wheat flour

FOR THE STUFFING:
¼ cup peanut or vegetable oil
2 medium yellow onions, coarsely chopped
6 cups coarsely chopped spinach, kale, or
    other hardy green
1 (15-ounce) can chickpeas, drained and
    rinsed
1 teaspoon salt
½ cup pomegranate molasses

According to tradition, this kibbeh laktin recipe was created by a Maronite monk to fool invaders who demanded that lamb kibbeh be served to them on a Friday during Lent, a day when meat is forbidden and only fish is consumed. The wily monk tricked his captors into believing that what they were consuming contained lamb when it was actually pumpkin. The monks at Saint Anthony of Qozhaya typically enjoy these kibbeh during Lent to honor the resourcefulness of that crafty monk. It can take a bit of practice to refine the technique of shaping and sealing the kibbeh laktin, which are similar to croquettes, with a nubbly bulgur wheat shell. Be patient with yourself and soon enough, you will perfect the technique.

This recipe can easily be halved. Kibbeh are typically served as an appetizer alongside dips or salads such as Hummus (page 21), Baba Ghanouj (page 20), Khyar bi Laban (page 18), or Tabouleh (page 22).

TO MAKE THE kibbeh: combine the onions, garlic, pumpkin puree, and bulgur in a medium bowl. Add the mint, allspice, salt, and flour and mix well. Cover and refrigerate for at least 1 hour. Transfer the dough to a clean work surface and knead until the mixture feels smooth and takes on a slightly glossy sheen, about 5 minutes. Set aside.

TO MAKE THE STUFFING: heat the oil in a large saucepan over medium heat. Add the onions and sauté until tender and aromatic, about 5 minutes. Add the spinach and chickpeas and sauté for 7 more minutes, or until the spinach is completely wilted. Stir in the salt and pomegranate molasses.

PREHEAT THE OVEN to 425°F. Line two rimmed baking sheets with parchment paper.

STIR THE CHILLED kibbeh mixture and add a few tablespoons of water if necessary to soften. With moistened hands, form the mixture into mounds the size and shape of eggs. With your index finger, make a hole in one end of each egg and spoon 1 tablespoon stuffing inside. Pinch the open end together to seal. (Remind yourself as you're preparing the rest of the kibbeh that this is repetitive, meditative work worthy of a Maronite monk.) Arrange the kibbeh on the prepared baking sheets and bake for about 25 minutes, turning halfway through, until golden brown. Refrigerate leftover kibbeh laktin in a covered container for up to 3 days. Unfortunately, they do not freeze well because they crumble once defrosted.

Kibbeh bil Sanieh

MAKES: 12 kibbeh slices; serves 4 to 6
PREPARATION TIME: 3 hours, plus overnight to soak the chickpeas

1 cup dried chickpeas
¾ teaspoon baking soda
1⅔ cups fine bulgur
Extra-virgin olive oil, as needed
1 medium yellow onion, coarsely chopped
3 garlic cloves, coarsely chopped
Juice of ½ lemon
2 teaspoons ground cumin
1 teaspoon ground allspice
1 teaspoon freshly ground black pepper
½ teaspoon cayenne pepper
1 cup finely chopped fresh flat-leaf parsley
Salt to taste

The monks at Saint Anthony of Qozhaya are especially fond of this kibbeh recipe. It feels celebratory, as if hosting a monastic pizza night. Unlike Kibbeh Laktin (page 24) that results in individual croquettes, this recipe sparks the solidarity of communal dining that the monks at Saint Anthony are so fond of. The key to producing kibbeh that isn't too crumbly is to knead the bulgur as if it were bread dough. After 5 to 10 minutes, it will hold together and become creamy. You can use your hands or a stand mixer with a paddle attachment. If you don't knead the bulgur enough, it will stay crumbly and the kibbeh will not hold together after being baked.

Bulgur is a whole grain that is packed with protein and other healthful nutrients. At the monastery, bulgur is derived from the wheat grown on terraces built into the side of the valley by the monks. They used to farm all the land themselves but over the centuries, they have offered it at no cost to local farmers, who have agreed to divide the harvest between themselves and the monastery in order to provide enough of a yield to support both entities. The monks also tap into their ancient agricultural wisdom to help the farmers manage their land in a way that benefits the entire community.

PUT THE CHICKPEAS in a large bowl, then pour in enough water to cover by 3 inches. Let soak overnight at room temperature.

DRAIN THE CHICKPEAS, transfer to a colander, and rinse for a few minutes under cold running water to remove any debris. Transfer to a large pot and cover with 3 inches of fresh water. Bring to a boil over high heat. Reduce the heat to medium, add the baking soda, and simmer until very tender, 1½ to 2 hours. Drain and, once they are cool enough to handle, use your fingers to remove and discard as many of the husks as possible. They should slip off very easily, and many will already have completely separated. Cut each chickpea in half using a sharp paring knife. Set aside.

Recipe continues

WHILE THE CHICKPEAS are simmering, line a colander with a double layer of cheesecloth or a clean kitchen towel. Add the bulgur and rinse it under cold running water until it begins to slightly soften, 3 to 4 minutes. Transfer the bulger to a bowl and add enough lukewarm water to cover it by 2 inches. Set aside at room temperature for 30 minutes. Line the colander with a fresh double layer of cheesecloth or another clean kitchen towel and add the bulgur. Gather the cloth around it, twist it at the top, and squeeze out the excess liquid. Set aside.

PREHEAT THE OVEN to 350°F. Generously grease a 12-inch round baking pan with olive oil.

PUT THE ONION, garlic, lemon juice, cumin, allspice, black pepper, and cayenne pepper in the bowl of a food processor and pulse until just combined. Add the bulgur and pulse until well incorporated. Transfer the mixture to a large bowl and add the chickpeas and parsley. Mix with your hands or a wooden spoon until incorporated. Season with salt.

TRANSFER TO A clean work surface and knead until the mixture feels smooth and takes on a slightly glossy sheen, about 5 minutes.

TRANSFER THE KIBBEH to the prepared baking pan and press it firmly with your hands until it is compressed and smooth. Drizzle with a generous amount of olive oil. Don't be bashful; there should be enough oil in the pan to cover the kibbeh with a thin slick. Using a sharp paring knife, slice the kibbeh into wedges that are about 2 inches wide at their base and then, beginning at the top of each triangle, gently score the surface of each section from top to bottom at a diagonal. Do not slice deeply enough to reach the bottom of the pan, only enough to form an indention. Bake until the surface is golden brown, 45 to 55 minutes. Serve hot or at room temperature. Leftovers will keep in a covered container in the refrigerator for up to 2 days.

Arak

Arak is the national drink of Lebanon and is still produced by the monks at Saint Anthony in the same way it has been for centuries. It is believed that arak, which means "perspiration" in Arabic, was invented using alembic distillation by the Levantine people living on Mount Lebanon in the twelfth century. Arak contains only two ingredients, anise seed oil and white grapes, preferably either the indigenous Lebanese varietals of Merwah or Obaideh. The grapes are harvested from mature vines that are primarily left to their own devices by the monks since the hot Mediterranean days, cool evenings, and well-drained, sandy soil are the ideal conditions for grapes to thrive. The grapes are typically harvested by the monks and fellow villagers in late September through October, then are crushed and fermented for three weeks. They are distilled in ancient copper pot stills along with the more coveted Moorish stills that were traditionally used for arak production. It is during the second distillation that the anise oil is added. Then the liquid is distilled a third time and stored in large clay amphoras, or arak stills.

Arak is high in alcohol, typically between 40 and 65 percent, and Lebanon is the only nation in the Levant region that has created an appellation system for its arak in the same way that Italy and France do for their wine. Lebanese arak is therefore the most desired due to the care the distillers take to produce a spirit that is authentic and of high quality.

Drinking arak is an art in itself. Traditionally, one part arak is combined with two parts water in a vessel called an ibrik. Because anise oil is not soluble in water, the tiny oil droplets scatter the light, turning the liquid into the milky white color that arak is known for throughout the world. The arak is then poured into small, ice-filled glasses and enjoyed with mezze or as an aperitif.

The monks appreciate arak not only for its flavor but also for its medicinal virtues. Anise is used as a treatment for colds and stomach ulcers, as well as a diuretic and appetite stimulant. Anise is believed to decrease blood sugar levels and also has antibacterial and anti-inflammatory properties.

Rishta

SERVES: 4

PREPARATION TIME: 45 minutes

1½ cups brown or green lentils

1 lemon, cut into wedges, plus more freshly squeezed lemon juice to taste

8 cups vegetable stock

2 tablespoons extra-virgin olive oil

1 large white onion, coarsely chopped

2 celery ribs, thinly sliced

1 large carrot, peeled and coarsely chopped

4 garlic cloves, finely chopped

2 cups broken pasta, such as pappardelle, fettuccine, tagliatelle, or lasagna noodles

1 bunch cilantro, finely chopped

½ teaspoon red pepper flakes

Salt and freshly ground black pepper to taste

Coarsely chopped fresh flat-leaf parsley, for garnish

Sour cream, for serving (optional)

Every monk at Saint Anthony seems to have their own version of rishta that they learned to prepare as children from the matriarch in their family. Comforting and healthful, rishta soup is considered humble peasant fare, a keystone recipe in virtually every Lebanese household. At Saint Anthony, they prepare their pasta dough from scratch, but for simplicity's sake, broken boxed pasta is a fine substitute.

PUT THE LENTILS in a colander and rinse under cold running water for a few minutes to remove any debris. Transfer to a heavy-bottomed pot and add the lemon wedges and stock. Bring to a boil over high heat, then reduce the heat to low. Partially cover the pot and simmer until the lentils are tender, 10 to 12 minutes.

MEANWHILE, HEAT THE oil in a large sauté pan over medium heat. Add the onion, celery, and carrot and sauté until the onion begins to turn a light golden brown, 5 to 7 minutes. Add the garlic and sauté until aromatic, about 2 more minutes. Once the lentils are tender, add the onion and garlic to the pot and bring to a vigorous simmer over medium-high heat. Reduce the heat to medium, add the pasta, cilantro, and red pepper flakes, and simmer until the pasta is tender, 7 to 9 minutes. Season with salt and black pepper and adjust the acidity with lemon juice.

SPOON INTO INDIVIDUAL serving bowls, garnish with parsley, dollop with sour cream (if using), and serve hot. The flavor of rishta continues to develop after it is prepared, and it will keep in a covered container in the refrigerator for up to 4 days.

Mehché Koussa

SERVES: 8
PREPARATION TIME: 1 hour

16 (4-ounce) yellow or green zucchini
¼ cup plus 2 tablespoons extra-virgin olive oil
2 large onions, finely chopped
5 garlic cloves, finely chopped
1¼ cups cooked long-grain rice

1½ pounds ground lamb
2 teaspoons ground allspice
2 teaspoons salt
1 teaspoon freshly ground black pepper
2 (15-ounce) cans diced tomatoes, undrained
3 cups chicken stock
1 tablespoon freshly squeezed lemon juice
Finely chopped fresh cilantro, for garnish

The monks at Saint Anthony don't consume meat at every meal, but they do enjoy it on Sundays and during feast day celebrations, which they often observe with the rest of the community. The Maronite liturgical calendar is populated by feast days that pay tribute to saints and other revered religious figures and acknowledges significant events in Maronite history. A feast day typically begins with Mass and virtually always culminates in a meal to honor the person or event being remembered. The feast includes recipes that are reflective of their season—robust comfort foods during the cooler winter months and light and refreshing dishes to cool down the fire on a sweltering summer day. Mehché koussa, a vibrantly colored dish, makes the most of the valley's summer zucchini harvest. Substitute ground beef, chicken, or turkey for the lamb. For a hint of sweetness, add ½ cup raisins to the lamb mixture before stuffing the zucchini.

USING A SMALL melon-ball cutter or an apple corer, hollow out each zucchini, working from both ends, removing all seeds and leaving shells about ⅓ inch thick. (The monks offer the pulp and seeds to their chickens, but if you're without a flock, either compost it or save it for another use, such as stirred into pasta sauce or risotto.) Set the zucchini shells aside.

HEAT ¼ CUP oil in a large, heavy-bottomed skillet over medium-high heat. Add the onions and sauté until translucent, 6 to 8 minutes. Add the garlic and sauté until fragrant, about 2 minutes. Transfer ½ cup of the onions and garlic to a large bowl, leaving the rest in the skillet. Add the cooked rice, lamb, allspice, 1½ teaspoons salt, and ½ teaspoon pepper to the bowl and stir well with clean hands or a wooden spoon. Stuff the prepared zucchini shells with the lamb mixture. Place the stuffed zucchini in a single layer on a rimmed baking sheet and cover with a dry kitchen towel.

ADD THE TOMATOES with their juices and the stock to the skillet with the remaining onions. Bring to a simmer over medium heat. Season with the remaining ½ teaspoon each salt and pepper. Arrange the stuffed zucchini in the tomato sauce, cover, and simmer until the zucchini is tender and the lamb is cooked through, 40 to 45 minutes, turning the zucchini over once about halfway through. Transfer the zucchini to a serving platter and spoon the sauce on top. Squeeze the lemon juice over the zucchini, drizzle with the remaining 2 tablespoons olive oil, and garnish generously with cilantro. Leftovers will keep in a covered container in the refrigerator for up to 3 days.

2.

Masbia

JUDAISM
BROOKLYN, NEW YORK, USA

"Then I grasped the meaning of the greatest secret that
human poetry and human thought and belief have to
impart: The salvation of man is through love and in love."
—*Viktor Frankl*

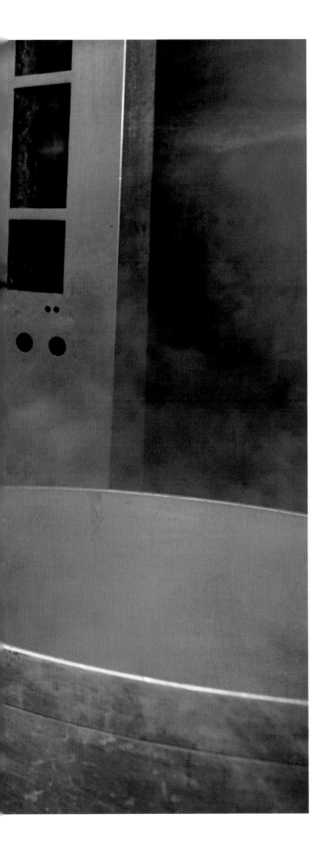

Rabbi Alexander Rapaport never stops working. If he's not networking, visiting members of the Orthodox Jewish community where he lives in Brooklyn, or shopping for ingredients at the vast kosher markets in New Jersey and New York, he's working to secure funding for Masbia, creating menus based upon the donations they receive each week with the cooks who staff the only kosher soup kitchen network in New York City. He greets many of the hundreds of people who visit Masbia each week for a hot meal and a bag of fresh and canned ingredients that they are sent home with after their dinner.

It's a daunting job, but Rabbi Rapaport relishes the role he plays in keeping his community fed. "It's important that we offer compassion to each visitor by treating them with kindness, with respect. We don't make people sign in like so many soup kitchens require. That strips a person of their dignity and makes them feel diminished." Rabbi Rapaport explains while busily shopping for vegetables at a nearby market to fill in the gaps that the day's donations cannot fill. "At Masbia, we invite people to sit down with their families at a table that has a tablecloth, that has ceramic plates, real silverware. We want them to linger, we don't want them to feel rushed. We take their order, we listen if they've had a difficult day, we make them feel heard, we want them to know that we see them and we value who they are. The biggest success we can have is when a family finishes their meal and instead of rushing off, they sit with the kids and help them with their homework right at the table. That's when we know we are doing our job. That's when we know they feel respected and loved."

Rabbi Rapaport takes many of the principles he's learned at the synagogue and applies them to Masbia. "Meals are served in the social halls of synagogues. Some synagogues have weekly meals, others only serve meals when someone is celebrating something, but either way, the food is about more than sustenance. It's about bringing people in the community together to share stories from our past, to discuss our current challenges, to make plans for the future. And the dishes that are served are filled with history. Often they are recipes passed down from previous generations, and woven into them is a story of struggle and a story of overcoming that struggle. These dishes always taste good because they are the dishes that got you or your ancestors over the hump, through the struggle."

The meals served at both Masbia and at the synagogue are always kosher, and meticulous attention is paid to following the rules. Rabbi Rapaport explains, "In Orthodox terms, kosher food means God's choice. The word basically means 'fit to eat,' and keeping kosher requires strict adherence to the rules that were established in the Torah. It's not simply about which foods are eaten and which are not, but it's about how they are prepared, how they are stored, how they are consumed. It's not a burden to eat kosher; it's a privilege for our Orthodox community."

The Hasidic community in Brooklyn, of which Rabbi Rapaport is a part, is a large and vibrant group of ultra-Orthodox Jews. The community has roots that can be traced back to the late nineteenth and early twentieth centuries, when a wave of eastern European Jewish immigrants arrived in New York City. Many of these immigrants were Hasidic Jews, who were attracted to the United States by the promise of economic opportunity and religious freedom. They settled in neighborhoods like Williamsburg and Borough Park, which became the center of Hasidic life in Brooklyn.

OPPOSITE
Rabbi Alex Rapaport and his brother,
Chef Berish Rapaport

" The biggest success we can have is when a family finishes their meal and instead of rushing off, they sit with the kids and help them with their homework right at the table. That's when we know we are doing our job. That's when we know they feel respected and loved."

The community is known for its strong cultural traditions, including a distinctive dress code, religious practices, and tight-knit social structure. The community's equally rich culinary traditions reflect its eastern European heritage and religious practices. Many traditional dishes are based on kosher dietary laws, which prohibit the consumption of certain foods and require strict separation of meat and dairy products. These culinary customs are central to their cultural and religious traditions and are enjoyed by families and friends at home, at communal events, and at the synagogue.

On a broader scale, the Jewish community in New York City is one of the largest and most diverse in the world, with roots that can be traced back to the mid-seventeenth century. Over the centuries, Jewish immigrants from a variety of countries and cultural backgrounds have made their home in New York City, contributing to its rich and vibrant cultural diversity.

Today, the Jewish community of New York City is estimated to number over 1.5 million people and includes a wide range of religious and cultural groups, such as Hasidic Jews, Modern Orthodox Jews, Sephardic Jews, Reform Jews, and many others. The community plays a significant role in the city's culinary, cultural, and intellectual life and is an integral part of its history and identity.

Running three soup kitchens in one of the busiest metro areas in America has its unique set of challenges, and Rabbi Rapaport draws inspiration from his Jewish faith. The underlying thread that stitches together the meticulous tapestry of tasks that Rabbi Rapaport must complete each day and the reason for his commitment to feeding those in need is personal. "My grandmother was a Holocaust survivor. Sugar made her vomit because the Nazis forced Hungarian Jews to go on a death march. They were walking through a sugar beet field and one of the young girls tore a leaf from one of the beet plants and ate it because she was starving. The Nazis shot her and, while she was still half alive, they made the others bury her."

Rabbi Rapaport continues, "But my grandmother was a fighter. She did end up in a camp, she lost everything, she went through unbearable, unspeakable things, but she was also resourceful, she was generous, she had an invincible spirit. One of the stories she would share at our Shabbat table was about when she and other girls on the march were forced by the SS into a barn. They had no food and they were starving. My grandmother smelled food being cooked and she snuck out of the barn, and there was a farmer there boiling potato peelings. She started to fill her pockets with them but the farmer saw her and said, 'These are for my pigs.' My grandmother said, 'I will be a pig. Please let me have them.' He relented and she took as many peelings as she could back to the barn to the others, a few of whom also went to gather their own. My grandmother told them to hide the peelings to avoid repercussions from the SS, but people were starving and they could not stop themselves. The SS officers did discover their food and took it all away. It was a hopeless moment, but my grandmother, always clever and resourceful, had hid her own peelings in the rafters. Once the officers were gone, she shared her treasure with everyone there. My grandmother and my grandfather, too, carried these memories with them to America. They never forgot the feeling of starvation, the devastation of it. They were always inviting people home, strangers who they knew were in need of a nourishing meal. Their generosity was infinite. Whenever I am feeling the stress that comes from running Masbia, I think of my grandparents, I think of those potato peelings, I think of the way my grandmother found the light of hope during her darkest hour. I think of all this. And I keep going."

OPPOSITE
Rabbi Rapaport shopping for Masbia
at a market in Brooklyn

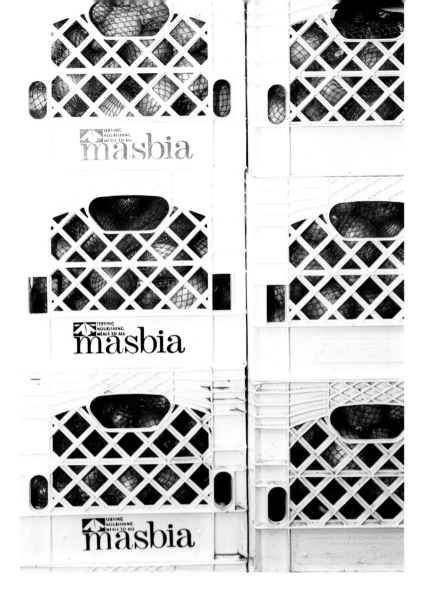

OPPOSITE
A rabbi at Masbia inspecting rice for sediment to adhere to kosher standards

ABOVE
Ingredient delivery at Masbia

RIGHT
Gala

Potato Kugel

MAKES: 1 (9-inch) pie or 6 muffin-size kugels
PREPARATION TIME: 1½ hours

Extra-virgin olive oil, as needed
6 (6-ounce) Idaho potatoes
3 large eggs
1 teaspoon kosher salt
½ teaspoon freshly ground black pepper
1 (8-ounce) white onion, cut into six wedges
Sour cream, to serve

Kugel is a traditional Ashkenazi Jewish dish popular on Shabbat and other Jewish holidays. The Yiddish word *kugel* comes from the German word of the same spelling that translates as a "ball" or "sphere." The original kugel was made from bread that became puffed and round when baked. About eight hundred years ago, Jewish cooks living in Germany replaced the bread with noodles. Over the centuries, countless other ingredients have been added, including raisins, cottage cheese, milk, caramelized sugar, cream cheese, cabbage, and carrots, to create a vast array of savory and sweet kugel recipes beloved by Jewish communities throughout the world. This potato kugel features a simple combination of potatoes, onions, and olive oil that create a fluffy golden interior complemented by a crunchy crust. Add grated zucchini or carrots, coarsely chopped baby spinach, or cottage cheese for variations on this endlessly versatile and comforting dish.

PREHEAT THE OVEN to 425°F.

POUR ENOUGH OLIVE oil into a 9-inch round baking dish or pie pan to fill it by ¼ inch, and also grease the sides of the dish. Place the baking dish in the oven to heat the oil while you complete the next steps.

FILL A LARGE bowl with ice water. Peel the potatoes, cut them lengthwise into quarters, and put them in the bowl of water to prevent oxidation.

HEAT AN ADDITIONAL ¾ cup olive oil in a saucepan over medium heat.

IN A MEDIUM bowl, whisk together the eggs, salt, and pepper; set aside.

DRAIN THE POTATOES and pat them dry with a kitchen towel. In a food processor fitted with the grating blade, process the potatoes and then the onion. Transfer the potato and onion strips to a large bowl and gently stir in the saucepan of warmed olive oil. Add the egg mixture and gently stir with a wooden spoon until incorporated.

WORKING VERY CAREFULLY to prevent the oil from splattering, remove the hot baking dish from the oven and spoon the kugel mixture into it in an even layer; smooth the top. Bake until the kugel is cooked through, slightly puffy, and crispy and golden brown on top, about 1 hour. Let it cool to room temperature, then loosen the edges with a knife and transfer to a serving plate. Serve with sour cream. The kugel will keep in a covered container in the refrigerator for up to 3 days.

Cholent

SERVES: 6

PREPARATION TIME: 12 to 14 hours

1½ pounds bone-in beef short ribs
1 teaspoon salt, plus more to taste
1 teaspoon freshly ground black pepper,
   plus more to taste
½ cup dried kidney beans
½ cup dried navy beans
½ cup dried cranberry beans
2 medium Yukon Gold potatoes, peeled and
   cut into 1½-inch chunks
1 large yellow onion, coarsely chopped
1 cup pearl barley
3 cups beef or chicken stock
1 tablespoon dark molasses
1 tablespoon honey
1½ tablespoons smoked paprika

Cholent is a slow-cooked, fortifying stew, often featuring succulent short ribs, a variety of beans, potatoes, and barley. These layers of flavor are subtly sweetened with honey and deepened with dark molasses. Cholent is thought to have developed during the Second Temple period in Jewish history, which lasted from 516 BCE to 70 CE. Over the centuries, cholent variations have emerged around the world as cooks within the Jewish diaspora incorporated the techniques and ingredients of their regions. To comply with Jewish laws that prohibit cooking during the Sabbath, which lasts from sunset on Friday to sunset on Saturday, cholent is prepared in a slow cooker or in a pot that is placed on an electric hotplate or "blech" (a metal sheet placed over stovetop burners) before the sun sets on Friday. It then slowly cooks throughout the night, developing its flavors and thickening into a glistening stew. The showpiece on the Sabbath table, the stew connects those who gather now to the past and to one another. This dish is inspired by a cholent recipe shared by Rabbi Rappaport from his brother, a chef who runs a kosher food market in New Jersey.

If you are not observing Shabbat, you can assemble the cholent in a Dutch oven or other large, heavy pot and bake, covered, in a 225°F oven for 12 to 14 hours.

SEASON THE SHORT ribs all over with the salt and pepper. Put all the beans in a colander and rinse under cold running water to remove any residue.

PUT THE POTATOES in a slow cooker, followed by the onion, and then the ribs. Sprinkle the barley over the ribs and then spoon the beans on top. Add the stock, drizzle with the molasses and honey, and sprinkle with the smoked paprika. Add enough water to cover everything by 3 inches. Cover the slow cooker and cook on low for 12 to 14 hours, stirring occasionally and adding additional water if the cholent becomes too dry as it cooks. Season with salt and pepper. Leftovers can be stored in a covered container in the refrigerator for up to 5 days or in the freezer for up to 1 month.

Corned Beef Sandwiches with Sauerkraut

MAKES: 8 sandwiches

PREPARATION TIME: 3½ hours, plus 10 days to cure the brisket

½ cup dark brown sugar
1¼ cups kosher salt
12 juniper berries
10 allspice berries
8 whole cloves

2 bay leaves
1 cinnamon stick
2 teaspoons black peppercorns
2 teaspoons brown mustard seeds
1½ teaspoons ground ginger
1 pound ice
1 (4½-pound) beef brisket, trimmed of fat and sinew
1 medium yellow onion, thinly sliced

2 celery ribs, thinly sliced
1 large carrot, peeled and thinly sliced
16 slices rye or pumpernickel bread, toasted
1 cup kosher nondairy Russian dressing, such as Lieber's
4 cups sauerkraut, store-bought or homemade (page 51)

The history of corned beef is stitched through the culinary traditions of cultures throughout Europe and the Middle East. It emerged when people began salt-curing meat for preservation purposes. *Corn* is an Old English word that initially denoted small, hard grains or particles. The word *corned* in corned beef is most likely in reference to the saltpeter (small grains of potassium nitrate) originally used to cure the beef. In order to be considered kosher, corned beef must be made from beef free from any forbidden substances, such as pork or shellfish, and must be prepared using utensils that are kept separate from nonkosher foods. In addition, corned beef must be made with a brine that does not contain any prohibited ingredients, such as vinegar made from wine that has not been produced according to kosher laws.

Jewish-style corned beef is made from kosher brisket that's also smoked for pastrami, the beloved staple of Jewish delis throughout New York City. Jewish delis in New York City have been serving corned beef for over a century and have played an important role in the city's culinary history. These delis, which are often family owned and operated, are known for their hearty and flavorful dishes, generous portions, and welcoming atmosphere. Despite facing challenges such as rising costs and changing dietary habits, Jewish delis in New York City continue to thrive and remain an integral part of the city's culinary landscape. Another deli staple, the Reuben, a corned beef sandwich with sauerkraut, is not kosher because it includes melted Swiss cheese. Rabbi Alex Rapaport enjoys his corned beef and sauerkraut sandwiches at his brother's kosher restaurant in New Jersey. They're a way to bring the brothers together to catch up on their busy lives. This recipe is rather complicated and requires quite a time investment (which is probably why Rabbi Rappaport does not make it himself!), but its ability to bridge the past and the present makes it a sandwich worth committing to!

IN A LARGE pot, combine 2 quarts water, the sugar, salt, juniper berries, allspice berries, cloves, bay leaves, cinnamon stick, peppercorns, mustard seeds, and ginger. Bring to a boil over high heat. Cook, stirring occasionally, until the sugar and salt have dissolved, about 5 minutes. Remove from the heat, add the ice, and stir until the ice has completely melted, about 5 minutes. If necessary, place the pot in the refrigerator until the liquid has reached 45°F.

PUT THE BRISKET in a heavy-duty 2-gallon plastic bag and carefully pour the brine into it. Seal the bag, lay it flat in a baking pan or on a rimmed baking sheet, and refrigerate for 10 days. Turn it over once per day to ensure that the brisket remains covered by the brine and is preserved evenly.

AFTER 10 DAYS, remove the brisket from the brine and rinse well under cold running water. Discard the brine. Put the brisket in a large pot, add the onion, celery, and carrot, and pour in enough water to cover by 1 inch. Bring to a boil over high heat, then reduce the heat to medium-low and simmer until the brisket is very tender and falls apart easily with a fork, 2½ to 3 hours. Transfer the brisket to a plate and, once it is cool enough to handle, cut into ⅛-inch-thick slices. Discard the other ingredients.

TO SERVE, TOP a slice of toasted bread with about 8 slices of corned beef. Spoon about 2 tablespoons Russian dressing over it, top with ½ cup sauerkraut, and then cover with a second slice of toast. Repeat to make 7 more sandwiches. Leftover corned beef can be stored in a covered container in the refrigerator for up to 4 days or in the freezer for up to 2 months.

How to Make Sauerkraut

Even though *sauerkraut* is a German word meaning "sour cabbage," the recipe is not from Germany. Its origins stretch all the way back to the Tatar era of China, which began in the early seventh century. It was the Tatars (sometimes called Tartars) who brought the tradition of fermenting thinly sliced raw cabbage with lactic acid with them to Europe. The highly nutritious dish was ideal for sustaining them on long journeys because it could be stored for months in ceramic jars that they carried with them on their campaigns through Europe. The Jewish people adapted their sauerkraut recipes to whichever region of the world they were living in, and it has become an important mainstay in the Jewish culinary repertoire.

Sauerkraut is naturally preserved through lactic fermentation. The fermentation process employed to make sauerkraut releases beneficial microbes that consume the natural sugars in the cabbage and convert them into lactic acid, which preserves the cabbage and transforms it into the pungent flavor bomb that enlivens so many Jewish recipes.

Making your own sauerkraut at home is a fairly simple process. The two main requirements are time and a high-quality ceramic fermentation crock with a tight-fitting lid. If you have both of these, along with a cool, dark space, you're well on your way to sauerkraut success. A fermentation crock is essential to kraut success and curtails health risks by minimizing unwanted yeast, microbes, and mold. It does this by creating an anaerobic environment that keeps contaminants and oxygen out of the crock while at the same time enabling the release of built-up carbon dioxide.

Before you begin, here are a few tips:

- Sauerkraut ferments more slowly in colder temperatures and faster in warm temperatures, but its storage space should never exceed 80°F or your kraut might have an off-flavor and squishy texture instead of that crisp bite that makes it so appealing.
- As you might guess, larger batches require more fermentation time than smaller ones.
- Begin taste testing after your kraut has been fermenting for about two weeks. The sour flavor intensifies and becomes more pungent with each passing day.
- As long as you vigilantly keep your kraut submerged in its brine, it can be stored in its fermentation crock and doesn't need to be refrigerated or canned.
- Colder temperatures, such as those found in a cellar or in the refrigerator, will essentially stop the fermentation process, so as long as it remains covered in brine and stored at a cool temperature, kraut will keep for at least three months and even as long as a year.

Sauerkraut

Fermentation crocks are available at specialty kitchen stores and online. Be sure to purchase one with a secure, tight-fitting lid. For this recipe, the crock should hold at least 4 quarts. Use fermentation weights to weigh down the kraut before sealing in order to ensure that the cabbage stays submerged in its brine.

MAKES: about 1 quart
PREPARATION TIME: 1 to 4 weeks (depending upon flavor preference)

2 (2½-pound) white cabbage heads
3 tablespoons kosher salt

REMOVE ANY OUTER cabbage leaves that are turning brown. Cut the cabbages in half lengthwise, then cut each half into quarters. Cut out the core portion from each quarter, then cut each quarter lengthwise into ⅛-inch-thick slices. In a large bowl, toss together the slices and the salt until well blended, then let it rest until the cabbage starts to release its juices, about 10 minutes. Squeeze the cabbage to release more juices, then let it rest for another 10 minutes, reserving the juices in the bowl. Repeat this process once more. At this stage, the cabbage should be quite limp and there should be 1 to 1½ cups of liquid in the bowl. Transfer both the cabbage and the liquid to a fermentation crock, packing it down as tightly as possible to release additional juice and to fully submerge the cabbage in the liquid. Place fermentation weights on top of the cabbage, seal the crock, and store it, undisturbed, at room temperature for at least 2 weeks. At this stage, taste the kraut. If its flavor has achieved what you're looking for, transfer the crock to a cool place such as the refrigerator or basement. If not, reseal and continue to ferment, tasting every week until it's just right. The kraut will keep for 3 to 12 months.

Smoked Salmon Spread

Jewish immigrants from Eastern Europe brought the tradition of fish curing with them to New York in the late nineteenth and early twentieth centuries. In Europe, a variety of fish was traditionally dry-cured by salting the fish directly. Jewish immigrants discovered a new preservation method when they arrived in the United States, whereby fish was wet-cured in brine and then cold-smoked. Because of the availability and affordability of Pacific Northwest salmon in America, lox (from the German word for salmon, *lachs*) became the most popular wet-cured fish variety. Since fish is pareve (neither dairy nor meat), it can be enjoyed with any meal.

COMBINE THE SALMON, scallions, dill, cream cheese, horseradish, lemon juice, salt, and pepper in the bowl of a food processor. Pulse a few times, then blend at medium speed until well combined, about 2 minutes. Stop the machine a few times to scrape down the sides. Use a spatula to transfer the spread to a serving bowl. Cover and chill for at least 2 hours.

GARNISH WITH FRESH dill and serve with crackers, crudités, or matzo, plus lemon wedges for squeezing. Leftovers can be stored in a covered container in the refrigerator for up to 5 days.

MAKES: about 1½ cups
PREPARATION TIME: 10 minutes, plus 2 hours to chill

4 ounces smoked salmon, coarsely chopped
2 scallions, both white and green parts, thinly sliced
Fronds from 2 dill sprigs, plus more for garnish
8 ounces cream cheese
1½ teaspoons prepared white horseradish
1½ tablespoons freshly squeezed lemon juice
½ teaspoon salt
½ teaspoon freshly ground black pepper
Crackers, crudités, or matzo, for serving
Lemon wedges, for serving

Tzimmes

Tzimmes is not only fun to say, but its Yiddish meaning playfully translates to "a big fuss." Tzimmes is ultimately a casserole with the similar texture of a thick stew. It's popular at Rosh Hashanah when a honey-infused dish is served to usher in and honor the new year, because sweet food symbolizes the hope for a sweet and joyful year ahead.

PREHEAT THE OVEN to 350°F.

BRING A LARGE pot of salted water to a boil over high heat. Reduce the heat to medium, add the sweet potatoes, and simmer for 10 minutes. Add the carrots and simmer until the carrots are fork-tender, about 10 more minutes. Drain in a colander. Cut the carrots into 1-inch chunks. Once the potatoes are cool enough to handle, peel them using your hands (the peelings should slip right off as long as the potatoes are still warm) or use a vegetable peeler. Cut the potatoes into 1-inch chunks.

IN A LARGE bowl, combine the potatoes, carrots, prunes, apricots, raisins, honey, orange zest and juice, lemon juice, cinnamon, and salt and mix well. Transfer to a 2-quart casserole dish, cover, and bake for 30 minutes, basting every 10 minutes. Serve warm. Tzimmes doesn't freeze well but will keep in a covered container in the refrigerator for up to 3 days.

SERVES: 4
PREPARATION TIME: 1 hour

¼ teaspoon salt, plus more to taste
2 pounds sweet potatoes (about 4)
1 pound medium carrots (about 9), peeled
1 cup bite-size pitted prunes
1 cup dried apricots
2 tablespoons black raisins
¼ cup honey
2½ teaspoons grated orange zest
⅓ cup freshly squeezed orange juice
2 tablespoons freshly squeezed lemon juice
1 teaspoon ground cinnamon

Pickled Beets and Onions

Hamutz is the Hebrew word for "sour," and the plural *hamutzim* is used to describe pickled vegetables in the Jewish culinary repertoire. Pickling vegetables is a sustainable way to transform older vegetables that might otherwise be discarded into a tantalizing condiment that infuses a meal with vibrancy and pluck. Hamutzim is a favorite at Masbia, where the cooks operate on a shoestring budget that necessitates working nimbly to ensure that nothing is wasted. Pickling is a way to stretch resources by saving something healthful and tasty for another day.

PUT THE BEETS in a large saucepan and pour in enough water to cover by 1½ inches; season with salt. Bring to a boil over high heat, reduce the heat to medium, and simmer until the beets are fork-tender, about 20 minutes. Drain. Once the beets are cool enough to handle, cut into ½-inch chunks.

WHILE THE BEETS are simmering, put the onion in a medium nonreactive bowl, pour in enough ice water to cover by 2 inches, and add 1 teaspoon salt. Let sit at room temperature for 25 minutes. Drain.

IN A LARGE bowl, toss together the beets, onion, olive oil, and vinegar. Season with salt and pepper and serve. Store leftovers in a covered container in the refrigerator for up to 1 week.

MAKES: about 2 cups
PREPARATION TIME: 30 minutes

1 pound medium red beets (about 6), peeled
Kosher salt to taste
1 small red onion, halved lengthwise and
    thinly sliced crosswise
2 tablespoons extra-virgin olive oil
⅔ cup red wine vinegar
½ teaspoon freshly ground black pepper

OPPOSITE
From top: Pickled Beets and Onions,
Hummus (page 21), Smoked Salmon
Spread (page 52)

ABOVE
Food delivery at Masbia

RIGHT
Matzo balls

Matzo Ball Soup

SERVES: 6
PREPARATION TIME: 4 hours

FOR THE MATZO BALLS:
1 cup matzo meal
¼ cup chicken schmaltz (see headnote)
4 large eggs, beaten
Leaves from 2 flat-leaf parsley sprigs, finely
    chopped

1½ tablespoons grated fresh ginger
¼ teaspoon grated fresh nutmeg
1 teaspoon kosher salt
¼ teaspoon freshly ground black pepper

FOR THE CHICKEN STOCK:
1 (5-pound chicken), cut into 8 pieces
2 large yellow onions, quartered
5 celery ribs, cut into 2-inch pieces

6 large carrots, 4 peeled and cut into 1-inch
    pieces, 2 peeled and shredded
1 large head garlic, cut in half crosswise
8 flat-leaf parsley sprigs, plus more
    chopped leaves for garnish
1 tablespoon black peppercorns
1 tablespoon salt

Matzo (also spelled matzoh) is an unleavened bread that is served during Passover when chametz (leavened bread) is forbidden because the Torah states that God told the Israelites to forgo leavened bread when they were fleeing slavery in Egypt. Matzo ball soup is an iconic comfort food for people of all backgrounds and cultures. Some prefer their matzo balls light and fluffy, while others relish a dense and chewy texture. The soup itself can range from a simple chicken broth to a more complex version that includes carrots, celery, and onions.

Today, matzo ball soup is an iconic fixture of New York's Jewish delis and a must-have dish at the Passover seder meal. It's also served at other holiday meals, such as Hanukkah and Rosh Hashanah, as well as at family gatherings and celebrations. At synagogues in Brooklyn, matzo ball soup is typically prepared by volunteers and served as part of a large meal or buffet. This recipe is a favorite of the members of Rabbi Rappaport's synagogue. Chicken schmaltz is rendered chicken fat. It's available from many butchers and specialty markets. You can substitute coconut or vegetable oil for the schmaltz, but it adds phenomenal flavor if you can source it.

FIRST, MAKE THE matzo ball dough. In a large bowl, gently stir together the matzo meal, schmaltz, eggs, parsley, ginger, nutmeg, salt, and pepper. Cover and refrigerate until chilled, at least 3 hours. This step is important because it will prevent the matzo balls from falling apart while they cook.

MEANWHILE, MAKE THE chicken stock. Combine 5 quarts water, the chicken, onions, celery, carrot pieces, garlic, parsley sprigs, and peppercorns in a large pot. Bring to a boil over high heat, then reduce the heat to medium-low, cover, and simmer gently until the chicken is cooked through, about 20 minutes. Using tongs, transfer the chicken pieces to a plate. Once the chicken is cool enough to handle, remove and discard the skin and bones, then shred the meat and store it in a covered container in the refrigerator until ready to use.

PARTIALLY COVER THE pot and continue simmering the stock until it has reduced by one-third, skimming to remove any scum that forms on the surface, about 2 hours. Strain through a fine-mesh strainer lined with cheesecloth and discard the solids. (If the stock isn't being used right away, let it cool to room temperature, then store in a covered container in the refrigerator for up to 3 days or in the freezer indefinitely.)

WHEN READY TO make the matzo balls, bring a large pot of water to a vigorous simmer over high heat. Roll the matzo dough into 1½-inch balls and carefully drop each one into the water after it is rolled. Once all of the matzo balls have been added to the pot, reduce the heat to medium and simmer until the matzo balls are cooked through and begin to sink to the bottom, about 20 minutes. Drain.

RETURN THE POT of stock to a boil over high heat. Add the reserved chicken meat, shredded carrots, and salt, reduce the heat to medium, and simmer until the carrots are tender, about 7 minutes.

TO SERVE, USING a slotted spoon, transfer 3 or 4 matzo balls to prewarmed bowls and ladle the soup on top. Garnish with parsley and serve immediately. Store leftover matzo balls and soup in separate covered containers in the refrigerator for up to 5 days.

Green Shabbat Dip

MAKES: about 1 cup
PREPARATION TIME: 10 minutes

2 large garlic cloves, coarsely chopped
¾ cup lightly packed fresh flat-leaf parsley leaves
¼ cup finally chopped walnuts
⅔ cup tahini
1½ tablespoons freshly squeezed lemon juice
½ teaspoon ground cumin
¼ cup extra-virgin olive oil
¾ cup ice water
½ teaspoon kosher salt

Shabbat, the Jewish Sabbath, is an important time for families to celebrate the spiritual aspects of life and deepen their relationships with one another. According to halakha (Jewish religious law), work and to-do lists and the endless tasks of our busy lives are set aside every week from a few minutes before sunset on Friday until sunset on Saturday. It's a time to feast, pray, share stories, and remember loved ones lost, and ultimately to engage in restful activities to honor the day, the Jewish heritage, and each other. Shabbat begins on Friday evening with the lighting of at least two candles and the reciting of a blessing. Three meals are enjoyed on Shabbat: dinner on Friday night, lunch on Saturday, and an afternoon dinner later that day. Each meal begins with a blessing called kiddush and features two loaves of challah. Challah is a yeasted egg bread similar in flavor, color, and texture to brioche. The challah is braided to symbolize the weaving of the industrious weekday mentality into a Shabbat state of mind. At sundown on Saturday, Shabbat concludes with a ceremony called havdalah. The festive period is filled with laughter, fellowship, remembrance, prayer, and beloved recipes passed down from one generation to the next. Spreads and dips are popular on the Shabbat table. They're enjoyed with challah, vegetables, pretzels, and, if they're as enticing as this refreshing green Shabbat dip, by the spoonful. This recipe has been in Rabbi Rappaport's family for decades and is a staple on their Shabbat table.

COMBINE THE GARLIC, parsley, walnuts, tahini, lemon juice, and cumin in the bowl of a food processor. Pulse a few times to begin incorporating everything, then pulse while adding the oil through the feed tube in a slow, steady stream. Continue to process until the dip is well incorporated but still slightly chunky, about 1 minute. Add the ice water in a steady stream while pulsing and then process until smooth. Season with the salt and transfer to a bowl. Cover and refrigerate until chilled. The dip will keep in a covered container in the refrigerator for up to 1 week.

Potato Latkes

MAKES: about 16 latkes
PREPARATION TIME: 30 minutes

1½ pounds large Idaho potatoes (about 6)
2 large eggs, beaten
3 shallots, finely chopped
2 tablespoons all-purpose flour (or matzo meal during Passover), plus more as needed
1 teaspoon kosher salt, plus more to taste
½ teaspoon freshly ground black pepper, plus more to taste
Vegetable oil, for frying
Applesauce and/or sour cream, for serving (optional)

Latkes are traditionally enjoyed during Hanukkah. This is the Jewish festival of lights honoring the recovery of Jerusalem after the Maccabean revolt against the Seleucis Empire in the second century BCE. Fried foods are popular during Hanukkah as a way to commemorate the miracle of just one day's supply of oil lasting long enough to keep the candles lit for eight days during the rededication of the Second Temple. The Yiddish word *latke* translates as "little pancake," and the basic recipe has many variations, including latkes made with zucchini, cottage cheese, and onions. Traditional potato latkes became popular in the nineteenth century when the potato arrived in Eastern Europe from South America. Latkes were traditionally fried in schmaltz (see page 57), but this recipe uses vegetable oil. Serve with applesauce or sour cream—or both!

SET A COLANDER over a large bowl and line the colander with a double layer of cheesecloth. Fill a second bowl with ice water.

PEEL THE POTATOES just before using to prevent them from browning. Grate the potatoes using either a box grater or a food processor fitted with the grating blade. If using a food processor, cut the potatoes into quarters lengthwise before grating. Transfer the grated potatoes to the colander, gather the cheesecloth around them, twist into a tight ball, and squeeze hard to release as much of the potato juice as possible. Let the potatoes rest over the bowl for 15 minutes to enable them to release additional juices. Squeeze the potatoes to release as much additional liquid from them as possible.

IN A LARGE bowl, combine the eggs, shallots, flour, salt, and pepper and stir until incorporated. Gently stir in the grated potatoes until they are moistened. If the batter is too runny, add a little more flour until the liquid resembles a dry cake batter.

HEAT 2 TABLESPOONS oil in a large nonstick skillet over medium-high heat. Working in batches so as not to crowd the pan, carefully drop 2 tablespoons of batter per latke into the oil. Fry until golden brown on one side, 3 to 4 minutes. Flip using a spatula and fry on the other side until golden brown and cooked through, 3 to 4 more minutes. Transfer to a paper towel–lined plate and season with salt and pepper. Add more oil as necessary to fry the remaining batches.

TRANSFER THE LATKES to a serving platter and serve hot with applesauce or sour cream. Latkes will keep in a covered container in the refrigerator for up to 2 days.

3.

Poblet Monastery

CISTERCIAN CATHOLIC
TARRAGONA, SPAIN

"Love is our true destiny. We do not find meaning of life by
ourselves—we find it with one another."
—*Thomas Merton, Cistercian monk*

The twelfth-century Cistercian monastery of Poblet has endured its share of hardship over the years as wave after wave of warring groups plundered their way through the vineyards and olive groves. Poblet has left its history of setbacks behind to develop into a monastery that boasts one of the most cutting-edge monastic gardening programs in the world. What the investment banker turned monk from Barcelona in charge of the vast gardens, orchards, and vineyards doesn't send to the monastery's kitchen or culinary training program for disenfranchised youth, he pickles or dehydrates for the Tarragonian winter.

The monastery, a UNESCO World Heritage Site, is a two-hour drive from Barcelona, on the southern border of Catalonia. Poblet is one of the largest and most complete Cistercian monasteries in the world. It towers above the valley as an imposing reminder of nearly nine hundred years of Spanish history, in all its illuminated triumphs and grievous defeats.

The abbey of the monastery rises up from the russet foothills of the Prades Mountains. Inside the abbey, alabaster statues of Christian icons watch over the ancient tombs of kings and queens who ruled for centuries over the legendary Kingdom of Aragon. Fra Borja Peyra, a former investment banker in his early forties with salt-and-pepper hair and a relaxed nature, details the conflicts the monastery has endured throughout its existence. It was closed altogether in 1835, when an edict from Prime Minister Juan Álvarez Mendizábal to confiscate all Church properties ushered in a dark time for the monasteries of Spain. Poblet was not spared. Pillaging transformed the grand complex, with its six-foot-thick battlement walls and intricately carved porticos, to ruins. Fortunately, many of Poblet's most valuable paintings, treasures, and furniture were safeguarded in private homes in the surrounding villages before a catastrophic fire ravaged what was left of the monastery.

Over a century later, Italian monks of the same Cistercian order reopened Poblet's doors after a painstaking restoration process initiated in 1940 to return the monastery to its original splendor.

Fra Borja smiles with a finger to his lips as he strolls along a cobblestone lane past lemon and hazelnut trees on this sunny but cool autumn morning. We stop to feed his chickens before ducking into the vast pantry to inspect the freshly harvested crates of persimmons and baskets heaped with almonds. Along the edge of the property, Fra Borja finds his stride in a garden that tumbles down the hillside to the olive and almond groves far below. He proudly explains that he is the monk in charge of the gardening program at Poblet, where they employ an amalgamation of ancient wisdom and modern technology to coax everything from tomatoes to beans to carrots from the region's fertile soil. Their goal is to be completely self-sustaining, with any excess distributed to the surrounding villages as a way to ensure that the time-tested kinship between the monks of Poblet and the people of Catalonia endures.

There is no sorrow in his voice as he discusses what had been vanquished, only optimism and possibility. "One of the things I'm working on that excites me most is a hydroponic growing system that I am installing in one of the greenhouses before winter sets in. If it's a success, we will be able to complement the preserved fruits and vegetables we serve during the winter months with fresh produce. It's a challenge for me because there are only a few younger monks now living at Poblet who can handle manual labor. I must balance my heavy workload with the care of the elderly monks who rely

" But this is what living in a monastic community is all about. It reflects society as a whole; to survive and to thrive, you must look out for one another."

upon us. But this is what living in a monastic community is all about. It reflects society as a whole; to survive and to thrive, you must look out for one another."

Fra Borja steps into an imposing stone room housing nothing but an intricate wooden rack upon which thousands of plump, ripe tomatoes are hung. He breaks one off the vine and bites into its taut red flesh, juice as vibrant as a tomato picked in the heart of summer dripping down his chin and fingers. He wipes his chin with the sleeve of his fawn-colored habit. "In Catalonia, this is a traditional way to preserve our tomatoes. Hanging them in this manner enables them to ripen to a sweet finish without spoiling. If we are fortunate, they will last us all winter long," he says as he runs his fingers through buckets of dried pinto beans and almonds.

He lifts up a sheet of burlap to reveal large glass jars of pickled vegetables prepared for the ensuing winter months and points to hundreds of fingerling potatoes and yellow onions carefully arranged on the cleanly swept stone floor. He says, "The cold floor preserves them long enough to carry us through the season. You don't need a root cellar, just a place brisk and dark enough to keep them in the game."

We walk to the refectory, where around thirty-five monks gather for their meals each day. A ray of sun beams down upon the long wooden tables, where settings of balsamic vinegar, olive oil, red and white wine, water, salt, and bread are carefully arranged for each monk. Poblet is renowned for its wine, especially its Pinot Noir, a tradition nearly as ancient as the monastery's eight hundred years.

Fra Borja explains that the handcrafted pottery in shades of chestnut, burgundy, and ecru was made by one of the monks. "Each one of us is encouraged to create something of value to be used at the monastery or sold in the gift shop to support the ethos of self-reliance that we encourage here." He picks up a ceramic wine goblet and inspects it before whispering, "I'm not sure if we are earning a profit from this monk's work, however. He breaks most of the pottery before he finishes firing it."

The resident chef of Poblet, Felip Abela, a silver-haired monk in his fifties, begins the lunch preparations in the next room. After a mushroom-foraging session and a trip to the herb garden just outside the basement kitchen's door to snip parsley, thyme, and sorrel for the meal, he begins to cook. There is a massive paella pan in one corner of the room tended by Felix and Sergi, two young men who look nothing at all like monks. The one wearing a backward baseball cap pours enough olive oil to coat the bottom of the pan and concocts a deep red sofrito of tomatoes, onions, garlic, and spices before his cooking partner, who sports a Barcelona football jersey, sifts in large spoonfuls of bomba rice. The rice hisses, filling the room with a toasty aroma coupled with the potent, nose-tickling scent of the sofrito. Fra Borja whispers that the young men are not residents of Poblet but troubled youth who are trained at the monastery to be cooks. The investment arms them with a skill the monks hope will transform their lives. The novice chefs share a few jokes in Spanish with their mentor, who has opened a jar of preserved pears that he slices thinly and arranges on a dehydrating tray, to be served with whipped goat cheese and fig syrup for dessert.

After a few hours of prepping and cooking, the monks file into the rectory for their meal. They are a noisy bunch, ribbing each other as they sip Poblet wine. Fra Borja sits next to a young monk who he explains will be assisting him with his hydroponic project. "We have big plans for the future," Fra Borja says before digging his fork into his plateful of paella. He sinks his teeth into a creamy roasted potato slicked with olive oil, then pops a slice of rack-dried tomato in his mouth. He closes his eyes and grins. "A Catalonian summer right here in my mouth on a cool autumn day. Life is good, in spite of my sacrifice."

OPPOSITE
Poblet Monastery

OPPOSITE
The culinary school at Poblet

RIGHT
Harvesting olives

BELOW
The vineyards at Poblet

Shrimp and Chorizo Paella

SERVES: 6
PREPARATION TIME: 2 hours

2 tablespoons extra-virgin olive oil
8 ounces chorizo, cut into ½-inch pieces
2 medium white onions, coarsely chopped
4 garlic cloves, finely chopped
1 (16-ounce) can crushed tomatoes
2 medium tomatoes, coarsely chopped

2 roasted piquillo peppers (see page 73), coarsely chopped
½ cup chopped fresh flat-leaf parsley, coarsely chopped, plus more for garnish
1 bay leaf
1 tablespoon smoked paprika
1 teaspoon Spanish saffron threads (see page 73), crumbled
1 cup bomba rice

1 cup dry white wine
6 cups fish stock
1 teaspoon salt
1 pound large shrimp, peeled (heads and tails left on, if desired) and deveined
Lemon wedges, for serving
Crusty bread, for serving

Every country claims a national dish, and for Spain it is paella. It graces tables from north to south and east to west, each incarnation reflecting the natural resources and gastronomic customs of the region. There are several steps involved in creating this paella, but they are not complicated. With a little patience, you will discover paella's irresistible character, as the Spanish have done for centuries. At the beginning of the cooking process, the foundational ingredients—onions, garlic, tomatoes, and spices—are combined. Give these elements time to commune and chat it up a bit until they form a thick paste called a sofrito. This is your flavor bomb and with it, you're well on your way to a paella championship.

The crusty layer of rice that forms on the bottom of the pan during the final stage of the cooking process is called the socarrat. It's discussed in this recipe's notes and is another crucial factor for a sublime paella. Although a paella pan is not necessary, a wide, shallow pan is preferred because it will allow a generous socarrat to form and also enable more balanced cooking. The flame should also be evenly distributed beneath the pan, which of course means that the ideal environment is a wood-burning fire, but in case you don't find yourself living in the ultimate paella fantasy world, use two stovetop burners beneath the pan as opposed to one.

This recipe calls for spicy Spanish chorizo and shrimp, but of course, any protein combination will suffice. Note that Spanish chorizo is a cured sausage, not to be confused with raw Mexican chorizo. Chicken, lobster, fish, and mussels are excellent backup plans. Chicken or vegetable stock (or even water in a pinch) are good swaps for the fish stock. If you keep all this in mind, you'll be well on your way to a lustrous paella—just channel the resident chef at Poblet, who advises, "Let paella wander around a bit, find its footing, develop a solid foundation all on its own. It knows what it's doing. It's been doing it in Spain since the beginning of time, or at least since good food became a part of what time is all about."

PREHEAT THE OVEN to 375°F.

IN A PAELLA pan or a large, shallow ovenproof skillet, heat the oil over medium heat. Add the chorizo and sauté until crispy and golden brown, 7 to 9 minutes. Transfer to a paper towel–lined plate and set aside.

Recipe continues

ADD THE ONIONS to the fat left in the pan and sauté until tender and caramelized, about 7 minutes. Add the garlic and sauté until tender and aromatic, about 2 minutes. Add the crushed and fresh tomatoes and piquillo peppers and bring to a low simmer, then add the parsley, bay leaf, smoked paprika, and saffron. Simmer until the sofrito is thick and caramelized, about 7 minutes. Add the rice and cook for 2 minutes while stirring continuously, then add the wine and 3 cups stock and bring to a boil.

SEASON WITH THE salt, reduce the heat to medium-low, and cook at a gentle simmer until the rice has absorbed nearly all of the liquid, about 20 minutes. Stir occasionally to prevent burning. Increase the heat to medium, stir in the reserved chorizo and remaining 3 cups stock, and bring to a simmer. Cook until the rice has absorbed nearly all of the liquid, about 10 minutes. Remove the bay leaf.

ADD THE SHRIMP, burying them as deep into the rice as you can, and transfer the pan to the oven. Bake for 20 minutes, or until the shrimp are bright pink and cooked through and the socarrat is crispy and dark caramel-red. Lightly cover the pan with aluminum foil and let rest at room temperature for 10 minutes. Garnish with parsley and serve from the paella pan for dramatic effect, alongside a bowl of lemon wedges and hunks of crusty bread. Leftovers will keep in a covered container in the refrigerator for up to 5 days.

Key Paella Ingredients and Tools

The first, and many would agree, most crucial element for a successful paella is the rice. The Spanish use a short, fat rice called BOMBA, which is similar to arborio should you not be able to locate bomba at your market. Long-grain rice will not do because the grain needs to be plump and ready to soak up all the flavor.

PIQUILLO PEPPERS are a specialty of northern Spain, where their name translates as "little beaks." These diminutive red jewels are prized for their sweetness and the depth of flavor they command when roasted. Piquillos are typically roasted, seeded, and sold in jars of brine. They are available in many grocery stores and specialty Spanish markets, but should you have trouble sourcing them, roasted red bell peppers make a good substitute.

SAFFRON is prized throughout the world for its unique flavor, the color it adds to a dish, and the backbreaking work required to harvest it. Saffron is the stamen of the crocus plant, and each purple flower produces only three precious threads of saffron, making the time and labor required to procure it highly intensive. Spanish saffron is not as prized as Iranian or Kashmiri saffron, but don't tell that to a Spaniard—they covet their saffron as much as they do their wine and siestas. Of course, nothing matches the flavor of authentic Spanish saffron, but in a pinch, 2 teaspoons ground turmeric will lend a similar color to this paella recipe.

One of the most crucial reasons to use a PAELLA PAN as opposed to a pan that is not as shallow and wide is for the socarrat, the irresistible layer of rice that caramelizes on the bottom of the pan during the final stage of cooking. This crusty flavor explosion is the thing that every paella lover will inspect (and wage war for) when the pan is set down in front of them. Give your paella time to develop its socarrat by letting the magic happen in the oven as long as it needs to.

Charred Artichokes with Caper-Bacon Dipping Sauce

SERVES: 4
PREPARATION TIME: 2 hours

FOR THE DIPPING SAUCE:
4 thick-cut bacon strips, cut into ½-inch pieces
Extra-virgin olive oil, as needed
2 garlic cloves, coarsely chopped
4 large egg yolks

1 tablespoon honey
1 tablespoon freshly squeezed lemon juice, plus more to taste
1 tablespoon capers
2 teaspoons Dijon mustard
½ teaspoon red pepper flakes
Salt and freshly ground black pepper to taste

FOR THE ARTICHOKES:
2 lemons, halved, plus 2 tablespoons freshly squeezed lemon juice, plus lemon wedges for serving
4 artichokes, stems and leaf tips trimmed
Extra-virgin olive oil, for drizzling
Salt and freshly squeezed black pepper to taste

Fra Borja grows artichokes in his vast vegetable garden. He harvests them in the late summer, then pickles half of them for the winter and stores the rest in a bed of hay for use throughout the autumn. They are grilled over an oak-wood fire until their leaves are a deep caramel color and their tips are charred. In his effort to reduce food waste at Poblet, Fra Borja composts the chokes and feeds the trimmed stems to his chickens. He also recommends feeding your chickens the discarded leaves once you've eaten off all the flesh, but if you don't have chickens, a compost pile will suffice.

At Poblet, the caper-bacon dipping sauce is made from pork trimmings left over from the restaurant's meal prep, but this recipe keeps it simple and uses thick-cut bacon instead. It's brightened with the addition of capers, infused with a hint of sweetness from the honey, and finished with a quick flash of pungency from the Dijon. It's an ideal companion for artichokes but also makes a sublime sandwich spread, chip dip, or baked potato filling.

FOR THE DIPPING sauce, fry the bacon in a medium sauté pan over medium-high heat until crispy and golden brown, about 5 minutes. Using tongs or a slotted spoon, transfer the bacon to a plate. Carefully pour the rendered fat from the skillet into a 1-cup glass measuring cup. Fill the remainder of the cup with oil. Set aside.

IN A BLENDER or food processor, puree the garlic and yolks on high speed until blended. With the blender running, add the bacon, honey, lemon juice, capers, mustard, and red pepper flakes through the feed tube and puree for 1 minute, then slowly add the bacon fat mixture in a slow, steady stream until a thick emulsion forms. Add a little water if necessary to achieve the desired consistency, which should be slightly

thicker than mayonnaise. Transfer to a bowl and season with additional lemon juice, if desired, and salt and pepper. (The dipping sauce can be made ahead and stored in a covered container in the refrigerator for up to 3 days or in the freezer for up to 3 months.)

FOR THE ARTICHOKES, fill a large, heavy-bottomed pot two-thirds with water and bring to a boil. Add the lemon halves and artichokes to the boiling water, reduce the heat to medium, and simmer until the artichokes are tender and their vibrant green color is slightly more muted, about 20 minutes. Pierce one on the stem end with a sharp paring knife to check for tenderness. Meanwhile, fill a large bowl with ice water. Transfer the artichokes to the ice bath using tongs. Once the artichokes are cool enough to handle, drain them and pat them dry with a paper towel. Using a paring knife, cut them in half lengthwise, then use the knife or a spoon to remove the feathery choke, along with any of the smaller, tougher leaves. Work carefully during this step to not damage the tender heart or outer leaves. Using your palm, flatten the artichokes slightly. Drizzle them all over with oil, sprinkle with the remaining lemon juice, and season with salt and pepper. Arrange them, cut-side up, on a rimmed baking sheet, cover with a clean kitchen towel, and set aside at room temperature for 30 minutes to allow the oil, lemon juice, salt, and pepper to soak into the leaves and heart.

PREHEAT A GRILL or stovetop griddle over high heat. Using tongs, arrange the artichokes, cut-side down, on the grill. Reduce the heat to medium and cook the artichokes until the surface is golden brown and slightly charred, 5 to 6 minutes. Flip them over and cook until the leaves are golden brown, 5 to 6 minutes more. Serve the artichokes on a large platter garnished with lemon wedges, with the dipping sauce in a bowl alongside.

Pan con Tomate

Pan con tomate, or tomato bread, proves that an iconic dish can sometimes be the simplest recipe to execute. In Catalonia, tomato bread is not only synonymous with the region's cultural heritage, but it proves the irrefutable fact that the highest-quality ingredients deliver the best possible flavors. At Poblet and throughout the surrounding region, the tomàquet de penjar ("hanging tomato") flourishes in the summer months and is preserved well into the winter by suspending it by its vines on wooden drying racks to prevent premature spoilage or damage to the flesh. The result is an impressive mosaic of tomatoes that sweeten as the winter closes in. This system helps stunt the maturation process and results in an extremely juicy tomato, ideal for pan con tomate. The hanging tomato variety is available at seed and garden stores throughout the United States and Europe and is highly recommended if, like the monks of Poblet, you crave the flavor of summer in the middle of a relentless winter. The ingredients in this recipe are very flexible, and the number of tomatoes required will depend upon how juicy they are. The objective is to add enough juice to each slice of bread to generously coat it. To engage your guests, serve them slices of grilled bread accompanied by the garlic, tomatoes, olive oil, and salt, enticing them to compose this iconic Spanish treasure themselves.

PREHEAT A GRILL or heat a cast-iron skillet over high heat until nearly smoking. Grill the bread until slightly charred on both sides. Rub one side of each slice with the cut-side of a garlic clove to infuse it with flavor. Slice open a tomato and rub its juicy innards over the garlic-rubbed side of the bread. Drizzle with your very best olive oil, season with sea salt, and serve immediately.

SERVES: 4
PREPARATION TIME: 10 minutes

4 thick slices crusty bread
2 garlic cloves, halved
4 very ripe, juicy Roma tomatoes
Extra-virgin olive oil, for drizzling
Sea salt to taste

Manchego, Ham, Mushroom, and Quince Turnovers

SERVES: 4
PREPARATION TIME: 45 minutes

1 tablespoon unsalted butter
2 garlic cloves, finely chopped
1 cup thinly sliced cremini mushrooms
2 frozen puff pastry rectangles, thawed in the refrigerator and kept chilled
4 thick slices Manchego cheese
4 thin slices Iberico ham
4 (¼-inch-thick) slices quince paste from a rectangular block
1 large egg, beaten

The fruit of the quince tree, or membrillo in Spanish, ripens around the grounds of Poblet long after summer fades. The monks harvest the quince with a brisk wind swirling around them, rustling the dried leaves in the vineyard that have turned amber and gold. A few pieces of fruit will be served that evening at dinner, tucked into a puff pastry triangle with a thick slice of jamón Ibérico. If you have trouble sourcing Iberico ham, prosciutto or even bacon can be used as a substitute. The monks at Poblet use cèpes or rovelló mushrooms in their turnovers, depending upon the season. Chanterelles, morels, or shiitakes would also make tasty substitutes.

PREHEAT THE OVEN to 375°F. Line a rimmed baking sheet with aluminum foil.

MELT THE BUTTER in a large sauté pan over medium heat. Add the garlic and mushrooms and sauté until the garlic is aromatic and the mushrooms are tender, about 5 minutes. Set aside to cool slightly. Cut the chilled puff pastry rectangles in half. Depending upon whether you would like your turnovers to be triangles or rectangles, place a slice of cheese on one half of a square, making sure that the filling leaves about 1 inch of the dough edge exposed. Top it with a slice of ham and a slice of quince paste. Spoon a quarter of the mushrooms and garlic on top. Using a pastry brush, wet the edges of the puff pastry with water. Fold the remaining dough over to form a turnover and seal the edges together by first pressing gently with your finger and then crimping with a fork. Using a spatula, transfer the turnover to the prepared baking sheet. Repeat with the remaining 3 turnovers. Brush the top of each turnover with the egg and bake until puffed and golden brown, 20 to 25 minutes. Serve hot or cold, depending upon your preference. The turnovers will keep in a covered container in the refrigerator for up to 3 days, but they taste best when enjoyed fresh.

Persimmon Harvest Salad

SERVES: 4
PREPARATION TIME: 15 minutes

FOR THE SALAD:
½ cup skin-on hazelnuts, pecans, or walnuts
3 persimmons, halved and thinly sliced
2 tart apples, such as Fuji or Granny Smith, cored, halved, and thinly sliced
1 cup packed arugula
Salt and freshly ground black pepper to taste
Torn fresh basil leaves, for garnish (optional)

FOR THE DRESSING:
1 teaspoon finely chopped fresh ginger
1 tablespoon honey
1 tablespoon sherry vinegar
1 tablespoon extra-virgin olive oil
1 teaspoon grated orange zest
1 tablespoon freshly squeezed orange juice

Spanish persimmons, which are referred to as kaki in Spain, are one of fall's sweetest offerings. They are a luscious, stone-free fruit with a taut, shiny skin resembling a tomato with the hue of a fiery Catalonian sunset. Persimmons are harvested at Poblet in the late fall when they are tender, vibrant peachy-orange, and at their peak of sweetness. The monks arrange them neatly in rows in wooden crates that line one entire wall of their cavernous pantry. Fra Borja eats them like apples, "at least one per day when they are in season," and also uses them as a basis for a pork loin marinade, transforms them into jam, and drizzles them with heavy cream sprinkled with torn mint leaves for one of the Poblet monks' favorite autumn desserts. He also makes a chutney that includes the persimmons and their blossoms. In this recipe, they're paired with fall flavors such as tart apples, toasted hazelnuts, and just enough honey to mellow out the sherry vinegar. Fra Borja closes his eyes when he takes the first bite of his daily persimmon. He chews slowly, swallows, and says, "The Greek name for persimmon is *diospyros*, which translates as 'fruit of the gods.'" Not opening his eyes, he takes another generous bite. It's clear that he agrees.

PREHEAT THE OVEN to 350°F.

ARRANGE THE HAZELNUTS in a single layer on a rimmed baking sheet and toast until light golden brown, 6 to 7 minutes. Set aside to cool to room temperature.

MEANWHILE, MAKE THE dressing. In a small bowl, whisk together the ginger, honey, vinegar, olive oil, orange zest, and juice until incorporated.

IN A LARGE bowl, combine the persimmons, apples, toasted hazelnuts, and arugula. Drizzle the dressing on top and toss gently to combine. Season with salt and pepper. Garnish with basil, if desired, and serve. Store leftovers in a covered container in the refrigerator for up to 1 day (after that the persimmons become mushy).

Marinated Olives and Almonds

SERVES: 4
PREPARATION TIME: 30 minutes

1 cup Marcona almonds
1 cup aromatic and flavorful olives, such as Farga, Morruda, Empeltre, or Arbequina, unpitted

4 garlic cloves, thinly sliced
3 or 4 (2-inch) strips lemon zest (see headnote)
1 teaspoon finely chopped fresh rosemary
½ teaspoon red pepper flakes
2 cups robust extra-virgin olive oil
Crunchy sea salt, such as Maldon, to taste

"When I need time for contemplation and meditation in the winter, I take my little rake outside with me and harvest olives. I mindfully rake them from their branches, listening to the sound of them dropping onto the canvas awaiting them below," say Fra Borja as he pulls a branch heavy with olives to his face and deeply inhales their aroma. The Arbequina olive trees that flourish in the alkaline-rich soil on the grounds of Poblet are harvested in November and December. They thrive in the long, hot days of the Mediterranean summer but are resilient enough to withstand a winter frost. This variety is dark brown, symmetrical, buttery in flavor, and quite a bit smaller than many of their counterparts. They have a gentle, peppery aroma with a subtle floral aftertaste. The monks at Poblet brine about one-third of their harvest in huge glass jars that are stored beneath burlap potato sacks to keep them in darkness during the brining process. The remaining bounty is pressed for olive oil, which the monks dip their bread into and drizzle over their food at every meal.

Tarragona is known for its Largueta almonds, with their distinctive, flat, elongated shape. The origin of this variety is unknown, but they are purely and distinctively Spanish. In this recipe, I have substituted Marcona almonds because they are similar and easier to source, but if you are able to find Largueta almonds, by all means use them. Almonds are typically harvested in the region in late August through September by spreading vast nets beneath the trees to catch the almonds that fall from their branches after ripening. The monks at Poblet know their almonds are ready to give way when the velvety, mossy-green drupe protecting the nut within splits open. Elsewhere, almonds are frequently harvested using a machine to shake the nuts from their branches, but at Poblet, the monks continue to harvest in the same way almond growers have done it for centuries, by hand-picking the almonds growing at the bottom of the tree and using a long wooden pole to shake those free near the top onto a net. The almonds are then left to dry in the hot summer sun before the net is gathered up and the almonds are distributed into bushel baskets. Spain is the second-largest almond producer in the world, and in Tarragona, they are vital for one of the region's most beloved recipes, romesco sauce, composed of garlic, hazelnuts, tomatoes, parsley, and almonds.

In this recipe, do not discard the flavorful cooking oil, but instead reserve it for dipping hunks of crusty bread just like the monks do at Poblet. Use a vegetable peeler to create the thick ribbons of lemon zest, being careful to not take too much of the astringent white pith along with it. Thyme is a good substitute for the rosemary.

COMBINE THE ALMONDS, olives, garlic, lemon zest, rosemary, red pepper flakes, and olive oil in a small saucepan and bring to a simmer over medium heat. Reduce the heat to low and gently simmer until the almonds are tender and the oil is aromatic, about 15 minutes. Remove from the heat and let them cool to room temperature.

DISCARD THE LEMON zest. Transfer the almonds, olives, and oil to a bowl and sprinkle with crunchy sea salt. They will keep in a covered container at room temperature for up to 1 week, but they're so good they will most likely not last for more than an afternoon.

Stuffed Cannelloni with Béchamel Sauce

SERVES: 6
PREPARATION TIME: 1½ hours

FOR THE CANNELLONI:
Butter, for greasing
Salt and freshly ground black pepper to
    taste
24 cannelloni
1 tablespoon extra-virgin olive oil
1 medium white onion, finely chopped
2 garlic cloves, finely chopped

2 tablespoons dry sherry
1 pound ground pork
½ cup chicken stock
1 cup ricotta
1 large egg
¼ cup ground skinless almonds
¼ cup plain bread crumbs
½ teaspoon red pepper flakes
¼ teaspoon grated fresh nutmeg
Chopped leaves from 2 thyme sprigs

FOR THE BÉCHAMEL:
2 tablespoons unsalted butter
2 tablespoons all-purpose flour
1⅓ cups whole milk
¼ cup ground skinless almonds
Pinch grated fresh nutmeg
Salt and freshly ground black pepper to
    taste
1½ cups shaved Manchego cheese

There is a culinary school at Poblet run by a Cistercian monk from Bolivia named Fra Pablo Flores. He's passionate about his work with disadvantaged youth from the region, who are invited to attend the school at no cost in exchange for completing tasks within the monastery such as cleaning, preparing meals for the monks and monastic guests, helping with the many harvests that take place throughout the year, and working in the gift shop. Stuffed cannelloni is one of the signature dishes the students are expected to master toward the end of their curriculum. Fra Flores says, "When I've tasted a perfect béchamel prepared by one of my students, I know they've mastered many things besides a cooking skill. They have also mastered patience and careful observation, skills they can carry with them into the world beyond the kitchen."

The small culinary school is situated near the main entrance to the monastery. Inside, there are rooms filled with the usual equipment one would find in a culinary school—refrigerators, ovens, industrial tables, pots and pans, speed racks lined with sheet trays. But there is also a small room near the front door containing three narrow beds, a few dressers, mirrors, and a sink. "Is this the boarding room for the students?" I ask Fra Flores. "No," he replies. It's where travelers are invited to stay." "For a fee?" I ask. He shakes his head no and says, "Any traveler passing through is invited to stay here for a few days if they are in need of shelter. They are invited to dine in the refectory with the monks and are treated as valued members of our community. It is the lesson of the Good Samaritan in the Gospel of Luke. We must always be willing to help someone in need. It should be one of our most valued rules in life."

PREHEAT THE OVEN to 400°F. Lightly butter a baking dish that is large enough to hold all of the cannelloni.

BRING A LARGE pot of salted water to a boil and add the cannelloni. Reduce the heat to medium to maintain a gentle simmer and cook until tender, 7 to 9 minutes. Line a rimmed baking sheet or large plate with a clean kitchen towel, drain the cannelloni, and arrange in a single layer to drain.

HEAT THE OIL in a large sauté pan over medium-high heat. Reduce the heat to medium-low, add the onion and garlic, and sauté until the onion is aromatic and caramelized, 8 to 10 minutes. Deglaze the pan with the sherry, scraping up the flavorful brown bits at the bottom of the pan. Add the pork and chicken stock, increase the heat to medium-high, and sauté until cooked through and the liquid has been absorbed, 12 to 14 minutes, stirring occasionally to prevent the onion from scorching. Remove from the heat and let it cool.

IN A SMALL bowl, combine the ricotta, egg, ground almonds, bread crumbs, red pepper flakes, nutmeg, and thyme and stir until well mixed. Stir in the pork and season with salt and pepper.

CAREFULLY FILL THE cannelloni with the pork mixture by spooning a portion into each side, making sure it meets in the middle (it's such a disappointment to discover that the middle of your cannelloni is unstuffed!). The mixture should fill the cannelloni but not bulge it. Arrange the cannelloni, side by side, nice and snug, in the prepared baking dish as you stuff them.

TO MAKE THE béchamel, melt the butter in a heavy-bottomed saucepan over medium heat. Add the flour, reduce the heat to medium-low, and stir constantly using a wooden spoon. The butter and flour will come together to form a runny, ivory-colored paste known as a roux. Keep stirring until the roux begins to form tiny bubbles, but do not let it turn golden brown. Increase the heat to medium and gradually add the milk in a slow, steady stream while stirring constantly. In about a minute, the roux should begin to boil. At this point, reduce the heat to medium-low and continue to stir until the roux thickens enough that a line is left behind the spoon when it runs through the roux, 3 to 4 minutes. Remove from the heat, stir in the ground almonds and nutmeg, and season with salt and pepper.

POUR THE BÉCHAMEL over the cannelloni in an even layer, sprinkle with the Manchego, and bake until the cheese is bubbling and golden brown, 20 to 25 minutes. Serve while hot and bubbly. Leftovers will keep in a covered container in the refrigerator for up to 3 days.

Chicken with Catalan Picada

SERVES: 6
PREPARATION TIME: 1 hour 15 minutes

FOR THE CHICKEN:

4 bone-in, skin-on whole chicken legs
Salt and freshly ground black pepper to taste
2 tablespoons extra-virgin olive oil
1 large yellow onion, coarsely chopped
3 garlic cloves, finely chopped
1 teaspoon finely chopped fresh ginger
¼ cup oloroso sherry (see headnote)
½ cup grated bittersweet chocolate, preferably 70%

1 teaspoon finely grated orange zest
¼ cup freshly squeezed orange juice
1 cup chicken stock
2 bay leaves
1 cinnamon stick
½ teaspoon red pepper flakes
¼ teaspoon ground cloves
Coarsely chopped fresh flat-leaf parsley, for garnish
Steamed rice or couscous (see page 331), for serving

FOR THE PICADA:

⅔ cup ground skinless almonds
½ cup bread crumbs
Salt and freshly ground black pepper to taste
Leaves from 5 flat-leaf parsley sprigs
1 teaspoon grated lemon zest
1 teaspoon anise seeds
½ teaspoon Spanish saffron threads (see page 73), crumbled
½ teaspoon red pepper flakes
½ teaspoon ground cinnamon
¼ teaspoon ground cloves
1 tablespoon extra-virgin olive oil
2 garlic cloves, finely chopped

This classic Catalonian dish is prepared often at Poblet by the cooks in the monastery's professional kitchen. It's served to the monks in their refectory as well as in the cantina to monastic visitors. The chicken sauce is essentially a Catalan version of mole, with a hint of bittersweet chocolate and blend of spices. Oloroso sherry, which is produced in the southern Spanish region of Andalusia, is a dark chestnut color and has a deep, nutty flavor. Feel free to substitute another dry Spanish sherry, such as palo cortado, raya, or amontillado should you have difficulty sourcing oloroso. Picada, essentially a Catalan pesto, will become your go-to for countless recipes. It's lovely tossed with pasta, added to salads, served as a vegetable dip, or slathered generously over thick, crusty bread.

SEASON THE CHICKEN all over with salt and pepper. Heat the oil in a large, heavy-bottomed sauté pan over high heat until it's shimmering. Reduce the heat to medium and add the chicken, skin-side down. Sear until golden brown, 4 to 5 minutes, then flip and repeat on the other side. Transfer the chicken to a plate. Add the onion, garlic, and ginger to the pan and sauté until the onion is aromatic and translucent, 5 to 6 minutes. Deglaze the pan by adding the sherry, scraping up the flavorful brown bits on the bottom of the pan. Increase the heat to high, add the chocolate, orange zest and juice, stock, bay leaves, cinnamon stick, red pepper flakes, and cloves and bring to a boil. Cook for 2 minutes, reduce the heat to medium-low, and return the chicken to the pan, skin-side down. Cover the pan and gently simmer for 15 minutes. Flip the chicken over and simmer for another 10 minutes. Season with salt and pepper.

MEANWHILE, MAKE THE picada. Preheat the oven to 350°F.

IN A SMALL bowl, combine the almonds and bread crumbs. Season with salt and pepper and evenly distribute onto a rimmed baking sheet. Bake until golden brown and aromatic, 6 to 7 minutes. Keep an eye on the mixture as it toasts to prevent it from burning. Transfer the mixture to the bowl of a food processor and add the parsley, lemon zest, anise seeds, saffron, red pepper flakes, ground cinnamon, and cloves. Heat the oil in a small sauté pan over medium-high heat. Add the garlic and sauté until aromatic, 3 to 4 minutes. Add the garlic to the food processor and pulse until everything begins to come together. Process on high until a paste is formed. If it is too dry and crumbly, add a little water to achieve a paste consistency.

TRANSFER THE PICADA to the chicken pan and stir until well incorporated. Gently simmer over low heat for 10 to 15 minutes, stirring occasionally to prevent scorching. Remove the cinnamon stick and bay leaves. Season with salt and pepper. Garnish with chopped parsley and serve alongside a heaping bowl of rice or couscous to soak up the unctuous sauce. Leftovers can be stored in a covered container in the refrigerator for up to 3 days.

Sangria

MAKES: about 4 quarts
PREPARATION TIME: 10 minutes, plus 2 hours to chill

2 oranges, thinly sliced and seeded
2 lemons, thinly sliced and seeded
1 pear, cored and thinly sliced
⅔ cup granulated sugar
2 (750-mL) bottles tempranillo or other high-quality Spanish red wine

½ cup triple sec
½ cup brandy
2 star anise pods
1 cinnamon stick
6 whole cloves
12 skinned almonds
3 (12-ounce) cans club soda or seltzer

It is said that the Romans invented the tradition of wine-making, but it was the Spanish winemakers of Catalonia whom they depended upon to stock their ancient cellars. Two millennia ago, Spanish wine from this region was transported to Rome in terra-cotta jugs from the port of Tarragona, then known as Tarraco. It was a robust trading route that survived for centuries until the Moorish conquest of territory in the early eighth century. Spanish wine production ceased in order to comply with the Islamic practice of abstaining from alcohol. The Frankish Empire conquered Barcelona in 801 and created a Christian buffer zone referred to as Marca Hispánica.

In 1151, the Count of Barcelona, Ramon Berenguer, founded Poblet and donated the monastery and its surrounding territory to the Cistercian monks of the Abbaye de Fontfroide in France. These early monks brought their Burgundian style of winemaking to Poblet, along with the unique single varietal Pinot Noir grape that is still cultivated in the monastic vineyards today. Even though the winery at Poblet now boasts a state-of-the-art production facility, the original, nearly nine-century-old winemaking equipment is still waiting to be rediscovered in one of Poblet's basements.

Poblet's contemporary winemakers still adhere to the noninvasive practices and natural yeast fermentation of their ninth-century Cistercian counterparts. Along with the original Pinot Noir grape, today's varietals also include several local grapes that reflect the terroir of the region, including garrut, grenache, trepat, and tempranillo. Predominant among these is trepat, a fragrant, low-tannin, highly acidic grape with a bright and peppery flavor.

Vineyards surround Poblet on all sides, glowing a fiery red in the autumn and painting the rolling fields in a blaze of electric green in the summer. The Abadía de Poblet is the only winery in Catalonia housed within a historical site, and while the monks typically drink their wine unadulterated, sangria is an elixir for flaming-hot summer days. Experiment with the fruit. At Poblet they add everything from figs and grapes to apples and limes. The almonds are not necessary, but since they flourish at the monastery, a handful is usually added because it's always a treat to discover an almond in your sangria. Hazelnuts or walnuts make fine substitutes.

COMBINE THE ORANGE and lemon slices, pear, and sugar in a large pitcher and, using a wooden spoon or a muddler, gently muddle for a minute or two. Set aside for 15 minutes to encourage the fruit to release their juices. Add the wine and stir briskly until the sugar dissolves, 3 to 4 minutes. Add the triple sec, brandy, star anise, cinnamon, cloves, and almonds and stir for a minute more. Refrigerate until chilled to give the flavors an opportunity to mingle. Taste and add more sugar if you desire a sweeter sangria. Just before serving, add the club soda and enough ice to fill the pitcher. Serve in festive glasses.

Panellets

MAKES: 30 to 35 panellets
PREPARATION TIME: 1 hour, plus overnight to chill

1 pound skinless almonds
2⅔ cups granulated sugar
½ teaspoon finely grated lemon zest
1 teaspoon freshly squeezed lemon juice
1 medium Idaho potato, boiled, skinned, and mashed well using a fork or potato masher
Salt to taste
1 cup pine nuts
2 large egg whites

These traditional Catalan almond sweets are served only once a year at Poblet, on Día de Todos los Santos, or All Saints Day, on November 1, a holiday of remembrance of deceased loved ones. They are enjoyed by the monks and are offered to anyone visiting the monastery. Panellets are tiny cookies or cakes made from equal parts almonds and sugar. This is the most traditional version of the recipe and is the one enjoyed at Poblet, but feel free to experiment with additional flourishes such as rolling the balls in shredded coconut, cocoa powder, or cinnamon sugar instead of pine nuts, or adding a bit of cocoa or espresso to the dough before chilling it. A glass of cava or Moscatel sherry typically accompanies these tantalizing little sweets.

IN THE BOWL of a food processor, blend the almonds on high speed until finely ground. Set aside.

COMBINE THE SUGAR and 1¼ cups water in a small saucepan and bring to a boil over high heat. Add the lemon zest and juice, reduce the heat to medium, and simmer until the sugar is dissolved and the liquid has reduced enough to form a syrup, stirring occasionally to prevent scorching. Remove from the heat and add the ground almonds, mashed potato, and a pinch of salt. Stir using a wooden spoon until well incorporated. Transfer to a bowl and cool to room temperature, then cover the bowl and refrigerate overnight.

THE NEXT DAY, preheat the oven to 375°F. Line a rimmed baking sheet with parchment paper.

USING YOUR HANDS, roll the chilled dough into 1-inch balls. Put the pine nuts in a small bowl. Put the egg whites in another small bowl. Dip each ball in the pine nuts and gently press on all sides to cover the ball. Using a pastry brush, lightly brush each ball on all sides with the egg white. Arrange the balls on the prepared baking sheet and bake until the pine nuts begin to turn a light golden brown, 5 to 6 minutes. Watch the panellets carefully to avoid burning the pine nuts. Transfer them to a plate and cool to room temperature. They can be kept in a covered container at room temperature for up to 3 days or in the refrigerator for up to 1 week.

4

Thikse Monastery

TIBETAN BUDDHISM
LEH, LADAKH, INDIA

"There is a saying in Tibetan, 'Tragedy should be utilized as a source of strength.' No matter what sort of difficulties, how painful the experience is, if we lose our hope, that's our real disaster."

—*Dalai Lama*

ABOVE
The monks of Thikse enjoying lunch

RIGHT
The many ways apricots are
processed

OPPOSITE
Thikse

In step with the rising sun, a young monk named Chodak is preparing yak butter tea in the sparse kitchen of Thikse, a Buddhist monastery perched atop a snowy 12,000-foot peak towering above a desert valley in Ladakh, a remote state in the Indian Himalayas that is a sanctuary for Tibetans in exile. He wears a crimson robe, has a large red birthmark on his left cheek, and his hair is shorn close to his scalp. Bells ring loudly in the distance signaling the call to prayer, but he is not distracted from his duties.

A beam of sunlight glints on the hammered copper pot filled with hot black tea, which he stirs with a wooden spoon as long as he is tall. The pot hangs from an iron tripod over a blazing wood fire. Chodak wears orange hunter's gloves to protect his hands from the flames that lick the sides. He sprinkles salt into the tea, then adds a large bowl of softened yak butter, milk curds, and toasted barley flour. He stirs methodically for several more minutes until the mixture is creamy, aromatic, and the color of almonds.

He strains the tea into a second copper pot sitting between his sandaled feet and ladles it into a long row of clay cups arranged on a shelf from one end of the kitchen to the other. A gong sounds just as the monk fills the last cup. The other monks file in from prayer, chattering to each other and sharing an occasional joke that makes a few of them double over with laughter. They range in age from four to ninety-three. Each one reaches for a cup of tea to warm them as they wait for their breakfast of barley dumplings stuffed with yak's cheese, purple carrots, and ginger. They carry their tea outside to sit beneath the sun that beams down upon them from a clear blue Himalayan sky. It is the start of another day at Thikse, and it begins just as it has for nearly four hundred years.

The Indian state of Ladakh is accessible by taking either a two-hour flight from Delhi, the plane nearly skimming the snowcapped Himalayas, or a daylong bus ride across the three highest drivable mountain passes in the world. Much of this drive is on a dirt road that I experienced with my hands clenched, white-knuckled, around the seat back handle of the rickety bus for nearly the entire 22 hours it took to get there. The high altitude of Ladakh has the potential to fell even the most stalwart of travelers. The anemic air robs them of their breath and seizes hold of their brain with a vice grip that pinches like a million bee stings.

Ladakh is the region where the Tibetans have found safe refuge from the Chinese forces that have occupied their homeland. They are free to live without persecution in this remote but majestic place. It is ringed by mountains capped with glaciers that never melt. In the winter, temperatures dip well below zero, the roads are blocked by snowfall, and the airport is open only for emergency landings. The state is closed off from the rest of the world until spring comes around once more.

The nearby town of Leh buzzes with energy when more hospitable weather finally rolls in. Buddhist monks in flowing red robes—called chougu in Tibetan—mingle with the rest of the Ladakhi population in markets that sell vegetables like daikon, potatoes, cabbage, and bulbs of ginger that farmers coax patiently from dusty, parched fields. The aroma of momos, or dumplings, frying in hot chili oil fills the brisk air. The whirring sounds of ever-spinning prayer wheels send the hopes and wishes of the Ladakhi people through the wind to the mountaintops crowned by ancient monasteries.

OPPOSITE
Yak butter tea production

" Traditions live on inside of us. We had to remind the people here how important it is to pass a legacy down to their children, to keep their spirits intact no matter how great the suffering. For hardship is only overcome by making the choice to live."

Trying to connect with the monks of Ladakh in advance of our visit proved futile; Tibetan Buddhist practitioners in these far-flung corners of the world are not generally on the internet. We had to wait until we arrived to determine which monastery we would visit. When we asked a monk in the marketplace which destination would be best, he responded without hesitation and with the infectious exuberance shared by most of the monks in Ladakh, "Thikse!"

The first monk we encountered the next morning as we climbed the steep stairs to Thikse, a white monastery seemingly tumbling down from a precipitous mountain peak, was the one we had met the day before. He enthusiastically pointed us in the direction of the kitchen before continuing down the stairs, red robe fanning out behind him in the wind. Encountering him and his perpetually grinning face seemed a good omen until we knocked on the kitchen door. We explained what we hoped to do and were told that we could not cook with the monks that day.

Disappointed, we began to walk away when the resident chef, an Indian Navy cook turned Buddhist monk called us back. He had salt-and-pepper hair and wore a silky black Members Only jacket. He stopped us and explained that the cooking was already done for the day, but we were more than welcome to come back in the morning. When we asked what time, he said without apology, "When the sun first begins to appear on the horizon."

I brought with me a bag of root vegetables the next morning as a token of gratitude. After the monks were assembled out in the sunshine, Chodak explained as he cleaned up his tea station that each monk rotates through all of the kitchen stations at the monastery except the cook. He stays where he is because, as Chodak said through a grin, "He is the best cook in Ladakh, and our momos would suffer without him."

Following the morning tea, we were invited to participate in the rest of the day's rituals. They included a mesmerizing drumming session while sharing handfuls of tsampa (roasted barley flour) and yak butter tea mixed into a shaggy dough. We were also allowed to prep for the day's meal with the chef, Jampa. The years of cooking at sea for a ship full of hungry sailors were evident in his deft knife skills; he made fast work of the daikon, cabbage, carrots, onions, garlic, and potatoes in front of him.

As Jampa prepared a thick batter for his momo wrappers, he explained that barley once flourished in the fields surrounding Thikse, but over time, the Tibetans who sought refuge in Ladakh lost the will to grow anything as the sorrow from losing their homeland engulfed them. The monks of Thikse and surrounding monasteries made it their mission to return barley to the fields. They encouraged the Tibetan population to take pride in growing it and to see it as a tradition they would one day pass on to their children. Jampa told us, "Traditions live on inside of us. We had to remind the people here how important it is to pass a legacy down to their children, to keep their spirits intact no matter how great the suffering. For hardship is only overcome by making the choice to live. In Ladakh, barley represents that decision."

Jampa filled each momo shell with a combination of fresh cow's milk cheese, onions, garlic, and spices. He said, "Spices help us stay alert to all of the beauty in the world." Once lunch was ready, dozens of monks spilled into the kitchen. They noisily filled their tin plates from the buffet of Tibetan delicacies before them. They ate outside under the blue Himalayan sky and scooped any leftovers into a dog dish shared by Thikse's three resident canines.

I asked the monk sitting next to me, a man in his mid-twenties named Tashi, about the dogs. He said, "We did not adopt them. They adopted us. Each one arrived by walking up the mountain to Thikse's door. You cannot turn away a living being in need, and they made the decision to honor us by living out their lives here. They are wise, good-natured dogs." I couldn't help but think that they must indeed be wise dogs. They made the choice, after all, to find their way to Thikse.

OPPOSITE
The morning prayer and drumming ceremony

Spinach, Ricotta, and Barley Momos with Ginseng-Yogurt Dipping Sauce

MAKES: about 30 momos

PREPARATION TIME: 45 minutes, plus 1 hour for the dough to rest

FOR THE DIPPING SAUCE:
1 cup Greek-style yogurt
2 teaspoons grated fresh ginseng or ginger
Salt to taste

FOR THE MOMOS:
2 cups all-purpose flour, plus more for dusting
¾ to 1 cup boiled water, kept hot
Salt and freshly ground black pepper to taste
8 cups spinach leaves
1½ cups ricotta cheese
½ cup cooked pearl barley
1 small red onion, finely chopped
1 garlic clove, finely chopped
Pinch red pepper flakes (optional)
½ cup chopped fresh flat-leaf parsley
Canola or peanut oil, for greasing
Sepen (page 107), for serving (optional)

Fried, steamed, or poached in hot soup, these juicy dumplings are on the menu in virtually every home and restaurant throughout Ladakh. The steamed variety are the most popular and are stuffed with any combination of meat, vegetables, or cheese.

I spoke to a chef in Ladakh's capital of Leh who served momos from his tiny kitchen consisting of a two-burner stove, a tiny sink for washing up, and a framed photograph of the Dalai Lama on a wall with a red patina. His four-table restaurant overlooked the city's main market, where Tibetan prayer flags, colorful yak wool blankets, and chunky turquoise rings and necklaces were sold. He told me that the main things to consider when making momos is first the dough, then the filling, and finally the preparation. He also assured me that no momo recipe is perfect because they are constantly shifting based upon each family's preferences and seasonal ingredient availability. "The dough is like a canvas for a painter. Use your imagination to create something beautiful," he said with a smile.

His momo recipe incorporates ricotta, spinach, and barley, three of the most popular ingredients in Thikse's momos. The dipping sauce is my own twist on the ginseng sauce I was served at the monastery. Tibetan ginseng is prized for its many nutritional benefits, including the promotion of cardiovascular health and the belief that it improves mood and increases mental alertness. It's available in many Asian markets, but feel free to substitute ginger if ginseng proves difficult to source. At Thikse, they also serve their momos with a fiery red pepper sauce called sepen, so feel free to add a little heat just as a Ladakhi monk would do.

TO MAKE THE dipping sauce, in a small bowl, stir together the yogurt and ginseng, then season with salt. Cover and refrigerate until ready to use. (The dipping sauce can be made up to a day ahead of time.)

TO MAKE THE momo dough, put the flour in a large bowl and create a well in the center. Add ¾ cup hot water in a steady stream. Don't worry about mixing it in as you pour it, but once it has all been added, stir it deftly with a wooden spoon. It will be crumbly at first, but this will give way to a smoother texture in the next step. The flour should be completely moistened by the water. If necessary, add a little more hot water, teaspoon by teaspoon, until it comes together without resistance. Knead the dough with your hands on a floured work surface. It should take on a smooth texture in 5 to 7 minutes. The most important thing during this stage is to keep the dough moist. Once the dough is pliable and bounces back when you poke it with your finger to only a subtle indentation, place it in a plastic bag or in a bowl covered with a damp kitchen towel. Let the dough rest at room temperature for 1 hour.

MEANWHILE, MAKE THE filling. Bring a large pot of salted water to a boil. Add the spinach and let it cook for 1 minute. Transfer it with a slotted spoon or a wire spider to a colander. Once it is cool enough to handle, tightly squeeze out the excess water. Coarsely chop the spinach, then transfer it to a medium bowl. Add the ricotta, barley, onion, garlic, red pepper flakes (if using), and parsley. Stir to combine, then season with salt and pepper.

NOW IT'S MOMO time. This next step is a little tricky, but it's easy to get into a rhythm after a few attempts. You will need a rolling pin, a tablespoon, a 3-inch biscuit cutter (a clean tuna can or a glass of about the same diameter would also work), and a steamer. Lightly oil one or two steamer trays.

ON A CLEAN work surface, roll the dough into a thin sheet, slightly less than ⅛ inch thick. Punch out circles using the biscuit cutter. Take one of the circles in your hand and fill its center with about 1 tablespoon of filling. Be sure to leave enough room along the edge to close your momo. Fold it over into a half-moon shape, then pinch the sides completely closed. If you'd like to add a decorative finish, begin at the top of the seal and gently pinch a small bit of dough and twist it slightly. Do this repeatedly all the way down. With a little practice, you'll find the shape that appeals most to you. As you finish each momo, place it on an oiled steamer tray. About 15 momos will fit on a tray, so a double steamer is ideal.

POUR ABOUT 2 inches of water into the base of the steamer and bring it to a boil. Place the filled steamer trays on top, cover, and steam until the dough is cooked through and the filling is hot inside, about 10 minutes.

SERVE THE MOMOS hot, with the dipping sauce and sepen, if you like. Leftovers will keep in a covered container in the refrigerator for up to 4 days.

Tangtse with Roasted Peanuts and Cilantro-Orange Vinaigrette

This salad is fresh and bright with a crunchy texture and a toasty finish thanks to the roasted peanuts. In Tibetan, this salad is referred to as tangtse, which means "cold vegetables." It's considered to be a food for long life and is served as an accompaniment to a wide variety of Tibetan dishes. Toss with soba or rice noodles to make it a main dish. Take it a step further by marinating chicken breast slices or deveined shrimp in additional vinaigrette before sautéing in peanut oil and then tossing into the salad. For extra vibrancy, add julienned green apple or green papaya for a Thai twist.

IN A LARGE bowl, combine the cabbage, carrot, daikon, and chile, if using.

IN A SMALL bowl, combine the citrus juices, orange zest, oil, cilantro, and honey and whisk vigorously with a fork until emulsified. Season with salt.

POUR THE VINAIGRETTE over the shredded vegetables and toss together until everything is glistening. Season with additional salt, if desired. Sprinkle with peanuts and serve family-style with a small bowl of lime wedges alongside. The salad should be eaten as soon as possible because this is when it's most crisp, but in a pinch, it will keep in a covered container in the refrigerator for up to 2 days. Just be sure to add the vinaigrette right before serving.

SERVES: 4
PREPARATION TIME: 30 minutes

½ head white cabbage, thinly sliced
1 large carrot, peeled and julienned
1 medium daikon radish, peeled and julienned
1 Thai chile (optional), seeded and finely chopped
Juice of 1 lime, plus lime wedges for serving
Juice of 1 small orange
1 teaspoon grated orange zest
1 tablespoon peanut oil
2 cilantro sprigs, finely chopped
1 tablespoon honey
Salt to taste
Roasted peanuts, coarsely chopped, for garnish

Sepen

MAKES: about 1 cup
PREPARATION TIME: 10 minutes

1 small white onion, coarsely chopped
3 garlic cloves, coarsely chopped
1 tablespoon finely chopped fresh ginger
3 long red chiles, such as Kashmiri, coarsely chopped
2 teaspoons ground cumin
1 teaspoon ground turmeric
¼ teaspoon whole red Szechuan peppercorns (optional)
Pinch asafoetida (optional)
2 Roma tomatoes, coarsely chopped
Salt to taste

This fiery condiment is never in short supply at Thikse, where the monks enjoy it with their momos, skyu, and thukpa. Every household, restaurant, and monastery in Ladakh has their own variation; this is the one used at Thikse. It's typically available at every meal, a small spoonful delivering a fiery mouthful of flavor. In Tibet and at Ladakh, sepen is traditionally made using Tibetan lhasa chiles, 4-inch-long peppers that transform from a lime green color to deep brick red as they mature. Lhasa peppers are hearty and slow-growing, ideal for the cool spring, summer, and fall Himalayan seasons. Sepen adds heat to milder Tibetan recipes such as momos, giving these recipes more character and depth. It also adds a vibrant hue to these dishes, which tend to fall into the brown section of the color spectrum. After the initial jolt of fire, sepen leaves behind a feeling of gratifying warmth, a valued commodity on a fiercely cold Himalayan day. Feel free to reduce the amount of chiles called for in this recipe should you desire a tamer incarnation. The optional Szechuan peppercorns infuse the sepen with a shot of electricity that enlivens the tongue the moment it hits it. Asafoetida is a naturally derived flavoring with a slightly sulfurous aroma that adds a deep, savory note to recipes. It's optional, but if you are able to source it, a generous pinch in this recipe is highly recommended. The sepen in this recipe is blended using a food processor, but feel free to use a mortar and pestle in the same way the Ladakhi monks prepare it.

IN THE BOWL of a food processor, combine the onion, garlic, ginger, chiles, cumin, turmeric, Szechuan peppercorns (if using), and asafoetida (if using) and pulse until just incorporated. Add the tomatoes and process on low speed until blended. Season with salt. Store sepen in a covered container in the refrigerator for up to 2 weeks.

Skyu

SERVES: 4
PREPARATION TIME: 1 hour

FOR THE NOODLES:
4 cups whole wheat flour, plus more as
    needed
1 teaspoon salt

FOR THE SKYU:
1 tablespoon unsalted butter
1 large yellow onion, coarsely chopped
3 carrots, peeled and coarsely chopped
2 celery ribs, thinly sliced

1 tablespoon finely chopped fresh ginger
2 garlic cloves, finely chopped
3 Roma tomatoes, coarsely chopped
2 teaspoons garam masala
2 teaspoons ground turmeric
½ teaspoon chili powder
1 cup fresh or frozen peas
1 cup lightly packed spinach leaves
1 cup heavy cream
Salt to taste
Coarsely chopped fresh flat-leaf parsley, for
    garnish
Sepen (page 107), for serving

Skyu is a fortifying stew the Thikse monks typically serve in the bitterly cold winter months when the air is so frigid within the walls at the monastery you can see your breath. The flour-based thumbprint noodles are similar in texture and flavor to Italian gnocchi. The stew's creamy texture and the vibrant medley of vegetables and cheerful golden color from the turmeric are a comfort even on the most unforgivingly cold day. When it's prepared at Thikse, the younger students love gathering around the kitchen prep table to produce them, their hands deftly working at lightning speed. Feel free to substitute the heavy cream with the same volume of full-fat coconut milk.

TO MAKE THE noodles, in a large bowl, combine the flour, 1½ cups water, and salt and stir until incorporated. Knead for 2 to 3 minutes until the dough comes together. It should be thick and quite dry and hold together well; if it's too runny, add more flour, bit by bit, until a thick dough is achieved. Divide the dough in half, transfer one half to a plate, and cover with a damp kitchen towel. On a clean work surface, roll the other half into a long rope about ¾ inch in diameter. Using a bench scraper or a butter knife, cut the rope into ½-inch sections. Using your thumb, press an indentation into each one until the

dough is about ¼ inch thick. Repeat with the remaining dough half. Cover the noodles with a damp cloth and set aside at room temperature while you make the soup.

IN A LARGE, heavy-bottomed saucepan, melt the butter over medium-high heat. Add the onion, carrots, celery, ginger, and garlic and sauté until the carrots are tender, 5 to 10 minutes. Add the tomatoes, garam masala, turmeric, and chili powder and sauté until the tomatoes have broken apart and the spices are aromatic, about 5 minutes. Add 6 cups water and bring to a boil over high heat. Reduce the heat to medium and simmer until the tomatoes are completely broken down and the liquid is a bright yellow color, about 10 minutes. Add the noodles, peas, and spinach and gently simmer until the noodles rise to the surface and have achieved al dente consistency, 7 to 9 minutes. Don't overcook the noodles or they will become gummy. Add the cream and continue to gently simmer for another 2 to 3 minutes. Season with salt, garnish with parsley, and serve hot with a small bowl of sepen alongside. Leftover skyu will keep in a covered container in the refrigerator for up to 3 days. The noodles will maintain their consistency if the skyu is reheated gently over medium-high heat.

Thukpa

Thukpa, or Tibetan noodle soup, is warm and comforting on a cold winter's day. What makes it unique is the addition of Thai chile for a flash of heat, soy sauce for a deeper savory flavor, and a handful of daikon to freshen it up. This recipe originated in eastern Tibet and is traditionally made with hand-pulled noodles and served with beef, mutton, or yak. Here, it has been simplified by swapping in egg noodles, but you can also use ramen noodles or any Asian noodle that you prefer. The recipe calls for an entire Thai chile, which will certainly infuse the recipe with heat. Feel free to reduce the amount for a tamer version. This fortifying soup is especially welcome on a sick day or, better yet, a snow day.

IN A LARGE pot, bring 3 cups water and the stock to a boil. Add the chicken pieces, onion, carrot, celery, ginger, garlic, chile, and soy sauce. Return to a boil, then reduce the heat to a low simmer, cover, and cook for 45 minutes. Using tongs or a slotted spoon, transfer the chicken to a plate and set aside to cool.

ADD 2 CUPS water, the lime juice, radish, and noodles to the pot and gently simmer, uncovered, until the noodles are cooked through, 7 to 9 minutes. Once the chicken is cool enough to handle, remove the meat from the bones, break it up into bite-size pieces, coarsely chop the skin, and return the meat and skin to the soup. Season with salt and pepper. Ladle the piping-hot soup into individual bowls. Garnish with scallions, a dollop of sour cream, and sepen if you enjoy a little (or a lot!) of heat. Leftovers will keep in a covered container in the refrigerator for up to 3 days.

SERVES: 4
PREPARATION TIME: 1 hour 15 minutes

2 cups chicken stock
1 (3- to 3½-pound) chicken, cut into 8 pieces
1 large white onion, coarsely chopped
1 large carrot, peeled and coarsely chopped
1 celery rib, coarsely chopped
1 tablespoon finely chopped fresh ginger
4 garlic cloves, finely chopped
1 Thai chile, seeded and finely chopped
1 tablespoon soy sauce
Juice of 1 lime
1 small daikon radish, thinly sliced
8 ounces egg noodles
Salt and freshly ground black pepper
   to taste
Sliced scallions, for garnish
Sour cream, for garnish
Sepen (page 107), for serving (optional)

Tingmo with Shapta

MAKES: about 12 tingmo; serves 4
PREPARATION TIME: 1½ hours, including 2 hours rising time

FOR THE TINGMO:
2 teaspoons active dry yeast
2 teaspoons granulated sugar
Vegetable oil, for greasing
1½ cups all-purpose flour, plus more for dusting
1½ teaspoons baking powder
½ teaspoon salt

FOR THE SHAPTA:
4 bone-in, skin-on chicken thighs
Salt and freshly ground black pepper to taste
3 tablespoons vegetable oil
1 large white onion, coarsely chopped
1 tablespoon finely chopped fresh ginger
3 garlic cloves, finely chopped
2 medium tomatoes, coarsely chopped
1 red bell pepper, seeded and coarsely chopped
4 green chiles, seeded and finely chopped
1 bunch scallions, thinly sliced, plus more for garnish
3 tablespoons soy sauce
2 cups chicken stock
1½ tablespoons tightly packed dark brown sugar
½ teaspoon red pepper flakes
Finely chopped fresh cilantro, for garnish

Tingmo is a savory, fermented steamed bun that is frequently paired in Tibetan cuisine with shapta, a sweet-and-sour soup with a bright flavor. The buns are similar in texture to the dough of a Chinese bean cake, and they love nothing more than to soak up the burgundy juices of the shapta. You will need a bamboo or stainless steel steamer to prepare the tingmo.

FOR THE TINGMO, whisk together the yeast, sugar, and 1 tablespoon room-temperature water and let rest at room temperature until the surface of the water is frothy, about 15 minutes. Lightly oil a large bowl. In a large bowl, sift together the flour, baking powder, and salt. Add ¾ cup water and the activated yeast mixture and stir together using a wooden spoon or spatula until the dough comes together. On a clean, lightly floured work surface, knead the dough until soft and uniform. Return to the bowl, cover with a damp kitchen towel, and let rest at room temperature until it has doubled in size, about 1½ hours.

DIVIDE THE DOUGH into 8 equal pieces and roll each one into a ball. On a clean work surface, roll each ball into a long rope about 1 inch thick. Gently roll each rope into a coil, in the same way you would a cinnamon roll, increasing the height ever so slightly with each pass. Transfer the tingmo to a steamer tray (or two trays, if necessary) and let rest until they double in size once more, 30 to 45 minutes.

POUR ABOUT 2 inches of water into the base of the steamer and bring it to a boil. Place the filled steamer tray(s) on top, cover, and steam until the tingmo are slightly puffy and have a matte rather than glossy surface, 17 to 20 minutes.

MEANWHILE, MAKE THE shapta. Season the chicken thighs all over with salt and pepper. Heat the oil in a large pot over high heat. Add the chicken and sear until golden brown on both sides and cooked through, 6 to 8 minutes per side. Transfer to a paper towel–lined plate and set aside. Reduce the heat to medium-high and add the onion, ginger, and garlic. Sauté until the onion is translucent, about 5 minutes. Add the tomatoes, bell pepper, chiles, and scallions and sauté until the tomatoes begin to fall apart, 5 to 6 minutes. Deglaze with the soy sauce, scraping up any flavorful brown bits from the bottom of the pan with a wooden spoon. Add the stock, brown sugar, and red pepper flakes and bring to a boil over high heat. Reduce the heat to medium and simmer until it thickens slightly, 10 to 12 minutes. Season with salt and pepper.

WHILE THE SOUP thickens, remove the chicken meat from the bones, shred the chicken, and coarsely chop the skin. Add the chicken and skin to the shapta and simmer for 5 more minutes. Ladle the shapta into individual serving bowls, garnish with chopped scallions and cilantro, and serve hot, alongside the tingmo. Dip the tingmo into the stew, allowing enough time for the buns to soak up the velvety juices before you eat it. The tingmo are best when enjoyed freshly made, but leftovers can be stored in a covered container in the refrigerator for up to 1 day. Leftover shapta can be stored in a covered container in the refrigerator for up to 3 days or in the freezer for up to 2 months.

ABOVE AND RIGHT
Lunch service at Thikse that includes
dal, rice, and vegetable curry

Dal and Black Rice

SERVES: 4
PREPARATION TIME: 1 hour 15 minutes

FOR THE DAL:
1 cup dried red lentils
1 tablespoon mustard oil or canola oil
1 medium yellow onion
2 teaspoons finely chopped fresh ginger
3 garlic cloves, finely chopped
2 teaspoons ground turmeric
1 teaspoon cumin seeds
1 teaspoon coriander seeds
1 teaspoon mustard seeds

2 Roma tomatoes, chopped
1 tablespoon unsalted butter
Salt to taste

FOR THE RICE:
1¾ cups black rice
½ teaspoon salt

TO SERVE (OPTIONAL):
Butter
Raita (page 260)
Quick pickles (see headnote)

Tibetans don't normally cook dal in their own country, but it has become a favorite recipe for those who are living in exile in India and Nepal. The chef at Thikse prefers to use masoor dal, or red lentils, because they cook faster than the green or black varieties. Rice typically accompanies dal, and at Thikse, Tibetan purple rice was served. Known as forbidden rice, it's similar to other black rice varieties found throughout southeast Asia. One benefit of black rice is that it contains less starch than brown rice and therefore cooks more quickly. In India, dal is often served with raita (page 260).

Pickles are another mainstay on the Indian lunch table. To prepare a quick pickle, thinly slice a cucumber and put it in a container with a tight-fitting lid. Add 1 tablespoon freshly squeezed lemon juice (or white vinegar for extra tanginess) and about ½ teaspoon salt. Shake vigorously and continue to add lemon juice and salt to taste. The pickles are ready instantly.

RINSE THE LENTILS under cold running water to remove any debris, then rinse again.

IN A LARGE, nonstick skillet, heat the oil over medium heat. Add the onion, ginger, and garlic and sauté until the onion begins to caramelize, about 5 minutes. Add the turmeric, cumin, coriander, and mustard seeds and continue to sauté until the spices are aromatic, about 3 minutes. Add the tomatoes and butter and stir until the butter is melted. Cover and cook for 5 minutes. Stir in the lentils, cover, and cook for 5 additional minutes. Add 3 cups water, turn the heat down to low, and cook until the lentils are soft and falling apart and the dal is thick and flavorful, about 35 minutes. Season with salt.

MEANWHILE, RINSE THE rice in a colander under cold running water for a few minutes. Combine the rice, salt, and 3 cups water in a medium saucepan and bring to a boil over high heat. Reduce the heat to low, cover, and cook until the rice is tender and the liquid is absorbed, 30 to 35 minutes. Remove from the heat and let rest for 10 minutes. Fluff with a fork before serving.

SERVE THE DAL with a generous spoonful of butter and a side of rice. Top with raita and pickles. Leftover dal, without the raita and pickles, can be stored in a covered container in the refrigerator for up to 3 days.

Son Labu

Pungent and spicy, with a flash of vibrancy from the Szechuan peppercorns and a pleasingly crunchy texture, these pickled radishes are ideal for a kick-in-the-pants flavor boost in soups, salads, lentils, and sandwiches. The monks at Thikse store the son labu in a cool, dark corner of the monastic kitchen, then use long wooden chopsticks to transfer the radishes to tiny red bowls for serving. They serve son labu with virtually every meal, not only for its probiotic virtues but also because it perks up every dish it meets. Son labu is not only pungently flavored, it's also powerfully aromatic. Don't be put off by this the first time you unseal your jar. With one taste, you'll instantly become enamored of the funk.

IN A LARGE colander set over a bowl or in the sink, combine the daikon radish, red radishes, and salt and toss until the salt is evenly distributed. Let sit for 1 hour in order for the radishes to release their juices, which will enable them to become more crunchy once pickled.

IN A SMALL bowl, combine the chiles, ginger, and black and Szechuan peppercorns. Add about one-quarter of the radishes to a large sterilized glass jar and top with about one-quarter of the chile mixture. Repeat these layers with the remaining ingredients. Combine the vinegar and 3½ cups water in a small saucepan and bring to a boil. Pour the hot liquid into the jar. If the liquid does not completely cover the radishes, add enough additional water to fully submerge them. Cool to room temperature, then seal the jar and place in the refrigerator. Chill for at least 2 days before serving to enable the radishes to ferment. Son labu will keep in the refrigerator for up to 3 weeks.

MAKES: about 2 quarts
PREPARATION TIME: 15 minutes, plus 1 hour to soak and 2 days to ferment

1 large daikon radish, peeled, quartered lengthwise, and thinly sliced
1 bunch red radishes, thinly sliced
½ cup kosher salt
10 to 12 dried Thai red chiles
1 (4-inch) piece ginger, peeled and thinly sliced
1 tablespoon black peppercorns
1½ teaspoons red Szechuan peppercorns
1½ cups distilled white vinegar

Poppy Seed Tsampa Pancakes with Apricot Syrup

SERVES: 4
PREPARATION TIME: 1 hour 15 minutes

FOR THE APRICOT SYRUP:
24 (4-ounce) apricots, pitted and cut into
    pieces (about 4 cups total)
¾ cup lightly packed light brown sugar
¾ cup granulated sugar
1 tablespoon grated fresh ginger
1 tablespoon freshly squeezed lemon juice
Salt to taste

FOR THE TSAMPA PANCAKES:
1½ cups barley flour
Unsalted butter, as needed
1 large egg
2 cups whole milk
1¾ teaspoons baking powder
½ teaspoon salt
¼ cup lightly packed light brown sugar
1 tablespoon poppy seeds
Crunchy sea salt, such as Maldon, for
    garnish (optional)

This recipe highlights two of the most important ingredients that the monks use at Thikse: tsampa (roasted barley flour) and apricots, the pride of Ladakh. Tsampa pancakes are the ideal landing pad for a drizzle of syrup made from the fruit that is so ubiquitous and beloved by the people of Ladakh. Himalayan apricots were introduced to Ladakh from central Asia over a century ago. The resilient tree is one of the few that is able to withstand the brutal Himalayan winters and the unforgiving, high mountain desert soil. In early spring, the heart-shaped leaves of the trees bear mirthful blush-pink blossoms that precede the apricots, which are ready to be harvested in the late spring.

The region boasts multiple varieties of apricots, providing an expansive flavor spectrum ranging from sour to sweet to bitter. Resourceful Ladakhis use every part of the apricot, transforming the fruit into everything from cookies and jams to chutneys and syrups. Dried apricots sustain people through the long, relentless winter when the region is cut off from the rest of India due to heavy snowfall. The kernels from apricot species that are not toxic (many apricot varieties throughout the world have toxic kernels and seeds) are ground into a flour that is added to bread; the seed within the kernel is enjoyed in the same way a handful of nuts would be. Oil is also extracted from the kernels and is undoubtedly the region's favorite moisturizer, buffering skin from icy windstorms that relentlessly blow down from the mountain peaks. There are entire stores in the Ladakhi capital of Leh devoted to the apricot and all of its riches. In the frigid pantry at Thikse, burlap bags overflow with the fruit in all its incarnations. In this recipe, the bright tartness of the syrup lifts the toasty notes of the pancakes and offers a sunny flash of color atop the cakes' deep chestnut hue.

FIRST, MAKE THE apricot syrup. In a heavy-bottomed saucepan, combine the apricots and brown and granulated sugars and muddle using a wooden spoon or a muddler. Cover and set aside at room temperature for 15 minutes to encourage the apricots to release their juices.

Recipe continues

PLACE THE PAN over medium heat and cook until the sugar begins to dissolve and the apricots begin to lose their shape, 5 to 6 minutes. Increase the heat to high, add 2 cups water, the ginger, and lemon juice and bring to a boil. Reduce the heat to medium-low and gently simmer until the apricots soften and dissolve into the liquid, about 10 minutes. Using a muddler or potato masher, break up the remaining solid apricot pieces until everything is incorporated. Increase the heat to medium-high and simmer until the syrup is reduced by about half and becomes thick, 18 to 20 minutes. Strain through a fine-mesh sieve and discard the solids, then season the syrup with salt. Cool until warm and serve immediately with the pancakes, or store in a covered container in the refrigerator for about 10 days or in the freezer indefinitely.

TO MAKE THE tsampa, in a large, heavy-bottomed sauté pan, roast the flour over medium-high heat, stirring constantly with a wooden spoon, until the flour begins to turn a light golden brown and is aromatic, about 5 minutes. Transfer the roasted flour to a rimmed baking sheet and spread into an even layer; set aside to cool to room temperature.

MELT 1 TABLESPOON butter in a small saucepan. Transfer the butter to a medium bowl, add the egg and milk, and whisk to combine. In a large bowl, sift together the tsampa, baking powder, and salt. Stir in the brown sugar and poppy seeds, then add the milk mixture and stir together until incorporated. The batter should be runny and slightly lumpy. If it is too runny, add a bit more tsampa; if it needs to loosen up, add a bit more milk. Melt about 1 tablespoon butter on a griddle or in a large skillet over medium-high heat. Using a ladle and working in batches so as not to crowd the pan, pour in about ⅔ cup batter per pancake and cook until tiny bubbles begin to form and the edges of the pancake become slightly dry and turn a very light golden brown, 2 to 3 minutes. Using a spatula, flip and repeat on the other side. The pancakes will take on a rich golden brown color. Transfer to a plate, cover with a dry kitchen towel, and repeat with the remaining batter, adding more butter as needed.

SERVE THE PANCAKES topped with a generous knob of butter and drizzled with ribbons of apricot syrup. If desired, sprinkle with sea salt to add a crunchy texture and to balance the sweetness of the syrup. The pancakes are best when enjoyed right away, but they will keep in a covered container in the refrigerator for up to 2 days.

Tsampa

Tsampa, roasted barley flour, is one of the most symbolically important ingredients in Tibetan Buddhism. Its use actually predates Buddhism, stretching back into ancient times, when animistic gods were worshipped in Tibet. It is traditionally flicked into the air as a symbol of celebration and joy and is especially important during festive occasions such as birthdays, weddings, and religious feast days. During the morning drumming ceremony at Thikse, the young novices carry vessels filled with tsampa from monk to monk, joyfully weaving their way through the rows, tipping their vessel to enable each monk to take as much tsampa as they would like. Other novices carry brass kettles filled with salty yak butter tea, pouring each monk a steaming cupful. Some of the monks stir some tsampa into their tea, relishing each fortifying, warming sip. Others pour a small amount of tea into their bowl of tsampa to form a ball of dough that they enjoy while chanting, the deep staccato of drums echoing through the red prayer hall adorned with brilliantly colored thangkas, silk appliques ornately ordained with paintings of deities and scenes from the life of the Buddha.

Saffron Rice Pudding with Walnuts and Ginger

SERVES: 4
PREPARATION TIME: 45 minutes

¾ cup long-grain white rice
4 cups whole milk
1 tablespoon honey, plus more to taste
¼ cup coarsely chopped walnuts, toasted
½ teaspoon finely chopped fresh ginger
4 to 6 saffron threads (see page 73)
½ teaspoon salt

Tibetans traditionally save their broken rice for rice pudding, a warming dessert ideal for a frigid day. Broken rice are fragments of rice grains that are broken in the field during harvest, or during the drying process, transport, or milling. Not only is broken rice less expensive, it also gives rice pudding a silkier texture. Long-grain rice has been substituted here because it is easier to source, but you should be able to find broken rice in most Asian markets. Saffron adds a tempting golden hue to this special treat.

RINSE THE RICE in a colander under cold running water for a few minutes.

IN A SAUCEPAN, bring the milk and honey to a gentle simmer over medium heat. Do not let it boil, as milk can scorch quickly. Stir in the rice, walnuts, ginger, and saffron, turn the heat down to low, and simmer gently until the rice has completely absorbed the milk, about 30 minutes. Stir frequently to prevent the rice from burning and sticking to the bottom of the pan. Remove from the heat and season with the salt. Drizzle with additional honey, if desired, and serve while still bubbling and hot. Leftovers will keep in a covered container in the refrigerator for up to 3 days; enjoy cold or reheated.

Yak Butter

Yak butter is a valuable commodity throughout the highlands of Tibet, Nepal, Bhutan, and India, where it's traded for spices, meat, wool, and other coveted items. It's produced from the milk of a female yak, called a dri in Tibetan. Her rich milk contains twice the amount of fat as cow's milk, resulting in a daffodil-yellow butter that is similar in texture to a soft cheese. Tibetans leave their dri's milk out to ferment overnight before transforming it into butter. The result is a tangy butter that forms the foundation of yak butter tea and many other Tibetan recipes.

Much like cow's milk, yak's milk is more flavorful in the summer months when the animals feast on fresh fields of green grass. The dri also produces more milk in the summer. This does not mean that there is a butter shortage in the wintertime, though, since yak butter will keep in a tightly sealed container at a cold temperature for up to a year.

Once the butter is exposed to air, it will form blue mold veins similar to Stilton cheese. Even rancid butter is valuable for Tibetan nomads, who use it to tan their yak and sheep hides. Some Tibetan nomads drink up to sixty mini cups of Tibetan yak butter tea to maintain their strength, keep warm, and stay hydrated during a long working day outdoors.

One of the most fascinating things that Tibetans do with their yak butter is carve it into elaborate sculptures representing different stages of Buddha's life. The creations are painted with vibrant vegetable dyes and presented at monasteries throughout Tibet as an offering to Buddha on January 15, the most auspicious day of the Tibetan New Year.

Yak butter tea is beloved by many Tibetans, including the monks at Thikse. They appreciate it for its nutty and salty-sweet flavor and its thick and creamy texture. Yak butter tea provides the calories, fat, and energy required to sustain themselves at such a high altitude. The ingredients are believed to enhance blood circulation, improve muscle and marrow strength, and encourage the production of regenerative fluids. All of these things are essential for people who live in the Himalayas because the high altitude slows both circulation and tissue and blood regeneration.

The recipe for yak butter tea varies throughout Tibet. In many regions, poorer, rural people do not own the yaks they milk each morning. They are required to turn over the butter produced after the milking to wealthier landowners. They can keep only the excess whey for themselves. As a result, yak butter tea is sometimes associated with affluence in Tibet, and yak milk tea is seen as the drink of the people since it is made from the butter's residual liquid.

The monks of Thikse are fortunate enough to have yak butter donated to them from nearby yak farmers and local villagers for most of the year. The monks prepare it by first brewing a dark, slightly bitter black tea called pu'erh. They then stir together roasted barley flour (tsampa), milk curds, and softened yak butter. The tea is poured on top and stirred together with chopsticks or a wooden spoon.

Yak butter tea is believed to trigger a symbiotic balance between the mind and body. For the monks of Thikse, it is the fuel required to sustain them through a day of prayer, cooking, farming, and meditating.

5

Kylemore Abbey

BENEDICTINE CATHOLIC
CONNEMARA, IRELAND

"The time is now. The time is for reflection on what we've lost in life, yes, but for what we have left in life too. It's time to begin to live life fuller rather than faster."

—*Joan D. Chittister, Benedictine nun*

Ireland's west coast, a 1,600-mile stretch of shoreline with staggering cliffs and camera-ready villages painted every shade of winsome, hums with industry. Here, creative food producers are transforming a once-tired repertoire of listless staples into a dynamic culinary awakening that is ever-flourishing and evolving. One of the coastal areas with less foot traffic is the remote region of Connemara, a wild tangle of alder, ash, and silver birch forests, dense hedgerows, jagged quartzite mountains known as the Twelve Bens and Maumturks, pristine lakes, deep fjords, vast heathlands, prehistoric bogs where peat has been sourced for fuel for thousands of years, and centuries-old fishing villages.

This region of County Galway is famed for its silver and white Connemara ponies, finely constructed tweed, and megalithic tombs. The remains of ancient monastic hermitages dot the landscape, haunting vestiges of the Catholic monks who first arrived in Ireland in the fifth century. These hermits and scholars settled in Connemara because they sought a remote corner of the island for prayer and contemplation.

Connemara, for all its enigmatic beauty, has proven over the centuries to also demand of its residents a tenacious resiliency, a stoic resolve to overcome periods of hunger, months of sodden cold, relentless rain, and lonely isolation. The Irish famine, which began in 1845 as a result of a fungal blight that decimated Ireland's potato crop, is the most ruthless attack nature unleashed upon the Irish in the modern era. The potato was introduced to Ireland from South America in 1509 and quickly became the nation's primary and, in many cases, exclusive crop. In Connemara, where tenant farmers did not own their own land and lived in poorly ventilated thatched houses and stone huts, subsisting on little but the potato and whatever could be harvested from the sea, the famine struck a devastating blow upon the population.

The ensuing starvation forced many to flee. Some ended up in crowded Irish workhouses populating the nation's larger cities. Others took their chance on one of the boats heading to America. For those who survived the famine in Connemara, decades of hardship followed. Reminders of this era of suffering haunt the landscape, resonating especially when one catches a glimpse of a long-abandoned stone tenant house, roofless, whispering of yesterday's sorrows. But they are also reminders for the Irish and the visitors who pass by of the fortitude and resourcefulness of the Connemara people.

Today, the inhabitants of this region celebrate their cultural and culinary heritage while proudly embracing the beguiling natural beauty that enticed an architect to construct one of Ireland's most illustrious architectural gems. At Kylemore Pass, a deep valley that divides the Twelve Bens in the south and Duchruach Mountain in the north, Kylemore Abbey emerges like a mirage in the mist, its shadow reflected in shades of amethyst, moss, and cobalt upon the silver waters of Lough Pollacappul located in front of it. Commissioned by its first resident, Mitchell Henry, in the mid-nineteenth century and constructed by architect James Franklin Fuller, this majestic building has been a family home, a school for girls, and today, an abbey for Benedictine nuns. In 1920, two dozen nuns, their order established in 1598, arrived at Kylemore from the Abbey at Ypres in Belgium, where they faced religious persecution after World War I. They found safe refuge at Kylemore and have made it their home ever since.

The sprawling building of Kylemore is home to a billiard room, a ballroom, a well-stocked library, and dozens of finely crafted bedrooms and living areas. The sumptuous interior of Kylemore is the polar opposite of the unadorned church next to the main building where the nuns

OPPOSITE
A Connemara pony

" One of our goals at Kylemore is to be useful, resourceful, and industrious. We have such a bounty here at Kylemore, and the nuns in my order derive great satisfaction from producing and from being able to sustain ourselves."

gather each day for prayers. The Benedictine order, established over 1,500 years ago, believes in stability, fidelity to the monastic way of life, prayer, hard work, and an investment in relationships and the community. At Kylemore, Mother Abbess Magdalena FitzGibbon says that she derives great joy from investing in her region, and that one of the ways her order does this has been to support the surrounding communities with the vast amounts of fruits and vegetables that are harvested from the sprawling gardens located on the grounds of the monastery.

As she strolls along the shore of Lough Pollacappul, Mother Abbess Magdalena inspects the fuchsia trees with their spiky red and royal purple blooms. "We will make fuchsia vinegar in a few weeks' time, but for now we are focusing on the elderberry berries because they are at their peak. We will make cordials and syrups, and Sister Genevieve will add elderberry blossoms to her soaps and shampoos. One of our goals at Kylemore is to be useful, resourceful, and industrious. We have such a bounty here at Kylemore, and the nuns in my order derive great satisfaction from producing and from being able to sustain ourselves."

Catholicism has had a foothold in Ireland since the fifth century. It's estimated that 87 percent of the population in the Republic of Ireland is Catholic, and while there are countless tales about the nation's patron saint, Patrick, introducing Catholicism to the country, it most likely preceded him. The early Catholic monks lived in humble stone huts shaped like beehives that to this day dot the Irish landscape. Eventually, monasteries were constructed, home to monks, nuns, and a treasure trove of valuable Church artifacts.

The Vikings plundered many of the Irish monasteries in the ninth and tenth centuries. Fortunately, there were monks and nuns who survived the persecution, escaping with both their lives and some of their monasteries' most precious treasures. Arguably, the most legendary was *The Book of Kells*, a resplendent illuminated manuscript featuring the four gospels, estimated to have been created by monks in the early ninth century. *The Book of Kells* is on display across the country from Kylemore at Trinity College in Dublin, but the nuns of Kylemore have treasures and a legacy of their own. The group of resilient, forward-thinking women who settled at Kylemore in 1920 have been dedicated stewards of the abbey and the three thousand acres of land that surround it ever since.

The award-winning restoration of the Victorian walled garden has garnered the nuns global acclaim and is one of the reasons 250,000 visitors find their way to Kylemore each year. But the industrious, visionary nuns would never dream of becoming complacent. Instead, they have spearheaded several restoration and managed-land projects that reflect their commitment to ecological sustainability. They are also committed to the well-being of the Connemara people, most recently reflected in a project they initiated to provide employment opportunities in the fields of tourism, crafts, energy, forestry, and the culinary arts for the local community.

In their workshops, they produce everything from marmalades, bread and scone mixes, and farmhouse chutney to lavender skin and lip balms, pottery, candles, and soaps scented with seaweed, rosemary, and lemongrass. Next door to the candle and soap workshop is the chocolate production room, run by an Australian nun, Sister Genevieve. She runs her thriving chocolate kitchen with graceful efficiency, embracing the ethos of her order: ora et labora, or pray and work. The chocolate produced by Sister Genevieve and the other nuns is beloved throughout Ireland and is one of the most popular tourist souvenirs. When asked what her most popular chocolate item is, Sister Genevieve immediately responds, "Sheep. Anything shaped like a sheep is a crowd favorite. This is Ireland, after all."

The chocolate is also sold in Kylemore's perpetually crowded café, which buzzes with the hum of locals and visitors. Mother Abbess Magdalena likes to visit the café in the mornings before the masses of people arrive. She prefers scones with clotted cream and berry compote. She politely, if not a bit sheepishly, agrees to have her photo captured while she enjoys a scone with her good friend Sister Mary. At one point, between bites of scone, Mother Abbess Magdalena leans in to whisper something to Sister Mary, who immediately starts giggling.

"What did you tell her?" I ask.

"I told her that this is making me feel more famous than Mick Jagger," she says with a grin.

OPPOSITE
The nuns enjoying teatime together

Pumpkin Scones

MAKES: about 16 scones
PREPARATION TIME: 30 minutes

4½ cups all-purpose flour, plus more for
   dusting
4 teaspoons baking powder
¾ teaspoon kosher salt
½ teaspoon baking soda
⅔ cup packed light brown sugar
2 teaspoons ground cinnamon
1 teaspoon ground ginger

1 teaspoon grated lemon zest
1 cup (2 sticks) unsalted butter, chilled and
   cut into ½-inch cubes
1⅓ cups pumpkin puree
2 large eggs, room temperature
¾ cup whole milk
½ cup hazelnuts, skinned, toasted, and
   finely chopped
2 tablespoons granulated sugar
Softened butter, for serving
Jam, for serving

At the café in Kylemore, fortifying sandwiches made with freshly baked sourdough, salmon quiche, warming lamb stew, and Kylemore's award-winning scones await hungry visitors. The scones have been voted more than once as the best in Ireland, and the bakers at the abbey take great pride in them. A basic scone is always available in the abbey's bakery, but other flavors reflect the seasons, including this deftly spiced pumpkin scone offered in the cooler autumn months. One universal key to producing a flaky, successfully risen scone is to make sure that the butter is well chilled before adding it to the dough. Cold butter will not completely incorporate into the dough, which is the result you should aim for because the tiny bits of butter will produce steam when heated in the oven, expanding the dough and encouraging it to rise. These scones are typically enjoyed smeared with golden Irish butter.

PREHEAT THE OVEN to 400°F. Line a rimmed baking sheet with parchment paper.

IN A LARGE bowl, sift together the flour, baking powder, salt, and baking soda. Add the brown sugar, 1 teaspoon cinnamon, ginger, and lemon zest and stir with a wooden spoon until incorporated. Add the cold butter and, using your fingers, mix it into the dry ingredients until it resembles large crumbs. Chill in the refrigerator while completing the next step.

IN A MEDIUM bowl, whisk together the pumpkin, eggs, and ½ cup milk. Pour the wet ingredients into the bowl with the dry ingredients, add the hazelnuts, and stir with a wooden spoon until just incorporated. The dough will be slightly lumpy. (At this point the dough can be stored in a covered container in the freezer for up to 1 month.)

STIR TOGETHER THE granulated sugar and remaining 1 teaspoon cinnamon in a small bowl until incorporated. Sprinkle flour on a clean work surface and knead the dough for about 1 minute. Do not overknead, which can result in a tough texture. Roll the dough about 1 inch thick, then use a 3-inch biscuit cutter (or a wide drinking glass or jar rim) to punch out circles. Transfer the scones to the prepared baking sheet. Gather up the scraps, roll out to 1 inch thick, and punch out additional circles. Brush the surfaces with the remaining ¼ cup milk and sprinkle with the cinnamon sugar. Bake until risen and golden brown, 14 to 16 minutes. Transfer to a wire cooling rack to cool a bit, then serve while still warm with softened butter—preferably creamy, rich Irish butter—and your favorite jam, if desired.

LEFTOVER SCONES DON'T freeze well, but they will keep in a covered container at room temperature for up to 3 days.

Connemara Steamed Mussels

SERVES: 4
PREPARATION TIME: 30 minutes

1½ pounds mussels
2 tablespoons unsalted butter
1 medium white onion, finely chopped
2 garlic cloves, finely chopped
4 plum tomatoes, coarsely chopped
2 tablespoons freshly squeezed lemon juice
1 (16-ounce) can or bottle IPA or other ale,
   plus more for serving

Leaves from 2 thyme sprigs
½ cup heavy cream
Leaves from 4 flat-leaf parsley sprigs,
   coarsely chopped
Salt and freshly ground black pepper
   to taste
Crusty bread or Irish Cheddar and Bacon
   Soda Bread (page 157), for serving
Lemon wedges, for serving

The region of Connemara is famed throughout Europe for its plump blue mussels. They are harvested on lines descending 25 meters into the deep, cool waters of Killary Fjord. The melding of ocean and fresh water that occurs in the fjord imparts the mussels with a singularly sweet flavor. Blue mussels have an impressively long culinary legacy in Ireland—their shells were discovered in eight-thousand-year-old prehistoric kitchens. The region celebrates the legacy of their mussels at the Connemara Mussel Festival, held each spring in the tiny coastal village of Tullycross. Mussels were traditionally roasted atop a bed of seaweed in this region, and this tradition is embraced at the festival. The nuns enjoy their mussels just like the rest of the locals, simmered with onions and garlic, sprinkled with lemon juice, and served alongside a loaf of crusty bread to sop up all the juices.

Be sure to run your mussels under cold running water and scrub them with a brush to remove any sand and debris. Remove them from the heat once they have all opened, and be sure to toss any that remain firmly shut since these are most likely unhealthy to eat.

RINSE THE MUSSELS under cold running water to remove any residue, then trim away any fibrous beards. Place any of them that are slightly open on a counter and give them a gentle tap. If they close up, they're suitable for consumption. Discard any that remain open.

IN A LARGE cast-iron skillet or heavy-bottomed saucepan, melt the butter over medium-high heat. Add the onion, garlic, and tomatoes and sauté until the onion is translucent and the tomatoes have broken down, 5 to 6 minutes. Add the lemon juice and IPA and scrape up any brown bits from the bottom of the pan. Bring to a simmer, then reduce the heat to medium and simmer until the liquid has reduced by about 1 inch, about 8 minutes. Add the thyme and mussels and cook until the mussels have opened, about 4 minutes. Stir gently a few times during this process to marry the mussels with the cooking juices.

ONCE ALL OF the mussels are opened (discard any that remain unopened), pour in the cream and sprinkle with the parsley. Season with salt and pepper. Continue to cook for 1 more minute, or until the cream is warmed through, stirring once or twice to distribute the juices.

DIVIDE THE MUSSELS and cream sauce into 4 bowls. Serve with large hunks of bread, lemon wedges and, to set a festive mood, pints of ale.

Lamb Stew with Sweet Potatoes

SERVES: 4
PREPARATION TIME: 1 hour 15 minutes

1 pound boneless lamb shoulder, cut into
    bite-size pieces
1 tablespoon all-purpose flour
Salt and freshly ground black pepper to
    taste
1 tablespoon vegetable oil
1 medium white onion, coarsely chopped
2 celery ribs, thinly sliced
1 large carrot, peeled and coarsely chopped
2 garlic cloves, thinly sliced
1 cup dry white wine, such as Pinot Grigio or
    Sauvignon Blanc

4 cups chicken or vegetable stock
1 cinnamon stick
1 large sweet potato, peeled and coarsely
    chopped
8 ounces cremini mushrooms, coarsely
    chopped
1 (15-ounce) can cannellini beans, drained
    and rinsed

TO SERVE
Toasted bread crumbs
Sour cream
Thinly sliced scallions
Crusty bread with butter

This simple stew is a favorite of the nuns at Kylemore on brisk, rainy Connemara evenings, preferably with a peat fire crackling in the background. The velvety sauce provides the perfect vehicle for chunks of succulent lamb shoulder. Stewing beef makes a fine substitute, but nothing quite compares to lamb, especially when paired with sweet potato, a generous splash of dry white wine, and a cap of toasted bread crumbs to soak up all those juices. Lentils or chickpeas make good substitutes for the cannellini beans. Don't forget the crusty bread for dipping.

IN A LARGE resealable plastic bag, toss together the lamb and flour until the meat is well coated. Season with salt and pepper and refrigerate until ready to use.

HEAT THE OIL in a heavy-bottomed saucepan over medium-high heat. Add the onion, celery, and carrot and sauté until the onion is translucent, about 6 minutes. Add the garlic and sauté until aromatic, about 2 minutes. Add the lamb and sear until it is golden brown on all sides, 5 to 7 minutes. Add the wine and bring to a boil over high heat, scraping up any brown bits that have formed on the bottom of the pot. Add the stock, cinnamon, sweet potato, and mushrooms. Reduce the heat, cover, and let the stew bubble away for 20 minutes, then add the beans and simmer until the meat and sweet potato are tender, another 25 minutes or so. Remove the cinnamon stick. Season with salt and pepper.

LADLE THE STEW into bowls, sprinkle with toasted bread crumbs, dollop with sour cream, sprinkle with scallions, and serve with crusty bread slathered with butter. Leftovers can be stored in a covered container in the refrigerator for 4 days.

Smoked Salmon, Asparagus, and Goat Cheese Frittata

Atlantic salmon, referred to as braden in Gaelic, is an indigenous Irish fish. Salmon runs through Irish rivers from late spring through the cooler autumn months. The smoked salmon at Kylemore is sourced from a smokery in Connemara that has supplied the abbey for decades. This breakfast frittata is inspired by the smoked salmon quiche sold in the abbey's café and enjoyed by the nuns on the weekends. Omitting the buttery crust results in a lighter meal, while the goat cheese fortifies it with tanginess. If asparagus isn't in season, replace it with whatever is, such as bell peppers, zucchini, or broccoli.

PREHEAT THE OVEN to 400°F.

MELT THE BUTTER in a 12-inch ovenproof sauté pan over medium heat. Add the onion and sauté until translucent, about 6 minutes. Add the garlic and sauté until aromatic, 1 to 2 minutes. Remove from the heat and stir in the parsley, salmon, and asparagus. Allow to cool for a few minutes, then add the goat cheese.

IN A LARGE bowl, beat the eggs, then whisk in the milk and season with salt and pepper. Pour the eggs into the pan and stir very gently for a few seconds to combine. Place the pan in the oven and bake until the edges of the frittata are puffed and golden brown and the eggs at the center have set, about 25 minutes. Serve while still hot with a handful of baby spinach, if desired, to add a few more greens to the start of your day. Leftovers can be stored in a covered container in the refrigerator for up to 3 days.

SERVES: 6
PREPARATION TIME: 35 minutes

2 tablespoons unsalted butter
1 medium white onion, coarsely chopped
1 garlic clove, finely chopped
2 flat-leaf parsley sprigs, finely chopped
8 ounces smoked salmon, cut into bite-size pieces
1 cup coarsely chopped asparagus
6 ounces goat cheese, crumbled
10 large eggs
3 tablespoons whole milk
Salt and freshly ground black pepper to taste
Baby spinach, for serving (optional)

Seaweed

On the vast ocean shores of Connemara, seaweed is everywhere, a tidal salad with unrivaled health benefits. Older farmers up and down the coast of western Ireland recall a time when seaweed was pulled in from the sea to dry upon their fields before being tilled into the soil. The modern world has little time for seaweed's virtues, and its veneration has waned with the encroachment of new technology and a faster pace of life, but at Kylemore Abbey, there are reminders all around of the time not so long ago when seaweed was a fundamental part of the cook and gardener's repertoire.

The lead gardener at Kylemore, Anja Gohlke, is proud of the contribution she is making to restoring the legacy of seaweed farming in Ireland. She says, "Our vegetables thrive here because of the seaweed. It's tilled into the rich Connemara soil and provides our crops with dense nutrition. They flourish because of the seaweed. It's a reminder of our past and a tribute to our resourceful ancestors, but it's also a cutting-edge technique that gardeners from all around the world are starting to wake up to that ushers us into a modern world."

Seaweed has the ability to heal an aching body. Seaweed's capacity to leach toxins from sore muscles, minimize the fluids that accumulate in the body, and replenish the system with rejuvenating minerals is another seaweed virtue. Ireland has a longstanding seaweed bath tradition, a practice stretching back all the way to ancient Roman times. At the start of the twentieth century, there were over three hundred public seaweed baths speckled throughout the nation.

As a growing number of seaweed advocates, including Kylemore's nuns who add seaweed to their recipes, strive to liberate seaweed from the association with destitution that arose during times of hardship, seaweed is once again being introduced into Irish kitchens, bathtubs, and gardens. Today, there is a renewed curiosity and appreciation for seaweed in Ireland. It is a tradition that is fundamental to the identity of the Irish people.

Seaweed, Beet, and Barley Salad with Whipped Goat Cheese Dressing and Hazelnuts

SERVES: 4
PREPARATION TIME: 1 hour

FOR THE SALAD:
2 large red beets, peeled and cut into bite-
   size pieces
2 large yellow beets, peeled and cut into
   bite-size pieces
2 tablespoons extra-virgin olive oil
Salt and freshly ground black pepper to taste
1 cup pearl barley
¼ cup finely chopped red onion
1 cup lightly packed equal amounts wakame
   and dulse
½ cup coarsely chopped hazelnuts, toasted

FOR THE DRESSING:
8 ounces goat cheese, room temperature
3 ounces cream cheese, room temperature
2 garlic cloves, coarsely chopped
1 tablespoon whole milk
2 teaspoons freshly squeezed lemon juice
½ teaspoon salt
¼ teaspoon freshly ground black pepper

This salad is a celebration of seaweed, its mild brininess an unexpected counterpoint to the earthy sweetness of the beets. The recipe calls for wakame, a slightly sweet, lime-green variety of kelp with a firm texture, and dulse, a brinier seaweed with a silky texture. If you have trouble sourcing either of these, any edible seaweed variety, such as hijiki, kombu, umibudo, or ogonori, will work. The heartiness, nutritional assets, and long shelf life of beets make them a mainstay of the Irish winter diet. Pair them with comforting and healthful barley, a handful of toasted hazelnuts, and a tangy goat cheese dressing and you've got yourself a salad to brighten the chilliest of winter days. Peeling and chopping the red beets before cooking will save you some kitchen stains.

PREHEAT THE OVEN to 400°F. Line a rimmed baking sheet with aluminum foil.

TOSS THE BEETS on the prepared baking sheet with the olive oil and season with salt and pepper. Roast until the beets are tender when pierced with a fork, about 40 minutes.

WHILE THE BEETS are roasting, combine the barley with 3 cups water and a generous pinch of salt in a small saucepan. Bring to a boil over high heat. Cover, reduce the heat to low, and simmer until the barley is tender and has absorbed all of the liquid, 25 to 30 minutes.

TO MAKE THE dressing, combine the goat cheese, cream cheese, garlic, milk, and lemon juice in the bowl of a food processor and process on high speed until whipped and fluffy. Season with the salt and pepper.

TO SERVE, IN a large bowl, toss together the red onion, seaweed, beets, and barley. Season with salt and pepper. Drizzle with the dressing and sprinkle with the hazelnuts. Serve immediately. This salad is best when enjoyed right away, but leftovers can be kept in a covered container in the refrigerator for up to 1 day.

Garlic and Nettle Soup with Chive Yogurt

SERVES: 4
PREPARATION TIME: 35 minutes

FOR THE SOUP:
Salt and freshly ground black pepper to taste
2 loosely packed quarts young nettle tops (wear rubber gloves when handling)
2 tablespoons unsalted butter
1 medium white onion, coarsely chopped
2 garlic cloves, coarsely chopped
10 (2-ounce) fingerling potatoes

1 celery rib, coarsely chopped
2 cups chicken or vegetable stock
2 bay leaves
4 thyme sprigs
1 tablespoon freshly squeezed lemon juice, plus more for seasoning

FOR THE CHIVE YOGURT:
1 cup Greek-style or whole-milk yogurt
Fresh chives, coarsely chopped
Salt to taste

Nettles really do sting! But if handled properly and harvested at the right time, their many virtues far outweigh their prickliness. In early spring, when their stingers are young and not potent, their flavor is sweetest. The trick is to use only the small leaves near the top of the plant and to wear rubber gloves during the harvesting and preparation process. Once they've been blanched, they're benign, nutritious, and flavorful. Use them in any dish that calls for spinach or, as the Irish used to (and some still do), to create a spring tonic that is prescribed to ward off arthritis and increase blood circulation.

The Irish used to use the fibrous nettle leaves to weave cloth bags and nets, fed wilted nettles to their livestock, and diluted nettles in water for a robust fertilizer in the fields. It was once believed that a patch of nettles indicated where the fairies lived, and even their sting was honored as protection from witchcraft and dark magic. At Kylemore Abbey, the nuns enjoy this nettle soup as often as possible during nettle season, not only for its earthy flavor but also for its many health benefits. This version is thickened with floury potatoes, enriched with butter and chicken stock, and garnished with chive yogurt for a tangy finish.

BRING A LARGE saucepan of salted water to a boil and prepare an ice bath. Wearing rubber gloves, carefully put the nettles in the boiling water and simmer for 2 minutes. Using tongs or a slotted spoon, transfer the nettles to the ice bath in order to shock them and prevent discoloration. Set aside.

MELT THE BUTTER in a large pot over medium-high heat. Add the onion and garlic and sauté until the onion is translucent and the garlic is aromatic, about 5 minutes. Add the potatoes and celery and sauté for a few minutes more, until the celery just begins to lose its color. Add the stock, bay leaves, thyme sprigs, and lemon juice and bring to a boil. Reduce the heat to medium, add the nettles, and gently simmer until the potatoes are tender, about 10 minutes.

MEANWHILE, IN A small bowl, whisk together the yogurt and chives with a few tablespoons of water for a slightly runny consistency. Season with salt.

USING TONGS, REMOVE the bay leaves and thyme sprigs from the pot, then transfer the soup to a blender, using caution to prevent splattering. Remove the cap from the lid of the blender and hold a kitchen towel over the hole while blending to allow the steam to escape. Blend at the lowest speed until incorporated, then increase the speed to its highest setting and purée until smooth. Season with salt and pepper and additional lemon juice, if desired. Serve the soup drizzled with the chive yogurt. Leftovers will keep in a covered container in the refrigerator for up to 3 days, but the soup will lose its vibrant color and deepen to more of a dark pine green.

Lamb Burgers with Creamy Red Cabbage Slaw and Rosemary Aioli

SERVES: 4
PREPARATION TIME: 45 minutes

FOR THE SLAW:
¼ cup mayonnaise
1 tablespoon extra-virgin olive oil
1 tablespoon apple cider vinegar
1 teaspoon mustard seeds
1 (1-pound) head red cabbage, cored, quartered, and thinly sliced
1 small red onion, halved and thinly sliced
1 green apple, cored and coarsely chopped

FOR THE ROSEMARY AIOLI:
1 tablespoon finely chopped fresh rosemary
1 garlic clove, finely chopped
Pinch salt
1 large egg yolk
2 teaspoons Dijon mustard
½ cup extra-virgin olive oil
1 tablespoon freshly squeezed lemon juice

FOR THE LAMB BURGERS:
1 pound ground lamb
2 teaspoons garlic powder
2 teaspoons onion powder
1 teaspoon ground cumin
Salt and freshly ground black pepper to taste
2 tablespoons vegetable oil
4 brioche buns
1 white onion, sliced
Quick pickles (see page 115)
Crunchy sea salt, such as Maldon, for garnish

A few of the nuns at Kylemore (I won't name names to protect the lamb burger–loving innocents) sometimes sneak away to the seaside village of Clifden, a 30-minute drive from Kylemore, to pop in to a pub for a pint and a lamb burger. Who can blame them? No one does lamb burgers better than Ireland, and the best way to prepare these is to have your butcher freshly grind the lamb meat before taking it home. Small family-owned butcher shops thrive in rural Ireland, supported by a population that values and invests in family-owned businesses. In this recipe, lamb is paired with a whimsical purple cabbage slaw that provides a welcome snap. The burger is slathered in rosemary aioli, a Provençal condiment with endless variations, its foundation being lemon, garlic, egg yolks, and olive oil. Make an extra-large batch and serve it drizzled over smoked salmon on bagels the next day or in a sandwich or even with roasted potatoes.

TO MAKE THE slaw, in a small bowl, whisk together the mayonnaise, olive oil, vinegar, and mustard seeds. In a large bowl, toss together the cabbage, red onion, and apple, then add the mayonnaise mixture and stir until everything is well coated. Set aside.

TO MAKE THE aioli, use a mortar and pestle or the back of a spoon to smash together the rosemary, garlic, and enough salt to form a paste. Stir together the egg yolk and mustard in a medium bowl, then add the garlic paste and stir to incorporate. Add about one-third of the olive oil in a slow, steady stream and whisk vigorously to emulsify the aioli. Once it reaches this stage, add the rest of the oil in the same slow, steady stream, pausing frequently to ensure that the aioli is thickening up properly. Once all of the oil has been incorporated, whisk in the lemon juice and season with additional salt, if desired. Cover and refrigerate until ready to use.

TO MAKE THE burgers, in a large bowl, combine the lamb, garlic and onion powders, and cumin and mix with your hands until just incorporated. Don't overmix or it will become stiff and lose some of its juiciness when cooked. Season with salt and pepper and form into four patties. Heat the vegetable oil in a large skillet over medium-high heat. Add the burgers and cook until done to your liking, flipping once to encourage browning on both sides, about 5 minutes per side for medium-rare.

MEANWHILE, SPLIT THE buns and toast them. Line the bottom of each bun with onion slices and pickles and spoon on a generous amount of aioli. Top with a burger and a spoonful of the slaw, or serve the slaw on the side for a less messy meal. Either way, be sure to sprinkle everything with sea salt for a crunchy finish.

Victorian Gardening

One of the primary reasons thousands of visitors make a pilgrimage to visit Kylemore Abbey every year is to stroll through the estate's sublime Victorian gardens. Lead gardener Anja Gohlke says, "Much like the Victorians themselves, their gardens were lavish, embellished with features and vegetation that inspired in visitors a sense of awe and wonder."

In Victorian England, it wasn't only affluent landowners who coveted a garden. The middle class also strove to re-create the characteristics of the era's gardens that flourished at the lavish estates. It was Kylemore's first owner who commissioned the property's gardens. They overflowed with the trademark features of Victorian gardens everywhere. There were glass houses for exotic trees such as banana and fig and indigenous varieties such as cherry, plum, damson, pear, and apple. There was a mushroom house and a gamekeeper's cottage, both of which, while no longer operational, have been well preserved to afford visitors an opportunity to experience the garden's former opulence, when it was essentially a community unto itself, with living quarters, a communal kitchen, and a dining hall for the workers.

Signature features of traditional Victorian gardens include ornamental wrought iron arches, neatly manicured gazebos, plaster fountains, ornate statues, bird baths, sundials, pedestals, urns overflowing with greenery and flowers, trellised walls covered with vines, lush borders bursting with neatly trimmed shrubbery, and expansive porches with swings for indulgent afternoons with nothing to do and nowhere to go. The Victorians often created geometric patterns in their gardens, and with the advancement of hybridization, they invented new cultivars of flowers, most notably dahlias and roses. There were greenhouses to shelter ferns, and flower and kitchen gardens that provided staff and families with seasonal bounties and meandering pathways that led curious visitors through the gardens.

The gardens at Kylemore might not be as elaborate as they once were, but they still comprise many acres of gardens, walled gardens, greenhouses, a monastic herb garden appreciated for its medicinal virtues, berry shrubs, fruit and nut orchards, and hedgerows blooming with escallonia, fuchsia, and rosehips. The gardens are diligently tended to by Anja Gohlke, who is never without her pruners and always has an endless list of tasks. "Sometimes the nuns join me in the gardens to harvest blooms for their communal house or fruit, herbs, and vegetables for their meals. I enjoy it when they're here because many of them have lived at Kylemore for decades and they always have so many garden stories to share with me. This is a big job that I have here, keeping this garden and these grounds thriving, but it's a legacy that I've inherited and I am grateful every day to be a part of Kylemore's history."

Rosehip Syrup

MAKES: about 1 quart
PREPARATION TIME: 2 hours

1 pound rosehips
Granulated sugar, as needed

At Kylemore Abbey, rosehips are frequently foraged from the surrounding hillsides and hedgerows. Rosehips are a member of the apple family, and in the early autumn they are to be discovered in abundance in rural Ireland. These teardrop-shaped, ruby-red gems are higher in vitamin C than oranges. They have been transformed for centuries into a syrup suitable for everything from pancakes and bread to waffles and scones. Rosehip syrup delivers a multisensory experience with its inviting floral aroma and delicately sweet flavor. The only trick with this recipe is to be sure to simmer and drain them a few times to remove the prickly hairs that accompany these Celtic beauties.

PREHEAT THE OVEN to 250°F.

CHOP THE ROSEHIPS as finely as possible or pulse them in a food processor. Put the rosehips in a medium saucepan, add 1½ quarts water, and bring to a boil. Reduce the heat to low and simmer gently for 20 minutes. Place a double layer of cheesecloth over a colander set inside a bowl and pour in the rosehips and cooking liquid. Drain for about 30 minutes. Reserve the liquid and return the rosehips to the saucepan, along with 1½ quarts fresh water. Bring to a boil again, then reduce the heat to low and simmer gently for another 20 minutes. Strain as above into the reserved liquid and discard the rosehips. Then, prepare a fresh double layer of cheesecloth and strain the liquid once more to remove all of the irritating little rosehip hairs.

WASH THE SAUCEPAN to remove any residual hairs. Measure the rosehip liquid and pour it back into the saucepan. For every 2 cups liquid, add 1 cup sugar. Bring to a simmer over medium heat and stir until the sugar dissolves. Increase the heat to medium-high and boil for 4 minutes, skimming any scum that forms on the surface. Carefully pour the syrup into a sterilized bottle or jar and seal it shut. The syrup will keep in the refrigerator for up to 3 months.

Sloe Gin Fizz

MAKES: 1 cocktail
PREPARATION TIME: 5 minutes

½ cup water
½ cup granulated sugar
1 ounce sloe gin
½ ounce freshly squeezed lemon juice
½ ounce simple syrup (see headnote)
4 ounces club soda

Sloe berries, from the blackthorn tree, thrive in the hedgerows of Connemara each summer, but these taut, amethyst-colored berries are not ready for harvest until after the first frost, which entices their sweet juices to emerge. The nuns harvest them each season in the same way that the Irish have for centuries.

If you want to make your own sloe gin, prick the berries with a needle to encourage their juices to flow or freeze them overnight and bash them with a rolling pin, before immersing in gin and sugar. The next part of the sloe gin recipe is the most challenging: waiting. To properly infuse your gin, give the sloes at least three months to work their magic in a cool, dark place, vigorously shaking the tightly sealed container about once a week to encourage the infusion. If they are harvested and infused at the right time (depending on when frost hits your region), the gin, with its amethyst or garnet hue depending upon how the light catches it, will be ready just in time for the holidays, when there is no better time to indulge in this regal spirit.

Of course, sloe gin is also available at many liquor stores, but if you're fortunate enough to discover sloes on your property, make your own. It will make your enjoyment of this sloe gin fizz, with its bubbly cap and jewel tone color, all the more virtuous.

FOR SIMPLE SYRUP, combine the water and sugar in a saucepan over high heat and bring to a boil while stirring occasionally. Reduce the heat to medium-low and gently simmer while stirring occasionally until the sugar is dissolved, about 10 minutes. Remove from the heat and cool to room temperature before using. It will keep in a covered container in the refrigerator for up to 1 month.

COMBINE THE GIN, lemon juice, and 1 teaspoon simple syrup in a cocktail shaker filled to the top with ice and give it a robust shake. Strain into a chilled highball glass and pour the club soda on top. Be a little wild with your pour to encourage the fizz.

A Hedgerow Harvest

There is no better way to explore the country-side of Ireland than with a basket in hand ready to receive the berries, nuts, and flowers that flourish there throughout the seasons. There is something wild, healthful, and tasty on hand during every season in Connemara, and the nuns at Kylemore take full advantage of nature's bounty. Foraging is a meditative practice that affords a moment of peace and contemplation in their frequently busy days.

There are sloes for gin, rosehips for syrup, fuchsia for vinegar, elderflowers for cordials, and elderberries for wine, spirits, and jams. There's wild garlic, nettles, chickweed, hazel-nuts, watercress, and blackberries. In the forests are mushrooms waiting to be noticed, and strewn along the seashore await dozens of varieties of seaweed. The nuns also transform their edible bounties into beauty care products, such as soaps, lotions, and balms that they sell in the gift shop.

There is something to be discovered during every season of the year in Connemara because it rarely becomes cold enough to quell growth, and it's a delight to anticipate what edible hillside, forest, or ocean feast awaits just around the sea-sonal bend. Syrups, spirits, jams, and cordials made from foraged foods make wonderful gifts because they not only taste sublime, but they embody the spirit of Ireland too.

Colcannon

Colcannon is a humble dish, prized by the nuns at
Kylemore because it reflects both their philosophy that less
is more and their desire for comfort food on cool and rainy
evenings. Colcannon, or cál ceannann in Gaelic, means
"white-headed cabbage" (although I use green in this version), and it's in virtually every Irish citizen's culinary repertoire. It's essentially mashed potatoes and cabbage. The
key is to add plenty of cream (or whole milk for a lighter
outcome) and butter for rich flavor and a velvety texture.
It's a versatile recipe that can be served as a side alongside
protein or on its own as a vegetarian main dish.

FILL A LARGE saucepan with water, season generously with
salt, and add the potatoes. Bring to a boil, then reduce the
heat to low and simmer until the potatoes are fork-tender,
about 15 minutes.

MEANWHILE, FILL ANOTHER large saucepan with water,
season generously with salt, and add the cabbage. Bring to
a boil, then reduce the heat and simmer until the cabbage
is tender, about 10 minutes. Drain the cabbage and return
it to the pan, then add 1 tablespoon butter and stir until the
cabbage glistens.

DRAIN THE POTATOES and slip off the skins while they are
still hot, then transfer the potatoes to a large bowl. In the
saucepan used to cook the potatoes, combine 3 tablespoons
butter, milk, and scallions and bring to a gentle simmer. Add
the mixture to the potatoes and beat until fluffy and smooth.
Stir in the cabbage and season with salt and pepper. Top with
at least 1 tablespoon butter and serve. Leftovers will keep in a
covered container in the refrigerator for up to 3 days.

SERVES: 4
PREPARATION TIME: 30 minutes

Salt and freshly ground black pepper
    to taste
4 large Idaho potatoes
1 small head green cabbage, about 1-pound,
    cored, quartered, and sliced into 1-inch
    strips
4 tablespoons unsalted butter, plus more as
    needed
3 tablespoons whole milk
2 scallions, thinly sliced

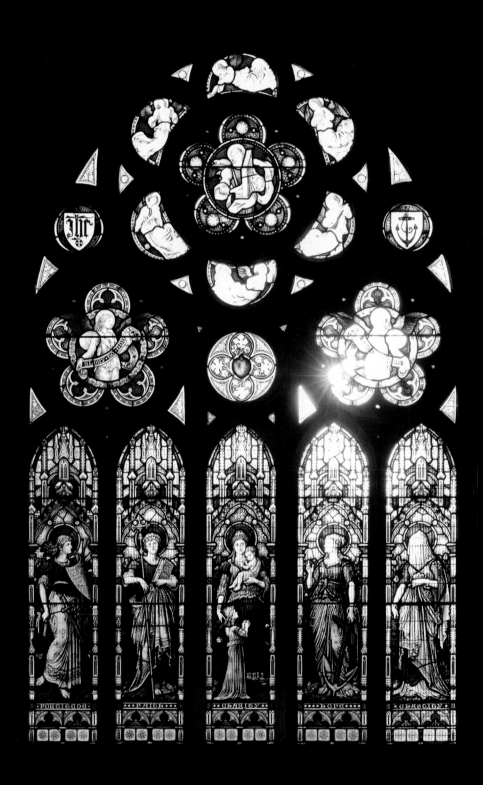

Irish Cheddar and Bacon Soda Bread

The homemade soda bread used for many of the sand-wiches served at Kylemore Abbey's café frequently arrives at the table still hot from the oven. Irish soda bread is one of the simplest and most pleasing bread recipes that has ever been concocted by a creative population with few resources. In this recipe, a mix of all-purpose and whole wheat flours is used, but feel free to use just all-purpose flour for a lighter texture. The buttermilk adds a subtle tanginess, and the bacon, cheddar, and scallions ratchet up the flavor, virtually making a slice of bread a meal onto itself. Soda bread is also baked frequently in the communal kitchen of the nuns, filling the century-old room with its comforting aroma.

PREHEAT THE OVEN to 425°F. Butter a loaf pan or rimmed baking sheet.

IN A LARGE bowl, sift together the flours, baking soda, and salt, then stir in the buttermilk. Add the bacon, cheddar, and scallions and bring the dough loosely together with a wooden spoon or your hands. On a floured work surface, gently knead the dough until it just begins to come together into a shaggy ball. Do not overwork it. Shape it into a loaf and place it in the prepared loaf pan, or shape it into a round and place it on the prepared baking sheet. Using a sharp paring knife, score the surface of the loaf with an X.

BAKE ON THE center rack until the surface is golden brown and a toothpick inserted in the center comes out clean, about 30 minutes, rotating the pan 180 degrees halfway through. Let the pan sit at room temperature for 5 minutes, then remove the bread and cool it on a wire rack for an additional 30 min-utes. Soda bread is best when eaten the same day, preferably slathered with creamy Irish butter.

MAKES: 1 loaf
PREPARATION TIME: 1 hour 15 minutes

Butter, for greasing and serving
2 cups all-purpose flour, plus more for dusting
2 cups whole wheat flour
1 teaspoon baking soda
1 teaspoon salt
1⅔ cups buttermilk
6 bacon strips, cooked until crispy and broken into bite-size pieces
1 cup shredded sharp cheddar cheese
4 scallions, thinly sliced

Salted Caramel Fudge Brownies

MAKES: 12 to 16 brownies
PREPARATION TIME: 45 minutes

¾ cup (1½ sticks) unsalted butter, plus more
    for greasing
6 ounces 60% dark chocolate, broken into
    pieces
⅔ cup cocoa powder

1½ cups granulated sugar
3 large eggs
2 teaspoons vanilla extract
1 cup all-purpose flour
½ cup store-bought melted caramel, kept
    warm until ready to use
Crunchy sea salt, such as Maldon, to taste

"Is it any surprise that it's the chocolate sheep that are the favorites? Everyone comes to Ireland for the sheep," asserts Sister Genevieve, the Benedictine nun from Queensland, Australia, who runs the chocolate program at Kylemore Abbey. Because she's an industrious nun, she also runs a soap-making operation in the former art room of the girls' school that closed at Kylemore in 2010. There she oversees the production of shampoo, soap, candles, balms, and creams that are infused with the botanicals that the nuns forage on the grounds of Kylemore Abbey. She sells these items, along with her chocolate truffles, squares, bars, and famed sheep in the gift shop. The result is a healthy source of revenue for the hardworking nuns who follow in the footsteps of their predecessors, who never sat idle but were instead always working, or always praying—and in the case of the Kylemore nuns, laughing quite a bit, too. These brownies were inspired by the brownies that are offered in the abbey's café. They incorporate the sea salt that is produced in Connemara from the cool Atlantic Ocean perpetually lapping at its shores. They are just as good, if not better, when consumed frozen because they do not freeze entirely but rather develop a chewy, fudge-like consistency.

PREHEAT THE OVEN to 350°F. Line the bottom and sides of a 9-inch square baking pan with parchment paper or aluminum foil, then grease the foil with butter to prevent sticking.

POUR ABOUT 3 inches of water into a medium saucepan. Set a large metal bowl over the pot, making sure the bottom of the bowl does not touch the water. Bring the water to a boil over high heat, then put the chocolate and butter in the bowl. Once the chocolate and butter begin to melt, whisk them together in order to emulsify the mixture. When it is fully emulsified and glossy, remove the bowl from the heat and add the cocoa, whisking until it is fully incorporated. Repeat with the sugar, then the eggs and vanilla, and finally the flour.

POUR THE BATTER into the prepared baking pan, drizzle it with the melted caramel, and sprinkle it with sea salt. Using a sharp knife or a toothpick, swirl the caramel and salt into the batter. Bake until a toothpick or fork inserted in the middle of the brownies comes out mostly clean (it's fine if there's a bit of batter on the toothpick or fork), 30 to 35 minutes. Cool to room temperature, then remove the brownies from the pan by lifting out the parchment or foil. Transfer the brownies to a plate (discard the parchment or foil), cover, and refrigerate until chilled. Cut into 12 or 16 rectangles and serve with a large glass of milk. The brownies will keep in a covered container in the refrigerator for up to 4 days or in the freezer for up to 1 month.

6

Abbey of Saint-Wandrille

BENEDICTINE CATHOLIC
NORMANDY, FRANCE

"Benedictine spirituality, after all, is life lived to the hilt.
It is a life of concentration on life's ordinary dimensions.
It is an attempt to do the ordinary things of life
extraordinarily well."

—*Joan D. Chittister, Benedictine nun*

The history of Fontenelle Abbey, also known as the Abbey of Saint-Wandrille, is the history of Normandy. The abbey was founded by Wandregisel (Saint Wandrille) in the year 649, in Rives-en-Seine. The Vikings raided Saint-Wandrille in the mid-ninth century and burned the church to the ground, but not before the monks were able to escape with its treasured relics. It was rebuilt again, only to be struck by lightning and destroyed once more just after it was consecrated in the early eleventh century. Undaunted, the monks rebuilt it, only to lose it to fire in the mid-thirteenth century.

It continued in this way for centuries. Its perpetual loss and rebirth became a symbol of resilience for the Norman people, who themselves endured their share of conquest. It became an esteemed center of learning for Catholic monks throughout Europe. They were drawn to this rural haven in northwestern France for its renowned library and its acclaimed schools of calligraphy, science, mathematics, and fine arts.

Several centuries later, just after the French Revolution, the abbey was sold at auction. Partial demolition was the fate of the church at this time, and the rest of the buildings were first used as factories and then sold to a local family. In the late nineteenth century, the property was restored to the French Benedictine monks. It was during this time that beloved traditions long abandoned, such as Gregorian chanting for which the monks are world renowned today, were revived. There was one more period of upheaval before the era of peace and industry that exists today. The entire monastic community was exiled in 1901 as a result of Prime Minister Pierre Waldeck-Rousseau's Associations Bill, which stemmed from his belief that clerical communities threatened the sovereignty of the republic. The monks spent the next three decades exiled in Belgium, finally returning in 1931.

The monks missed not only their monastery, but also the culinary traditions of their beloved Normandy during their time away. Its 370 miles of coastline and fertile green, windswept countryside where free-range sheep and cattle graze, pear and apple orchards flourish, and hazelnut and walnut trees thrive, have shaped a distinctive cuisine that has mesmerized gourmands for centuries. Oysters and mussels from the Atlantic Ocean, brown trout and salmon from the meandering rivers, rich cream and buttery cheeses from the cows and sheep, cider and Calvados from the apple trees all make up the tapestry of an ancient culinary history as distinctive as Saint-Wandrille—and as resilient, too.

"Many of the dishes the monks enjoy today at Saint-Wandrille are the same recipes that the cooks here have used for hundreds of years. Why change something that is as close to perfect as human beings will achieve here on earth?" It's a fair question from Father Philippe Chopin, administrative director for this Benedictine monastery. When the menu consists of dishes like rabbit in cider, duckling à la Rouennaise, mussels à la crème, escalope à la normande, andouillette d'Alençon, and estouffade, there's no reason to evolve. Before anyone thinks that these are everyday dishes for the monks, Father Chopin clarifies: "Our daily meals consist of simpler things, like salads made from vegetables and herbs grown in our garden, cheese from nearby dairy farms, honey from our bees, herbal teas from our medicinal garden, and on Sundays we have wine and beer, brewed right here at the monastery." Father Chopin pauses and then smiles. "As I hear myself describe our everyday meals, I do realize that even those are quite splendid."

But before one begins to think that the life of a monk at Saint-Wandrille is nothing but idyllic, Father Chopin stresses, "The Rule of Saint

" Many of the dishes the monks enjoy
today at Saint-Wandrille are the same
recipe that the cooks have used here
for hundreds of years."

Benedict states that we must be industrious and support ourselves through communal activities that generate revenue." There is a retreat center with fifteen rooms that house fifty men and fifty women when they're at full capacity. There is also a dining hall that serves 36,000 meals per year to guests who travel to the monastery from every corner of the world. The popular gift shop at Saint-Wandrille is another testament to industry. The shelves are stocked with products made by the monks, who look to the traditions of the past but also keep on eye on the future to produce everything from beeswax candles, lavender syrup, and pear and apple cider to hazelnut scones, herbal teas, honey, and even cleaning products such as floor polish made from beeswax, a tradition that was revived once the monks returned from their exile in 1931.

Another tradition from the past that has been revived in recent years is beer brewing. Today, Saint-Wandrille is the only monastery producing beer in France. "Our beer brewing custom began in the ninth century. There is evidence of hops being cultivated here at that time. But it wasn't until Saint Hildegard, the abbess of Bingen in the eleventh century, that the use of hop beer became popular. Beer was brewed here for several centuries, but the knights who returned from the Crusades during the Middle Ages developed a taste for wine during their travels. Beer became a relic of the past for hundreds of years."

But in their perpetual quest to be self-sufficient and industrious, the monks decided to revive the tradition of brewing in 2016. They have a testing team of four monks and a professional brewer, an uncle of one of the monks who was trained by the beerologist Hervé Marziou. They needed to overcome several challenges during their brewing journey. One was to configure a modern brewing system into the medieval monastic buildings. But after a few fits and starts, the monks at Saint-Wandrille are proudly brewing beer once more, embracing a tradition that began here 1,100 years ago. Their most popular beer is a light amber-colored blonde ale with a subtle spicy caramel flavor made from four different French hop varieties. They haven't attempted to grow hops on monastic grounds, but Father Chopin says that project is certainly on the horizon. "Like everything at Saint-Wandrille, brewing beer survives because the monks here are forever looking to the past to revive these old traditions. They trust in the past to create a strong foundation for the present and to ensure a positive future. Our commitment to our traditions and to Saint-Wandrille itself makes us resilient and ensures we will endure no matter what tomorrow may hold."

OPPOSITE
The monastery's brewmaster

RIGHT
Saint-Wandrille beer

ABOVE
The fields surrounding
Saint-Wandrille

RIGHT
Radishes

OPPOSITE
The exterior of Saint-Wandrille

Egg Salad with Potatoes and Apples

SERVES: 6 as a side dish
PREPARATION TIME: 45 minutes

½ teaspoon salt, plus more to taste
24 small waxy potatoes, such as fingerling
  or Red Bliss
1¼ cups unsweetened apple juice
2 tablespoons apple cider vinegar
2 Granny Smith apples
Juice of ½ lemon

¼ cup heavy cream, chilled
¾ cup mayonnaise
1 tablespoon Calvados
1 teaspoon garlic powder
1 shallot, finely chopped
6 large eggs, hard-boiled (see page 292),
  peeled, and thinly sliced
Leaves from 2 flat-leaf parsley sprigs, finely
  chopped
½ teaspoon freshly ground black pepper

Some 750 apple varieties grow in Normandy, with over 50 of them used to make a dry cider coveted throughout the region. The cider is sometimes distilled into the renowned Norman brandy known as Calvados, which elevates this salad with its complex dance of bitter and sweet. If you have trouble sourcing Calvados, you can substitute another brandy variety or return to its origin with a dry hard cider. The monks at Saint-Wandrille enjoy this salad during the Norman apple harvest season between September and December; the apples offer a tangy crunch that is tempered by the creamy eggs and earthy potatoes. The original recipe from the monastery includes bittersweet Bulmer's Norman cider apples, but Granny Smith or another tangy apple variety is a fine substitute. The monks use their own homemade apple syrup (sold in the monastic shop) to sweeten the salad, but honey is substituted here since apple syrup can be challenging to find.

FILL A LARGE, heavy-bottomed pot with water, season generously with salt, and add the potatoes. Bring to a vigorous boil, then reduce the heat to medium-low and simmer until the potatoes are just tender enough to be easily pierced with a fork or paring knife, 18 to 20 minutes.

WHILE THE POTATOES are simmering, bring the apple juice to a boil in a small saucepan over high heat. Continue to boil it until reduced by half, about 10 minutes.

DRAIN THE POTATOES and slip off the skins while they are still hot. Cut the potatoes into ¼-inch-thick rounds. Transfer to a large bowl and gently toss the potatoes with the vinegar.

PEEL, CORE, AND quarter the apples, then cut each quarter crosswise into ¼-inch-thick slices. Put the apples in a medium bowl and toss with the lemon juice to prevent them from browning.

PREPARE THE DRESSING by whisking together the cream, mayonnaise, Calvados, and garlic powder in a medium bowl. Stir in the shallot, then pour the dressing over the potatoes. Add the apples, eggs, parsley, salt, and pepper and gently stir everything together using a spatula. The salad is best consumed immediately, when the apples are their brightest and the parsley is lively, but it will keep in a covered container in the refrigerator for up to 2 days.

Buckwheat Crepes with Spinach, Fried Eggs, Bacon, and Neufchâtel

MAKES: 6 crepes
PREPARATION TIME: 20 minutes, plus 2 hours to chill the crepe batter

1 cup buckwheat flour
1 cup 2% or whole milk
2 large eggs
1 tablespoon unsalted butter, melted
½ teaspoon salt

Vegetable oil or nonstick cooking spray, for greasing
12 ounces Neufchâtel cheese, cut into 12 equal slices
¾ cup packed baby spinach leaves
¾ cup crumbled cooked bacon, kept warm
6 large eggs, fried with yolks slightly runny, kept warm

Buckwheat arrived in Normandy in the Middle Ages and has been esteemed for its nutty aroma, hearty texture, and slightly tart flavor ever since. Buckwheat crepes, also known as galettes, are a mainstay at the bustling cafés throughout Normandy and Brittany, where they are folded into neat little squares that temptingly reveal at their epicenters the stuffing within. They are consumed with gusto by tourists and locals alike for breakfast, lunch, dinner, and late-night snacks, preferably washed down with a glass of crisp, dry Norman cider. Buckwheat is gluten-free, which makes it a welcome choice for those with a gluten intolerance. For centuries, the monks at Saint-Wandrille sourced their buckwheat flour from a local watermill that ground this hearty grain for the community each day. Today, the monks must forgo freshly ground buckwheat flour since the mill shut down decades ago.

A crepe pan is preferable for preparation, but a nonstick skillet will also work. Be sure the pan is heated thoroughly before preparing the first crepe and be patient with yourself. If this is your first time making crepes, the first few attempts can prove frustrating. But forge ahead and soon this delightful treat will become a mainstay in your home, just as it is at Saint-Wandrille. The trick is to quickly flip the crepe using either a silicone spatula or a large offset spatula once the batter is covered in tiny bubbles and the edges have just begun to set and have turned a light golden brown. With practice, you might even be able to flip the crepe using nothing but a deft flick of the wrist holding the pan like the monks at Saint-Wandrille do.

Stuffed crepes (galettes complètes) are endlessly versatile. Additional stuffing ideas include asparagus and goat cheese drizzled with a high-quality balsamic vinegar, charred radicchio and smoked ham with a potent soft cheese such as Taleggio, roasted butternut squash with pumpkin seeds and Parmesan, smoked salmon with capers and cream cheese, roasted chanterelles or porcinis with caramelized shallots, roasted garlic and thyme, crab or shrimp with wilted scallions, béchamel and grated lemon zest, and the ridiculously indulgent (and deliriously good) combination of Nutella and sliced bananas for dessert. For this recipe, if you have trouble sourcing Neufchâtel cheese, swap it out for any semi-soft, bloomy-rind cheese such as Brie, Camembert, or l'Explorateur.

Recipe continues

IN A LARGE bowl, whisk together the flour, milk, eggs, melted butter, and salt until incorporated. Cover the bowl with a damp kitchen towel and refrigerate for at least 2 hours. This step will prevent your crepes from becoming chewy and will reduce the chance of breakage when they are cooked.

PREHEAT A CREPE pan or small nonstick skillet over medium-high heat until a drop of water flicked on it sizzles upon contact. While the pan heats, thin the batter by stirring in a little water until incorporated. It should be as runny as a thin cake batter. Use more water for thinner crepes and less for a thicker result. Wad up a paper towel, dip it in the oil, and carefully grease the pan (or spray it).

LADLE ABOUT ⅓ cup batter into the center of the pan and swirl the pan to ensure the batter is distributed evenly; it should thinly coat the surface. Once the surface of the crepe is covered in tiny bubbles and the edges have begun to set and have turned a light golden brown, 1 to 2 minutes, gently use a silicone spatula or offset spatula to release the edges of the crepe from the pan and, as quickly as you can, flip it over. Continue to cook until the surface looks dry and the crepe releases easily from the pan, 1 to 2 minutes more. Using the spatula or by tipping the pan, transfer the crepe to a clean plate. Wipe away any residual batter from the pan using a paper towel, allow the pan to reheat, grease it, and repeat the process until all of the batter has been used; you should get 6 crepes. If you won't be serving the crepes right away, wrap them in plastic wrap and refrigerate for up to 1 day until you're ready to use them.

TO COMPLETE EACH crepe, heat the crepe pan or skillet over medium heat. Place a cooked crepe in the pan and heat it up on one side, about 1 minute. Place two slices of Neufchâtel in the center of the crepe and top it with about 2 tablespoons spinach, 2 tablespoons crumbled bacon, and a fried egg. Fold the sides of the crepe over the filling to form a square. Continue to warm the crepe until the ingredients are heated through, 2 to 3 minutes. Serve right away.

Camembert on Toast with Pears, Hazelnuts, and Salted Caramel

MAKES: about 14 toasts
PREPARATION TIME: 30 minutes

¾ cup granulated sugar
¾ cup heavy cream
⅓ cup salted butter, cut into ½-inch cubes, room temperature
¼ teaspoon crunchy sea salt, such as Maldon, plus more for garnish
1 baguette, cut on the diagonal into 14 (¾-inch) slices
14 ounces Camembert, cut into 28 slices
2 pears, cored, halved, and thinly sliced lengthwise
½ cup coarsely chopped hazelnuts, toasted

Cheese is a mainstay at the monastic table of Saint-Wandrille, and two or three options are usually served at every meal. For holidays or festival days, more lavish Norman cheese varieties such as Le Crémeux du Mont-Saint-Michel or Brillat-Savarin would be served, but on most days, Camembert graces the table. Camembert might be considered a more pedestrian cheese due to its wide availability throughout many parts of the world, but the complex flavor and silken texture of genuine AOC (special designation of origin) Camembert from Normandy is quite extraordinary. The milk used to make genuine Camembert, which is named after a small village in Normandy, is sourced from brown and white Normande cows that spend their days grazing beneath the apple trees in the lush green pastures of the region. Their aromatic milk is what gives Camembert its slightly grassy, mildly fruity flavor, with a hint of wild garlic and an earthy afternote.

Salted butter caramels are one of Normandy's most iconic sweet treats. This recipe includes a method to make salted butter caramel sauce, but if you're looking for a store-bought substitute, seek out the brand Salidou, a decadent and utterly perfect caramel sauce from La Maison d'Armorine in Brittany. If you decide to make your own, it's sure to become a go-to favorite topping for ice cream, pancakes, and waffles, or even enjoyed on its own by the heaping spoonful.

Hazelnut trees flourish on the grounds of Saint-Wandrille, and the monks harvest the nuts from August through October. They snack on them throughout the year and include them in monastic mainstays like tarts, cookies, and breads. This easy-to-assemble recipe celebrates so many of the ingredients that define the unique characteristics of Normandy. Serve it for breakfast or as an afternoon pick-me-up or late-night snack.

Recipe continues

TO MAKE THE caramel sauce, heat the sugar in a small, heavy-bottomed saucepan over medium heat. Heating sugar can be finicky work, but the trick is to not stir it, to let it come to a languid bubbling on its own, and to monitor it closely to prevent it from scorching. The sugar will begin to liquefy and slowly turn from white to light golden brown to a medium amber color, about 6 minutes total. Once it reaches this color, remove from the heat.

WHILE THE SUGAR liquefies, heat the cream in another small saucepan over medium heat, whisking occasionally to prevent it from scorching; do not let it come to a boil. Once it's hot and tiny bubbles are forming on its surface, about 3 minutes, remove from the heat.

ONCE THE SUGAR is ready, carefully pour about 2 table-spoons of the hot cream into the sugar while whisking until it's incorporated. Continue to whisk in the rest of the cream until it is incorporated. Add the butter, a few cubes at a time, and whisk until incorporated. Stir in the salt. Pour the caramel into a glass jar and let it cool to room temperature, then cover and refrigerate for up to 1 month (although it's very doubtful it will last that long!).

PREHEAT THE OVEN to 350°F.

ARRANGE THE BAGUETTE slices on a rimmed baking sheet and bake until they are just toasted, about 4 minutes. Do not let them get too toasty at this stage, because they will need to be heated for a few more minutes to melt the Camembert. Remove from the oven and top each one with 2 slices of Camembert. Return to the oven and toast until the cheese has melted and is oozy and bubbling, about 5 minutes.

WHILE TOASTING, REHEAT the caramel sauce by placing the jar in a saucepan filled with enough water to come two-thirds of the way up the side of the jar. Bring the water to a simmer over high heat. The sauce should begin to melt once the water is simmering. Remove from the heat and carefully remove the jar from the pan using tongs or a kitchen towel.

ARRANGE THE TOASTS on a serving platter, top each one with a few pear slices, drizzle with warm caramel sauce, garnish with hazelnuts, and sprinkle with crunchy sea salt. Serve immediately.

Courgettes à la Crème

Normandy is the region in France with the highest use of land reserved for agricultural purposes. With nearly 70 percent of the region devoted to vegetable and wheat crops, it's no surprise that so many recipes from Normandy showcase vegetables. Zucchini are planted in the spring at Saint-Wandrille. They grow throughout the hot Norman summers alongside a variety of other vegetables, including broccoli, carrots, yellow squash, cauliflower, field peas, green beans, leeks, lamb's lettuce, chard, kale, Brussels sprouts, onions, parsnips, and cabbage. This recipe is a mainstay at Saint-Wandrille throughout the harvest season from June through late September; the delicate flavor of zucchini is especially beloved by the monks when it's thinly sliced into ribbons and then gently cooked in heavy cream. The only thing to be mindful of when preparing this dish is to not overcook the zucchini. It's ready as soon as the ribbons are tender. Feel free to substitute other herbs such as dill or thyme for the parsley.

MELT THE BUTTER in a large sauté pan over medium heat. Add the garlic and sauté until aromatic, about 2 minutes. Add the zucchini ribbons, parsley, and lemon zest and sauté until the ribbons are tender, about 5 minutes. Add the cream and simmer while gently stirring to prevent scorching until the sauce begins to thicken, about 3 minutes. Do not let the cream boil; reduce the heat if it begins to simmer too vigorously. Season with the salt and pepper, sprinkle with additional parsley, and serve hot. This dish is best enjoyed right away but will keep in a covered container in the refrigerator for up to 1 day.

SERVES: 4 as a side dish
PREPARATION TIME: 30 minutes

2 tablespoons unsalted butter
2 large garlic cloves, minced
6 (6-ounce) zucchini, peeled and cut lengthwise into ribbons using a vegetable peeler
Leaves from 4 flat-leaf parsley sprigs, finely chopped, plus more for garnish
1 teaspoon grated lemon zest
⅔ cup heavy cream
½ teaspoon salt
¼ teaspoon freshly ground black pepper

Grilled Oysters with Lavender Mignonette

SERVES: 6
PREPARATION TIME: 45 minutes, plus
2 hours if resting the mignonette before
serving

1 tablespoon lavender buds
2 tablespoons minced shallot

¼ cup champagne vinegar
½ teaspoon grated lemon zest
⅓ cup freshly squeezed lemon juice
⅓ teaspoon freshly ground black pepper
18 large oysters, such as Saint-Vaast or
    Isigny
Lemon wedges, for serving

Oysters from Normandy and the neighboring region of Brittany are renowned for their fleshy texture, iodine-rich health benefits, and nutty, slightly metallic flavor. Two of the most coveted varieties are the voluptuous Saint-Vaast and Isigny oysters, both of which are ideal for grilling. Tourists and locals slurp oysters alongside the region's famed oyster beds, flinging the shells back into the ocean. The monks at Saint-Wandrille embrace a more sustainable approach by scrubbing oyster shells clean, crushing them into a coarse powder, and incorporating it into their compost and gardening soil. The calcium additive is an age-old way to balance soil pH levels, aid in plant enzyme formation, strengthen cell walls, and improve nitrate intake. This results in more robust and flavorful vegetables with a terroir that hints of the briny sea. About once a year, the monks grill oysters over the applewood branches that fall to the ground and are collected for memorable culinary occasions like this one.

Lavender flourishes in a regal amethyst wave alongside the pale, creamy yellow Caen stone (limestone) walls of the monastery. It's transformed by the monastic bees into lavender honey and incorporated by the monks into scones, biscuits, tea, syrup, jam, and in the case of this recipe, an elegant lavender mignonette.

FOR THE MIGNONETTE, bring ½ cup water to a boil in a small saucepan over high heat. Remove from the heat, add the lavender, cover, and let steep for 30 minutes. Strain through a fine-mesh strainer, reserving the liquid and lavender separately. Mince enough lavender to measure 1 teaspoon. Combine the lavender liquid, minced lavender, shallot, champagne

vinegar, lemon zest and juice, and black pepper in a small bowl and stir until incorporated. Ideally, cover and refrigerate for 2 hours to enable the flavors to mingle, but serve it right away if pressed for time.

ADD APPLEWOOD BRIQUETTES (or whichever wood you are using) to a grill, set the grate about 5 inches above, and preheat the grill.

WHILE THE GRILL is heating, scrub the oyster shells with a brush under cold running water to remove residue. Use only live oysters that are heavy and filled with liquid. They should either have tightly sealed shells or, if their shells are partially open, they should clamp shut when tapped. Discard any oysters with broken or open shells that do not respond when tapped or those that do not have liquid inside. Once the grill is heated and the oyster shells are clean, carefully line up the oysters on the grate using a pair of tongs. Cover the grill, open the vents, and grill the oysters until the shells begin to open, 8 to 10 minutes. Take a peek at about 8 minutes to check if any of the oysters are ready. Wear an oven mitt or protect your hand with a dry kitchen towel and use tongs to begin removing the oysters that are ready to prevent them from overcooking. Use an oyster knife, paring knife, or screwdriver to pry open the oyster shells, being careful not to spill the oyster juice. Sever the muscle that connects the shells, discard the top shells (or reserve to pulverize for a garden additive), and arrange the oysters on the half-shell on a serving platter. Serve hot, with the lavender mignonette and lemon wedges alongside. Store any leftover mignonette in a covered container in the refrigerator for up to 3 days.

Butternut Squash Potage with Toasted Pumpkin Seeds and Crème Fraîche

SERVES: 6
PREPARATION TIME: 1½ hours

2 (1½-pound) butternut squashes, peeled, seeded, and cut into 1½-inch chunks
2 medium yellow onions, quartered
3 tablespoons extra-virgin olive oil
6 large garlic cloves, peeled
1 Granny Smith apple, peeled, cored, and cut into 1-inch chunks
1½ quarts low-sodium vegetable stock
¾ cup dry white wine

1 bay leaf
1 thyme sprig, plus chopped fresh thyme for garnish
¼ teaspoon red pepper flakes (optional)
¾ cup crème fraîche, plus more for serving
1 teaspoon salt
½ teaspoon freshly ground black pepper
Toasted pumpkin seeds, for garnish
Crunchy sea salt, such as Maldon, for garnish
Sourdough bread, for serving

Like so many beloved recipes throughout France, the origin story of potage begins with peasant culinary traditions from the medieval era. Potage is essentially a thickened vegetable stew that is cooked low and slow with aromatics and then blended to create a deeply flavorful soup. It was traditionally cooked over an open fire and blended by hand, but an oven and blender come in handy for the contemporary cook who is looking for healthful comfort food. Grains such as barley, amaranth, or farro are sometimes added either before or after the potage has been blended, and meat eaters can stir in shredded cooked chicken, lamb, or crispy pancetta after it is blended. Potage is a cherished recipe at Saint-Wandrille throughout the year, its versatility making it an ideal vehicle for whatever has been harvested from the garden that day, but it's especially welcome in the fall and winter. This butternut squash potage is enticing for both its earthy-sweet flavor and its lively apricot color. Tangy crème fraîche gives it a lift, while the roasted apple lends a subtle, zesty finish. Add a handful of croutons (see page 292) for an additional layer of substance and texture.

PREHEAT THE OVEN to 400°F.

IN A LARGE roasting pan, toss the squash chunks and onions with the oil until everything is glistening. Bake for 10 minutes. Add the garlic cloves and apple chunks and continue to bake until the squash is very tender when pierced with a fork, about 25 minutes more.

TRANSFER TO A large pot and add the stock, wine, bay leaf, thyme sprig, and red pepper flakes (if using). Bring to a boil over high heat, reduce the heat to medium, partially cover, and simmer until the liquid has reduced by one-third, about 35 minutes. Add the crème fraîche and stir until incorporated. Season with the salt and black pepper. Remove the bay leaf and thyme sprig and carefully transfer the potage to a blender. Remove the cap from the lid of the blender and hold a kitchen towel over the hole while blending to allow the steam to escape. Blend, beginning at the lowest speed to prevent splattering and eventually increasing the speed to high, until the potage is smooth and thick. If the texture is too thick, adjust by stirring in water, 1 tablespoon at a time, until the desired consistency is achieved—but don't forget that the trademark of potage is its thick consistency. Some cooks strain potage through a fine-mesh sieve at this point for a smoother texture, but it seems to align more with its rustic peasant origin story if it's left a bit rough around the edges.

TO SERVE, LADLE the potage into prewarmed bowls, dollop with crème fraîche, garnish with toasted pumpkin seeds, and sprinkle with thyme and crunchy sea salt. Serve alongside a rustic loaf of sourdough bread. Store leftover potage in a covered container in the refrigerator for up to 3 days.

Beer-and-Honey-Glazed Pork Loin with Roasted Apples

SERVES: 4
PREPARATION TIME: 1 hour

1 cup dark beer, such as porter or stout
2 tablespoons honey
1 tablespoon apple cider vinegar
2 large garlic cloves, minced
1 (2-pound) pork tenderloin
1 teaspoon kosher salt
½ teaspoon freshly ground black pepper
1 large white onion, coarsely chopped
8 tablespoons (1 stick) salted butter, chilled and cut into ½-inch cubes
2 (5-inch) rosemary sprigs
1 bay leaf
3 sweet-tart apples, such as Gala, Empire, or Fuji, cored and quartered (unpeeled)
Coarsely chopped fresh flat-leaf parsley, for garnish

On the day a priest is ordained at Saint-Wandrille, committing to a life of poverty, obedience, and chastity, he is allowed to choose what the dinner menu will include that evening. Pork loin is a favored choice. It's a good day for everyone since all of the priests and monks indulge collectively. A little more wine is served than usual that evening, and the meal often concludes with a glass or two of Calvados. This recipe is much easier to prepare than its nuanced flavors might suggest. Be sure to select a dark beer such as a stout or porter because it will result in an irresistible caramelized glaze that's rounded out by the honey and tempered by the tanginess of the apples. Serve with your favorite comforting carb; at Saint-Wandrille, fluffy mashed parsnips or roasted celery root are the vegetables of choice.

PREHEAT THE OVEN to 350°F.

IN A LARGE bowl, whisk together the beer, honey, vinegar, and garlic. Put the pork loin in a large roasting pan and season it all over with the salt and pepper. Scatter the onion and butter evenly around the pork, pour the glaze over the top, and add the rosemary sprigs and bay leaf. Cover loosely with aluminum foil. Roast for 10 minutes, then scatter the apples around the pork and cover again with the foil. Continue to roast until an instant-read thermometer inserted into the center of the pork reads 160°F, about 25 more minutes.

DISCARD THE ROSEMARY sprigs and bay leaf. Use a slotted spoon to transfer the onion and apples to a bowl and cover with foil to keep warm. Transfer the pork loin to a serving platter, reserving the juices in the pan, and let it rest for at least 5 minutes, flipping once with tongs to evenly distribute the internal juices.

WHILE THE PORK rests, set the roasting pan over two stovetop burners and reduce the liquid over high heat, scraping up any brown, flavorful bits at the bottom of the pan, 8 to 10 minutes. The sugars in the beer and honey should result in a thick, glistening glaze.

TO SERVE, CUT the pork into ½-inch slices and spoon the onion and apples around it. Drizzle the glaze over everything, garnish with parsley for a pop of color, and serve. Store leftovers in a covered container in the refrigerator for up to 3 days or in the freezer for up to 1 month.

Chicken Normandy

SERVES: 6
PREPARATION TIME: 1½ hours

2 tablespoons vegetable oil, or more as needed
6 bone-in, skin-on whole chicken legs
Salt and freshly ground black pepper to taste
4 ounces bacon lardons
1½ cups coarsely chopped yellow onion
2 celery ribs, thinly sliced
3 garlic cloves, minced
1 tablespoon all-purpose flour
2½ cups dry hard cider
1½ cups chicken stock
1 bay leaf
2 thyme sprigs
⅔ cup crème fraîche
Coarsely chopped fresh flat-leaf parsley leaves, for garnish
Lemon wedges, for serving
Crusty bread, for serving

Early Sunday evenings at Saint-Wandrille include Gregorian chanting performed by the monks for locals who have witnessed this calming tradition every week from the time they were small children. Visitors from around the world are also there to experience this monophonic sacred song in Latin embraced by Roman Catholic monks since it was first developed in the ninth and tenth centuries, a few hundred years after Saint-Wandrille was founded. Those who bear witness marvel at how such a refined sound is born from unaccompanied voices mingling in such a captivating way.

After their singing session concludes, the monks gather for Sunday supper, a meal typically more elevated than those during the rest of the week. Chicken Normandy reflects the same humble yet beguiling nature of a Gregorian chant. Serve these chicken legs with their crispy gold skin, bathed in a luxuriously creamy sauce, right in the casserole dish, family-style—just as the monks do at Saint-Wandrille. Serve with pasta, rice, or mashed potatoes.

PREHEAT THE OVEN to 350°F.

HEAT 2 TABLESPOONS oil in a Dutch oven over medium-high heat. Season the chicken legs all over with salt and pepper. Place 3 chicken legs, skin-side down, in the pot and fry until golden brown and crispy, about 5 minutes. Flip the legs over and fry for another 5 minutes. Using tongs, carefully transfer to a paper towel–lined plate. Repeat with the remaining legs, adding more oil, if necessary. Add the bacon lardons to the pot and fry until they have released most of their fat and are beginning to turn golden brown. Remove them using a slotted spoon and drain on a second paper towel–lined plate. Reduce the heat to medium, add the onion and celery, and sauté until the onion is translucent, about 5 minutes. Add the garlic and sauté until aromatic, about 2 minutes. Add the flour and stir for 1 minute. Add the cider and stir until the liquid begins to bubble, about 1 minute. Add the stock, bay leaf, and thyme sprigs and bring to a simmer. Return the chicken legs, skin-side up, to the pot. Cover and transfer to the oven. Braise for 40 minutes.

TRANSFER THE CHICKEN legs to a plate and cover loosely with aluminum foil to keep warm. Add the crème fraîche to the pot and whisk over medium heat until it is incorporated. Continue to stir the sauce occasionally until it is bubbling and thick enough to coat the back of a wooden spoon, about 5 minutes. Remove the bay leaf and thyme sprigs. Season with salt and pepper.

RETURN THE CHICKEN, skin-side up, to the pot to showcase their crispy gold skin, along with the fried bacon. Garnish with parsley and serve with lemon wedges and crusty bread for sopping up the sauce. Leftovers can be stored in a covered container in the refrigerator for up to 4 days or in the freezer for up to 1 month.

Saint-Wandrille Tonic

When Saint Benedict of Nursia established the Montecassino Abbey in southern Italy in the early sixth century, he wrote in the *Rule of Saint Benedict*, "Before all things and above all things, care must be taken of the sick." Benedictine monks have remained committed to this edict ever since. At the heart of most Benedictine monasteries throughout the world is the medicinal herbal garden, where herbal remedies have been concocted for the monastic community and local population. The monks of Saint-Wandrille have tended to their medicinal garden since the monastery was founded in 649. The botanicals in the herbal remedies they create for countless ailments are sourced either exclusively from the medicinal garden or are blended with those foraged from the hillsides and forests that flourish on the vast monastic property. Rosemary, balsam thyme, sage, honeysuckle, elderberry, juniper, bay laurel, lovage, lemon verbena, garlic chives, and wild fennel are only a few of the edible plants the monks use to concoct their elixirs (and their homemade digestifs and aperitifs).

This cocktail pays homage to the monastic commitment to these medicinal gardens and to Normandy's most celebrated spirit, Calvados. If you have difficulty sourcing it, substitute another high-quality brandy.

RUB THE RIM of a highball glass with the orange peel, then add it to the glass, along with the rosemary and ginger. Muddle gently using a muddler or the back of a spoon. Transfer the orange peel, rosemary, and ginger to a cocktail shaker, along with the Calvados, bitters, and enough ice to fill the shaker. Shake vigorously. Strain back into the highball glass and fill the rest of the glass with tonic water. Garnish with the orange peel and rosemary sprig.

MAKES: 1 cocktail
PREPARATION TIME: 5 minutes

1 (2-inch) orange peel (avoid the white pith)
1 (4-inch) rosemary sprig
1 (¼-inch-thick) piece ginger, peeled
2 ounces Calvados
2 drops bitters, such as Peychaud's
Tonic water, as needed

7

Eihei-ji Temple

ZEN BUDDHISM
FUKUI PREFECTURE, JAPAN

"Just as the great ocean has one taste, the taste of salt,
so also this teaching and discipline has one taste, the taste
of liberation."

—*Gautama Buddha*

Eihei-ji is a renowned temple of the Sōtō school of Zen Buddhism, located in Fukui Prefecture in northern Japan. The temple was founded in 1244 by the Japanese Buddhist monk Eihei Dōgen, who was also the founder of the Sōtō school and is considered one of the greatest Zen Masters in history. He established Eihei-ji as a headquarters of the Sōtō school after his return from studying Zen in China. The temple remains a critical center of Zen practice and education to this day.

Zen Buddhism is a branch of Mahayana Buddhism that originated in China and was brought to Japan in the thirteenth century. It emphasizes the practice of meditation and mindfulness as a means of gaining insight into the nature of existence and realizing one's own potential for enlightenment. Zen also stresses the importance of direct experience and personal realization, rather than relying solely on religious texts and doctrine. It values simplicity, humility, and self-discipline and aims to cultivate a state of inner peace and wisdom.

Eihei-ji was built atop a gently rolling hillside in the dense cedar forests that surround it (some of the trees are as ancient as the temple itself). The remote location of the temple enables the monks and nuns who live there to focus on their daily Zen practice far from the distractions and temptations of densely populated urban centers. The name Eihei-ji means "Temple of Eternal Peace."

The region experiences four distinctive seasons. In the fall, the Japanese maples and ginkgo trees surrounding the temple blaze fiery red and orange. In the spring, the cherry blossoms bloom, perfuming the mountain air with the scent of optimism and hope. In the summer, the moss-colored boulders ringing the temple foundation turn a vibrant electric green. And in the winter, the grounds are covered in a blanket of rejuvenating white snow, snowflakes gently fall-ing from the cool gray sky, covering the heads of the Buddhist statues nestled serenely into the landscape.

The monastery follows the strict traditional monastic practices of Sōtō Zen, including zazen (sitting meditation), manual labor, liturgical chanting, and study of Buddhist scriptures. It is a place for intensive Zen training and spiritual growth for the 250 monks and nuns who live there and for thousands of annual visitors who come to experience the traditional practices and teachings of Sōtō.

The temple provides accommodations for overnight guests, who participate in the daily routines of the community and attend meditation and religious services. Guests are invited to experience Zen bathing during their stay at Eihei-ji. Zen bathing is considered a form of meditation and self-reflection, where the bather washes away the stress and impurities of the body and mind, symbolizing a cleansing of the spirit. This bathing practice is done in a tradi-tional Japanese onsen or hot spring, with the use of natural hot water, and is typically performed in silence and in accordance with specific Zen teachings and rituals.

The guests also enjoy traditional shojin ryori cuisine, a vegetarian philosophy of eating that originated in Japan during the Kamakura period. This style of cooking is based on the Buddhist principle of ahimsa, or non-harm, and requires monks to abstain from eating meat, fish, or other animal products. The food is prepared follow-ing the principle of ichi ju san sai, or "one soup, three sides," plus rice and pickles. The main ingredients used in shojin ryori cuisine include soybean products, such as tofu, miso, and yuba,

" Buddha said that the mind precedes all mental states. Mind is the chief; all mental states are mind-wrought. This suggests that the state of the mind while cooking can greatly impact the experience and outcome."

and vegetables, such as Japanese white radish and burdock root. Tofu is an important source of protein for the monks. Strongly flavored ingredients such as garlic, onions, and ginger are typically avoided in shojin ryori cooking because they are thought to conjure negative emotions.

Alcohol is avoided, and on certain days, fasting is expected from noon until the dawn of the following day as a way to practice self-control. The goal of shojin ryori cuisine is to purify the body and mind through mindful food preparation and consumption.

The strict daily routine of the monks at Eihei-ji begins at 3:30 a.m. or 4:30 a.m. in the winter, when they perform meditation, read, and chant sutras. For breakfast, they have a bowl of rice gruel with pickles. Afterward, they complete various tasks, like cleaning, weeding, and snow shoveling. The floors and corridors have been kept smooth through daily cleaning for centuries. The monks then continue with more reading and chanting. Dinner at 5 p.m. is simple and follows a set ritual, where the placement of the bowl and utensils is of utmost importance because it reflects the teachings of Zen itself. The placement varies depending upon the ingredients, meal being served, and time of day. After dinner, the monks either participate in a zazen session or listen to a lecture before retiring to bed at 9 p.m. Every five days, the monks shave each other's heads and take baths.

The person who is responsible for cooking at Eihei-ji is known as the tenzo. At Eihei-ji, cooking and meditation are not separate. They hold equal value as important forms of cultivation. The monks believe that careless cooking without considering others is not considered a form of cultivation. At the temple, the tenzo is someone with high spiritual aspirations who carries out the work in the kitchen with care, not delegating it to others. Doing so would result in missing out on the opportunity for spiritual growth.

The kitchen at Eihei-ji is cavernous and has an industrial aesthetic that diverges from the rest of the temple, which hums with a serene energy, its meticulously handcrafted pillars, staircases, and ornately framed doorways reflecting the tranquil nature of the monks themselves. In contrast, the kitchen is a lively place that buzzes with the intensity of any busy kitchen. At the various stations, the tenzo and his apprentices work on multiple dishes. The smoky aroma of dashi floats past a monk chopping cabbage heads in one corner of the kitchen and a monk peeling ginkgo nuts in another. At the heart of the room, rice and tofu are always in some state of preparation, and just beyond the kitchen's ornately carved cedar doors, red and black lacquered plates are being arranged on a massive wooden serving station in preparation for lunch. There is the faint aroma of toasted sesame seeds in the air and the hiss of oil hitting a pan. The cooks quietly move with industrious efficiency, guided by a timeworn routine made up of small but meaningful habits.

The tenzo at Eihei-ji prefers to be referred to by his title rather than his name. He says it is his duty, his daily practice, the rituals of the kitchen, and the care and commitment he has for others that is of value to him. He pauses for a moment from his current task of deftly chopping fresh ginkgo nuts. Without looking up he says, "Buddha said that the mind precedes all mental states. Mind is the chief; all mental states are mindwrought. This suggests that the state of the mind while cooking can greatly impact the experience and outcome." He grins briefly and knowingly before quietly returning to the task at hand.

OPPOSITE
A monk ascending the stairs at
Eihei-ji Temple

OPPOSITE
Eihei-ji Temple

RIGHT
Umeboshi (pickled plums) and
takuan (pickled daikon radishes)

BELOW
The kitchen at Eihei-ji Temple

Namasu

Namasu consists of refreshing daikon and carrots pickled in rice vinegar. The original recipe, which typically contained meat or fish, was brought to Japan from China in the eighth century. This version is a component of most of the monks' meals at Eihei-ji. Yuzu is a citrus fruit that infuses namasu with a tart astringency similar to grapefruit, a flash of tangy sharpness akin to lemon, and a delicate floral aroma. Lemon can be substituted if you have trouble sourcing yuzu.

IN A COLANDER set over a large bowl, toss together the daikon, carrots, and yuzu peels. Add the salt and stir gently to incorporate. Set aside at room temperature for 25 minutes.

MEANWHILE, IN A medium bowl, whisk together the yuzu juice, vinegar, 1 tablespoon water, and sugar until the sugar is dissolved. Using your hands, gently squeeze out any additional liquid from the daikon, carrots, and yuzu peels, being careful not to mangle the daikon and carrots. Add the daikon and carrots to the rice vinegar liquid and toss until incorporated. Garnish with toasted sesame seeds, if desired. Serve at room temperature or chilled; namasu is best when the vegetables are fresh and crisp, although it will keep in a covered container in the refrigerator for up to 2 days.

SERVES: 4 to 6 as a side dish
PREPARATION TIME: 30 minutes

1 (14- to 16-inch) daikon radish, peeled and julienned
2 (6-ounce) carrots, peeled and julienned
Peel and juice of 1 yuzu
2 teaspoons kosher salt
3 tablespoons rice vinegar
1 tablespoon granulated sugar
Toasted sesame seeds, for garnish (optional)

Gomashio

Gomashio is a flavorful condiment made from sea salt and black or golden sesame seeds. The word translates as "salt and pepper" to describe the color contrast between the black sesame seeds and the white salt. The sesame seeds are unhulled, which means their shells are not removed. This adds a subtle bitterness to the gomashio. It's sprinkled over many dishes throughout Japan, including plain rice, sekihan (rice with red beans), and onigiri (rice balls). It's a standard fixture in Buddhist shojin ryori cuisine. Sometimes the salt is smoked before it's mixed with the sesame seeds for a more complex flavor. For a sweet alternative, sugar is stirred in before it's served. In coastal areas, the salt is sometimes swapped out for dried dulse or wakame for a brinier flavor note and a healthful iodine boost. Gomashio is traditionally ground using a Japanese mortar and pestle known as a suribachi, but any mortar and pestle or even a spice grinder can be used.

PREHEAT THE OVEN to 325°F.

SPREAD OUT THE sesame seeds in an even layer on a rimmed baking sheet. Toast until aromatic, about 10 minutes, shaking the baking sheet every 3 to 4 minutes to ensure even toasting. Transfer the sesame seeds to a clean, dry plate and cool to room temperature, about 15 minutes. Using a mortar and pestle or a spice grinder, combine the toasted sesame seeds and the salt and either pulverize or pulse in the grinder until it reaches a texture similar to coarse sand. Use immediately or store in a covered container in a cool, dark place for up to 1 week.

MAKES: 1 cup
PREPARATION TIME: 30 minutes

1 cup raw, unhulled black or golden sesame seeds
1 tablespoon flaky sea salt, such as gray Celtic, or crunchy sea salt, such as Maldon

Okayu

SERVES: 4

PREPARATION TIME: 1 hour 20 minutes

⅔ cup Japanese short-grain rice

3 cups water (or 1½ cups water plus 1½ cups stock or dashi)

½ teaspoon crunchy sea salt, such as Maldon

Okayu is a comforting dish of slowly cooked rice porridge that serves as the foundation for many meals at Eihei-ji. It requires only two ingredients, rice and water, which makes it not only an economical dish to serve dozens of monks in training but a nutritious and easily digestible one, too. Okayu is an omnipresent dish through all stages of life in Japan. It's usually one of the first solid meals an infant experiences and is a comforting meal served to the elderly in their final stages of life. At Eihei-ji, it's usually served with Namasu (page 198), Gomashio (page 199), and umeboshi, pickled plums. Other ideas include thinly sliced scallions, a runny poached egg, smoked salmon or other smoked fish, thinly sliced radishes, and nori flakes, with each one arranged in a separate bowl. For something sweeter, top with honey or brown sugar. If you'd prefer a more flavorful okayu, replace half the water with vegetable stock or dashi. Use polished, short-grain sushi rice (haku-mai), which is widely available in most grocery stores or specialty markets. Okayu is similar to the Cantonese rice porridge dish congee but has a thicker texture. If you prefer a looser version, increase the volume of water or stock. In Japan, okayu is traditionally prepared in a glazed clay pot called a donabe because of its ability to evenly circulate heat, but any heavy-bottomed pot will do.

PUT THE RICE in a colander and rinse it under cold running water until the water runs clear. This step will remove any excess starch, resulting in a less gummy okayu.

COMBINE THE RICE and 3 cups water in a heavy-bottomed pot, cover, and let sit at room temperature for 30 minutes. Keep covered and bring the water to a boil over medium-high heat. Reduce the heat to medium-low and gently simmer until the rice has broken down and the okayu is thick and creamy, about 30 minutes. Remove from the heat and let rest for 15 minutes.

SEASON WITH THE salt, spoon the okayu into prewarmed bowls, and serve. Leftover okayu can be stored in a covered container in the refrigerator for up to 3 days. It does not freeze well.

Homemade Tofu

MAKES: about 2 cups
PREPARATION TIME: 2 hours, plus 12 hours to soak the soybeans

3 cups dried soybeans
1 tablespoon gypsum (calcium sulfate) or nigari (magnesium chloride)
½ cup distilled water

Tofu was invented by the Chinese around 100 BCE and was introduced to Japan by Zen Chinese priests in the eighth century. Eihei-ji would have been one of the first places to begin using tofu in the country, and it is still enjoyed by the monks there 1,300 years later. Tofu is made from fermented soybeans and is appreciated for its silken texture as well as for the protein it adds to their strict plant-based diet. In the seventeenth-century *Shokin Ryori Kondate Shu (A Collection of Courses in Shojin Cuisine),* over 90 percent of the recipes featured tofu. Several dishes included kouya, or dehydrated tofu, and nearly all of them called for yuba, or sheets of dehydrated tofu skin. Many recipe titles referenced animals, such as tanuki (raccoon dog), shigi-yaki (roast snipe), and ganmodoki (mock goose), as the shojin chefs attempted to re-create the look and flavor of meat using tofu.

To make tofu, soybeans and water are combined to produce soy milk, then a coagulant is added to separate the curds and whey in the same way that cheese is made. The coagulant is typically gypsum (calcium sulfate) or nigari (magnesium chloride), both of which are available in Asian specialty markets. Tofu has a neutral flavor, and the only taste is derived from the coagulant being used. Gypsum is slightly salty and nigari has a subtly bitter flavor. Both options will result in firm, velvety tofu.

The only special equipment you need to make tofu is a tofu mold (available in Asian markets). Once you've collected your coagulant and tofu mold, you're on the way to silky tofu and will soon discover that store-bought tofu is no comparison to fresh homemade tofu.

PUT THE SOYBEANS in a colander and rinse under cold running water for several minutes to remove any residue. Transfer the soybeans to a large bowl and cover with cold water by 3 inches. Loosely cover with a kitchen cloth and soak the soybeans at room temperature for 12 hours.

DRAIN THE SOYBEANS in a colander and transfer to a food processor. Add 8 cups fresh water and pulse until chunky. Increase the speed to high and blend until creamy and frothy on the surface.

LINE A FINE-MESH strainer with a double layer of cheesecloth, set it over a large bowl, and set aside. Transfer the soybean mixture to a large, heavy-bottomed pot and bring to a gentle simmer over medium heat, stirring frequently with a wooden spoon to prevent scorching. If it begins to simmer too vigorously, turn the heat down and stir to settle the liquid; do not let it boil. Scrape the surface free of any foam that develops.

STEAM WILL BEGIN to rise from the surface in 12 to 15 minutes and the milk will become very foamy and begin to inch its way up the sides of the pot. Keep a close eye on it because foam development can happen very quickly. Once this happens, remove from the heat immediately to prevent the liquid from burning and strain through the prepared cheesecloth-lined strainer. Let it drain and cool undisturbed for at least 1 hour. Clean the pot in order to use it in the next step.

Recipe continues

CAREFULLY BRING TOGETHER the edges of the cheesecloth and then twist it firmly to form a tight ball in order to drain as much of the liquid as possible from the solids. The solids (okara in Japanese) can be discarded—or, better yet, incorporate it into stir-fries, use it as a spread for sandwiches, sprinkle it on salads or soups, or eat it by the spoonful because it's very tasty.

BRING THE SOY milk to a simmer over medium heat once more, stirring frequently with a wooden spoon to prevent it from burning the bottom of the pot. Do not let it boil. Turn the heat down to low once steam begins to form on the surface and simmer gently for 5 minutes, stirring frequently. Remove from the heat and scrape away and discard any skin that has formed on the surface.

IN A SMALL bowl, combine the coagulant and distilled water and whisk with a fork until the coagulant has dissolved and a slurry has formed. Vigorously stir the soy milk with a wooden spoon for 15 seconds, then add one-quarter of the coagulant and stir for another 5 seconds. Remove the spoon from the pot, then sprinkle another one-quarter of the coagulant over the surface of the soy milk. Cover the pot and wait for 4 minutes. Gently stir the top of the soy milk for a few seconds, then sprinkle another one-quarter of the coagulant over its surface. Cover the pot for 5 minutes. Gently stir the soy milk for a few seconds, then add the rest of the coagulant. Cover for a final 4 minutes. At this stage, the solids and liquid should have begun to separate in the same way that curds and whey separate during the cheesemaking process. The liquid should be a tawny yellow color and the solids should be ivory.

LINE A TOFU mold with four layers of cheesecloth and position it over a bowl that is large enough to hold all of the liquid. Using a ladle, begin pouring the curds and whey into the mold in stages. Gently press the curds with the back of the ladle after each drainage to remove additional whey from the curds. Let the curds drain for a few minutes before adding the next portion. Be patient in the same way that the tenzo would be in the kitchen of Eihei-ji. This is quiet, meditative work.

ONCE ALL OF the curds have been drained, pour the whey into a container, cover, and refrigerate. Whey is packed with nutrients and has a similar tanginess to buttermilk. The monks at Eihei-ji enjoy it as a healthful beverage, but it can also be added to soups and sauces to brighten their flavor. Set the tofu mold back over the bowl and arrange the excess cheesecloth over the curds like you're wrapping a gift. After the cheesecloth is securely in place, place about 2 pounds of weights (such as canned goods) on top and gently press them down. Let the tofu rest and drain at room temperature for about 30 minutes, or a little less if you prefer softer tofu. Remove the weights and refrigerate the mold and tofu until the tofu is chilled enough to cut into cubes or slices. It's now ready to be baked, fried, grilled, steamed, or enjoyed as is. If you don't eat it all right away, store the remainder in a container with enough cold water to cover it by an inch or two. Cover and refrigerate for up to 3 days.

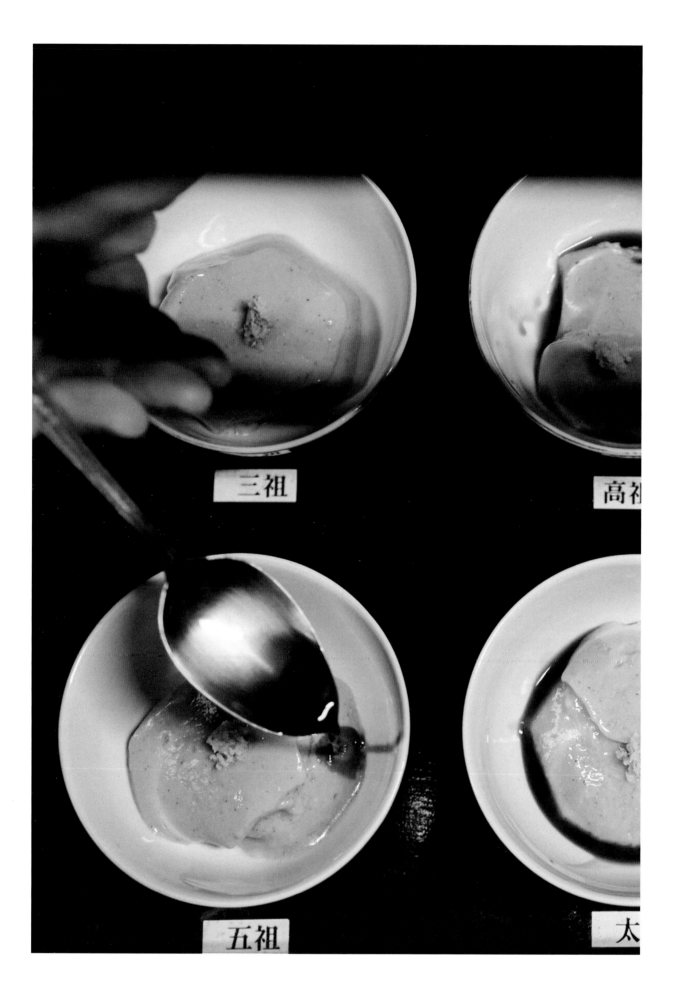

三祖　　　　高祖

五祖　　　　太

Ankake Dofu

SERVES: 4
PREPARATION TIME: 15 minutes

12 ounces firm tofu, store-bought or
    homemade (page 203), cut into 8 even
    cubes
2 ounces dried kombu
1 tablespoon potato starch
1 cup dashi
¼ cup dark soy sauce
1½ teaspoons granulated sugar
Wasabi paste, for serving
1 tablespoon grated fresh ginger
2 scallions, thinly sliced

Ankake dofu is served at virtually every meal at Eihei-ji. Ankake translates as "covered or poured sauce," which in this case is a velvety dashi broth poured atop silken cubes of firm tofu. Every bite is packed with the savory flavoring of umami. In ankake dofu, the pleasurable, slightly meaty flavor is attributed to the kombu, dashi, and soy sauce. Kombu is a seaweed variety that is frequently added to the recipes at Eihei-ji. The tenzo at Eihei-ji recommends rinsing the kombu well under cold running water before it is used to remove any residual sea salt.

Dashi, a hardworking stock made from dried bonito flakes or a combination of kombu and bonito, forms the flavorful backbone of miso soup and many other Japanese recipes. It's the easiest way to add savory depth to a dish and can be purchased at Asian grocery stores and many supermarkets. Potato starch, or katakuriko, is a common thickener in Japanese recipes and transforms the gentle dashi broth into a silky sauce that clings seductively to the tofu. Katakuriko is widely available at Asian markets, but if you have trouble sourcing it, arrowroot, cornstarch, or tapioca starch can be substituted. The tenzo recommends whisking the sauce vigorously immediately after adding the slurry in a slow, steady stream to prevent lumps from forming.

IN A MEDIUM saucepan, combine the tofu, kombu, and 1½ cups water. Bring to a simmer over medium-high heat, then reduce the heat to low and gently simmer while you prepare the broth.

IN A SMALL bowl, whisk together the potato starch and 2 tablespoons water to form a slurry; set aside. In another medium saucepan, combine the dashi, soy sauce, and sugar and bring to a simmer over medium-high heat. Stir with a wooden spoon until the sugar is dissolved. Reduce the heat to medium, add the potato slurry, and whisk vigorously until the liquid begins to thicken, about 30 seconds. Remove from the heat.

REMOVE THE TOFU from its liquid using a slotted spoon and evenly divide into 4 bowls. Pour the broth over the tofu and garnish each serving with wasabi paste, ginger, and scallions. Serve while warm. Ankake dofu does not store well and should be enjoyed immediately.

Sataimo no Nimono

SERVES: 4
PREPARATION TIME: 50 minutes

8 Japanese taro roots
2 teaspoons salt
1 tablespoon vegetable oil
3 cups dashi
½ cup sake
1½ tablespoons sugar
1½ tablespoons dark soy sauce
1½ tablespoons mirin
Yuzu or lemon peel, to serve

Taro root is enjoyed by the monks at Eihei-ji for its subtle sweetness, which complements the savory depth of the dashi it is gently simmered in for sataimo no nimono. This recipe includes sake, but because the monks at Eihei-ji do not consume alcohol, they substitute rice wine vinegar with a low alcohol content that cooks off during the simmering process. Feel free to use rice wine vinegar if you like, but the sake does elevate and round out the flavor a bit more than the vinegar.

Taro is a starchy root vegetable that is prized for its dense texture and for the way it absorbs the other flavors in a dish. The tenzo at Eihei-ji uses Japanese taro, known as sataimo, which is slightly smaller than other taro varieties. The tenzo advises that the taro root be blanched before it's added to the sauce. This step will remove its bitterness as well as the slime that forms on its surface once it is cut. Blanching also helps prevent scum from forming on top of the broth during the simmering process. He also advises that the taro pieces be lightly coated in oil before they are simmered in the sauce to lock in their flavor. This dish is traditionally garnished with yuzu peel, which is similar to lemon but with a slightly more pungent flavor; if you have trouble sourcing yuzu, lemon can be substituted.

RINSE THE TARO roots under cold running water to remove any residual sediment. Trim both ends, then remove the thick skin using a vegetable peeler. Cut each taro root into bite-size pieces, transfer the pieces to a bowl, sprinkle with the salt, and gently toss until the pieces are evenly salted.

BRING A LARGE pot of water to a vigorous boil. Add the taro pieces and blanch until just tender, about 5 minutes. Drain in a colander and rinse for 30 seconds under warm running water to remove any sliminess. Rinse the pot, then return the taro to it. Drizzle with the oil and gently toss until the pieces are glistening.

ADD THE DASHI, sake, and sugar to the pot and bring to a simmer over medium-high heat. Reduce the heat to low and gently simmer for 5 minutes, then add the soy sauce. Simmer until the sauce reduces by about half and the taro is very tender, 15 to 20 minutes. Add the mirin and remove from the heat.

REMOVE THE TARO root from the pot using a slotted spoon and divide evenly into 4 bowls. Ladle the sauce on top and garnish with yuzu peel. Store any leftovers in a covered container in the refrigerator for up to 3 days.

Eihei-ji Cabbage Rolls

MAKES: 8 cabbage rolls
PREPARATION TIME: 1 hour

½ cup dark soy sauce
⅓ cup mirin
4 tablespoons thinly sliced scallions
1 tablespoon minced fresh ginger
2 teaspoons grated lemon zest
Salt, as needed

1 (8-ounce) lotus root, peeled and cut into
⅛-inch slices
8 large napa cabbage leaves
1 quart dashi
1 cup (½-inch) firm tofu cubes, store-bought
or homemade (page 203)
½ cup coarsely chopped canned and
drained ginkgo nuts

In keeping with the Zen Buddhist commitment to leading a zero-waste lifestyle, these cabbages rolls are a vehicle for whatever leftover vegetables remain at the end of the week. This recipe features homemade tofu, steamed lotus root, and ginkgo nuts. Lotus root adds a snappy texture and has a special significance in Zen Buddhism, as it represents purity of the mind, body, and spirit and detachment from physical desire and materialism. In Zen Buddhism, the ginkgo tree represents vitality, long life, and hope. Ginkgo trees are considered holy and are often found at temples and other places of worship. In keeping with his commitment to cooking in step with the growing season, the tenzo at Eihei-ji uses fresh ginkgo nuts when they are in season. In this recipe, canned ginkgo nuts are used.

IN A SMALL bowl, whisk together the soy sauce, mirin, 2 tablespoons scallions, 1½ teaspoons ginger, and 1 teaspoon lemon zest; set the sauce aside.

BRING A LARGE pot of salted water to a boil over high heat and prepare a large ice bath. Add the lotus root slices to the boiling water and blanch until crisp-tender, about 5 minutes. Using a slotted spoon, transfer to the ice bath. Return

the water to a boil and add the cabbage leaves. Blanch for 30 seconds, then gently remove using tongs or a slotted spoon and transfer to the ice bath. Once the lotus root and leaves are cool, drain and pat dry with a clean kitchen towel.

POUR THE DASHI into the base of a steamer (or into a pot or wok if using a bamboo steamer). Bring the dashi to a gentle simmer over medium heat, then reduce the heat to low.

WHILE THE DASHI heats up, arrange the cabbage leaves, interior-side up, in an even layer on a clean work surface. Evenly divide the tofu cubes among the leaves, placing them lengthwise on the leaf. Top the tofu with the chopped ginkgo nuts and the lotus slices, then drizzle with about 2 teaspoons reserved sauce. You should have about half the sauce left over for drizzling over the rolls before serving them.

FOLD THE BOTTOM and top of each cabbage leaf over the filling, then fold in the sides to form a tight roll around the ingredients. Arrange the cabbage rolls, seam-side down, in the steamer tray, cover, and place the steamer tray over the simmering dashi. Steam the rolls for 15 minutes. Remove from the heat and, once the rolls are cool enough to handle, arrange them on a serving platter. Drizzle with the remaining sauce, garnish with the remaining 2 tablespoons scallions, 1½ teaspoons ginger, and 1 teaspoon lemon zest and serve warm. The rolls are best enjoyed right away, but leftovers will keep in a covered container in the refrigerator for up to 1 day before getting soggy.

PREVIOUS
The tenzo preparing cabbage leaves
for Eihei-ji Cabbage Rolls with
ginkgo nuts

Nimono

This rustic dish, which is essentially a Japanese hot pot, is a favorite at Eihei-ji because it is the perfect vehicle to honor whatever vegetables are in season. Nimono has a rich flavor that deepens over time, making this one of those dishes that tastes even better the day after it's prepared. Although it's rare to use oil in shojin ryori cuisine, the monks make an exception for its inclusion in this dish because of the nutty flavor that toasted sesame oil imparts.

Burdock root is a popular ingredient in Japan, where it's referred to as gobo. It's appreciated for its high fiber content, which aids in digestion, and the earthy flavor it imparts to a dish. It is quite fibrous and firm when raw but softens easily when simmered in broth. The tenzo at Eihei-ji uses fresh bamboo shoots for his nimono, but this recipe calls for canned to make it more convenient. Feel free to vary the vegetables in this soup; suggestions include parsnips, turnips, lotus root, rutabaga, napa cabbage, and enoki mushrooms.

IN A WOK or large sauté pan, heat 1 tablespoon oil over medium heat. Add the burdock and carrots and sauté until just tender, about 5 minutes. Transfer the burdock and carrots to a large pot. Add 1 quart water, the dashi, soy sauce, rice wine vinegar, and sugar to the pot and bring to a boil over high heat. Reduce the heat to low and add the daikon, bamboo shoots, and mirin. Cover and simmer gently until the vegetables are tender and the nimono is deeply aromatic, 35 to 40 minutes. Add the scallions and remaining 1 tablespoon sesame oil and simmer for 5 more minutes. Remove from the heat and ladle into bowls, or serve communally with the steaming pot at the center of the table. Leftover nimono will keep in a covered container in the refrigerator for up to 3 days.

SERVES: 4
PREPARATION TIME: 1 hour 20 minutes

2 tablespoons toasted sesame oil
1 (8-ounce) burdock root, peeled and cut into ¼-inch slices (about 1½ cups)
2 (6-ounce) carrots, peeled and cut into ¼-inch slices
1 quart dashi
2 tablespoons dark soy sauce
2 tablespoons rice wine vinegar
2 teaspoons granulated sugar
1 (4-ounce) daikon radish, grated
1 (8-ounce) can bamboo shoots, drained
2 tablespoons mirin
2 scallions, thinly sliced

Shiro Goma Dofu

MAKES: about 16 portions
PREPARATION TIME: 15 minutes, plus 2 hours to chill

Vegetable oil or nonstick cooking spray, for greasing
¼ cup kudzu powder, cornstarch, or potato starch
2 cups plus 2 tablespoons warm water
⅔ cup tahini

Goma dofu is a hallmark of shojin ryori temple cuisine, and no proper ceremonial meal would be complete without this elegant indulgence at the end of it. The name goma (sesame) dofu (tofu) is misleading because this sweet delicacy isn't tofu at all. Instead, it contains sesame paste, water, and kudzu powder, which is used as a thickening agent in the same way that cornstarch or potato starch would be used. It has a similar slightly elastic texture and sheen to tofu, hence the name. The sesame paste adds a slightly sweet, nutty flavor, and it's therefore enjoyed by the monks at Eihei-ji at the end of their ritualized dining ceremony. There are three varieties of goma dofu. The version in this recipe is made with white (shiro) sesame seeds; then there's kuro goma dofu, made with black sesame; and shiro kin goma dofu, which is white and gold sesame.

This dish is served without a garnish, but if you would like to add a flourish, black or red bean paste would add an additional layer of sweetness, or for a more savory bite, consider soy sauce and wasabi. This recipe calls for tahini because it is easier to source, but the traditional shojin ryori goma dofu recipe contains the Japanese sesame paste neri goma. The difference is that tahini contains hulled sesame seeds, whereas unhulled seeds are used in neri goma. Of course, if you wanted to follow the centuries-old goma dofu recipe, you could grind the sesame seeds by hand using a mortar and pestle until a paste is formed. This painstaking task was traditionally given to the novice monks at the temple. The repetitive work was thought to build character and strengthen their resiliency.

It's important to remember with this recipe that like the practice of Buddhism itself, it might not be perfect right away. It's a bit tricky to achieve the ideal sheen and texture, but be patient with yourself and if you enjoy the flavor, keep trying and eventually, like the Eihei-ji monks and their daily practice, you will get there.

GREASE A 9-INCH square baking pan.

IN A SMALL saucepan, combine the kudzu powder and 2 tablespoons warm water and whisk vigorously to form a smooth paste. Whisk in the remaining 2 cups warm water and the tahini until smooth and incorporated. Bring to a gentle simmer over medium heat, whisking frequently to prevent lumps from forming. The liquid will begin to thicken quite quickly as it heats up. After about 3 minutes of whisking and heating, it will start to turn from a milky color to a more translucent shade. Continue heating and whisking until it is the texture of a thickened pudding, 8 to 10 minutes. Once it reaches this stage, carefully pour the hot liquid into the prepared baking pan. Gently tap the dish on the counter a few times to ensure the surface is as even and smooth as possible. Let it cool to room temperature, then refrigerate until chilled, about 2 hours.

USING A PARING knife, slice the goma dofu into squares and serve. Goma dofu will keep in a covered container in the refrigerator for up to 3 days.

OPPOSITE
A traditional monastic lunch

8

Saint John's Abbey

BENEDICTINE CATHOLIC
COLLEGEVILLE, MINNESOTA, USA

"There are those who seek knowledge for the sake of knowledge; that is curiosity.

There are those who seek knowledge to be known by others; that is vanity.

There are those who seek knowledge in order to serve; that is love."

—*Saint Bernard of Clairvaux, Benedictine monk*

The first thing a visitor notices about Saint John's Abbey, located in the midst of the seemingly endless corn and soybean fields of central Minnesota, is the bell banner. Standing at 112 feet, this massive concrete structure, built by renowned Hungarian architect Marcel Breuer (who built only two of his otherworldly masterpieces in the United States), can be seen up to a mile away. Inside the church, an entire honeycombed wall of stained glass panels, designed by the monk Bronislaw Bak, was once the largest stained glass piece in the entire world.

These landmarks might hint at an ostentatious place where prestige and status reign supreme, but this is central Minnesota. Nothing could be further from the truth.

"As Benedictines, we embrace the philosophy of humility and compassion, for our community and for the world as a whole," explains Brother Aelred Senna, a former teacher from New Mexico who found his way to Saint John's twelve years ago. Brother Aelred works at the renowned publishing house located on the monastic grounds and oversees the monastery's expansive menu and culinary program. With over 133 active monks and priests residing at Saint John's, cooking three meals a day, plus feast days, special events, and holidays, is no small task, but Brother Aelred undertakes it with enthusiasm. "I love my community and I love being busy. There is really no better place for me on earth than right here, right now."

Saint John's was established in 1856 by Benedictine monks from Saint Vincent Archabbey in Latrobe, Pennsylvania, who primarily spoke German. The region, now known as Collegeville, Minnesota, is located along the Mississippi River and defined by its glacial lakes, wetlands, oak savanna, prairie, and abundant pine and hardwood forests. The monks called the area schoenthal, or beautiful valley. The monastery quickly grew and in 1857 encompassed Saint John's Preparatory School, Saint John's University, and

Saint John's School of Theology and Seminary. In 1961, the Hill Museum and Manuscript Library was established, which today houses the world's largest archive of ancient manuscript photos from around the globe on microfilm and digital.

The expansive grounds of the abbey (over 2,700 acres) include barns, herds of cattle, a butcher shop, a smokehouse, a chicken house, vegetable gardens, cornfields, root vegetable cellars, a potter's studio, and a flour mill. Over the years, as the university expanded, the self-sustaining lifestyle of the monks diminished a bit. But the enthusiasm for industriousness and productivity remained. Today, it is one of the rare monasteries in the world that continues to grow as opposed to contract.

Vestiges of the older buildings still remain, including a coop that houses carrier pigeons once trained by a monk with a passion for this ancient tradition. There's a thriving woodworking studio, where monks produce much of the furniture for the schools and abbey. There's a cider press and a painting studio filled with massive canvases created by the monk Jerome Tupa, whose work has been supported by the National Endowment for the Arts. There are greenhouses, a bountiful garden growing dozens of varieties of vegetables, an apple orchard, apiary, and a maple syrup production facility. There's an enormous bakery where Johnnie bread is produced. It is a rye and whole wheat flour bread that is coveted throughout central Minnesota for its crusty exterior, tangy flavor, and malty aroma. It was first produced using the abbey's own flour by Brother William Baldus in the 1890s.

Brother Aelred eagerly embraces the traditions brought to the monastery by monks who

OPPOSITE
The honeycomb stained glass
window in the abbey designed by
architect Marcel Breuer

" Much like the rest of the world, we are a global community at Saint John's and I value that so much, that acceptance of one another, the embrace of differences, and the realization that in the end, we all desire the same things: solidarity, joy, shelter, safety, sustenance."

have relocated from around the world. They are attracted to Saint John's partly because it's a large, industrious monastery within a lively university community that affords countless vocational opportunities. But another reason is that it strikes a fine balance between being a forward-thinking institution rooted in the history of Catholicism and the region. "I love learning about Mexican dishes from Brother Pedro, who recently joined us from Mexico City, and I'm learning to make kimchi from Brother Sung-ho, who arrived a few years ago from Seoul. Much like the rest of the world, we are a global community at Saint John's and I value that so much, that acceptance of one another, the embrace of differences, and the realization that in the end, we all desire the same things: solidarity, joy, shelter, safety, sustenance."

"Do you ever miss being a teacher?"
Brother Aelred contemplates this question for a few minutes before smiling and then responding, "I sometimes miss teaching, but should I want to teach again, there are opportunities for me here. What I love about being in a monastic community is just that, the community. In the modern world, in these nuclear families, we can sometimes feel isolated, and I have come to realize that this individualistic approach to living does not work well for me. In a community like this one, each person has their strengths, everyone contributes their talents and their efforts, and there is always someone to turn to for guidance and support. This is invaluable to me. I wish the rest of the world worked in this way; I think it used to, but unfortunately, we lost this in so many parts of the world as we modernized. I hope we will start to see that it does indeed take a village and that there is happiness, contentment, love, and solidarity to be discovered there."

ABOVE
Honeycomb

RIGHT
"Johnnie Bread" made from a combination of whole wheat and rye flour.

OPPOSITE
The squash harvest in the monastic greenhouse

Beef and Mushroom Wild Rice Casserole

SERVES: 8 to 10
PREPARATION TIME: 1 hour

3 cups chicken or beef stock
1 cup wild rice
Salt and freshly ground black pepper to taste
4 tablespoons unsalted butter, melted, plus more for greasing
3 tablespoons extra-virgin olive oil
1 pound ground beef

1 leek, rinsed well and thinly sliced
2 celery ribs, thinly sliced
1 small fennel bulb, thinly sliced
4 garlic cloves, finely chopped
2 tablespoons freshly squeezed lemon juice
1½ cups coarsely chopped cremini or white button mushrooms
2 tablespoons tomato paste
2 cups lightly packed baby spinach, coarsely chopped
½ teaspoon red pepper flakes

Leaves from 4 flat-leaf parsley sprigs, coarsely chopped
1½ cups bread crumbs
Leaves from 4 thyme sprigs
1 teaspoon grated lemon zest
1 teaspoon garlic powder
1 teaspoon ground ginger
⅔ cup grated Parmesan cheese
Crunchy sea salt, such as Maldon, for serving
Sour cream, for serving

Wild rice is as ubiquitous in central Minnesota as camping in the summertime and bonfires on the lakeshore. Its mahogany color and nutty-sweet flavor makes it a favorite in soups and casseroles, which are called hot dishes in Minnesota. It's highly nutritious and contains generous levels of fiber, vitamin B6, magnesium, and iron. Despite its common name, wild rice is in fact a species of grass that thrives in the shallow lakes and gentle streams of Minnesota, Michigan, and Canada. In Minnesota, it's been harvested for centuries by Indigenous communities, who refer to it as manoomin and consider it a sacred ingredient. Indigenous tribes historically harvested it in canoes, gliding softly into a wild rice bed, tipping the grain heads into the canoe, and, using two sticks called flails or knockers, threshing the grains into the canoe. It is traditionally stored in tightly woven cedar bark pouches and enjoyed in a wide variety of dishes, such as being boiled in venison stock and maple syrup or consumed as a puffed rice sweet. Brother Aelred's favorite way to prepare it is by using it as a base for this comforting casserole.

IN A MEDIUM heavy-bottomed pot, bring 2 cups stock and 1 cup water to a boil over high heat. Reduce the heat to medium, add the rice, cover, and simmer until the liquid has been completely absorbed and the rice is tender, 40 to 45 minutes. Keep an eye on the rice as it cooks to prevent scorching. Fluff the rice with a fork, season with salt and pepper, and let it sit at room temperature for 15 minutes.

MEANWHILE, PREHEAT THE oven to 400°F. Butter a 9-by-13-inch casserole dish.

HEAT THE OIL in a large sauté pan over medium-high heat. Add the beef, leek, celery, and fennel and sauté until the celery and fennel are tender, about 6 minutes. Add the garlic and sauté until aromatic, about 1 more minute. Deglaze the pan with the lemon juice, scraping up the flavorful browned bits at the bottom of the pan. Add the mushrooms and sauté until tender, 4 to 5 minutes. Add the tomato paste and stir until it turns a deep red color, 3 to 4 minutes. Add the spinach, red pepper flakes, and remaining 1 cup stock and bring to a simmer over medium heat; cook until the spinach has wilted, 2 to 3 minutes. Season with salt and pepper.

IN A LARGE bowl, combine the rice, vegetables, and parsley and gently stir until incorporated. In a small bowl, combine the bread crumbs, thyme, lemon zest, garlic powder, ginger, melted butter, and Parmesan. Season with salt and pepper. Transfer the rice mixture to the prepared casserole dish, then evenly distribute the bread crumb mixture on top. Bake until the bread crumbs are golden brown and the casserole has been warmed through, 25 to 30 minutes. Let it cool for a few minutes, then garnish with a sprinkle of crunchy sea salt and a dollop of sour cream and serve.

Skillet Bratwurst and Sauerkraut

Up until a few years ago, Saint John's hosted a fiddling contest that attracted fiddlers and violinists from every corner of the country to a contest of skill that played out over the course of one noisy, jubilant weekend, fueled by icy-cold German beer and bratwurst. Bratwurst is a staple of central Minnesota summers, a tradition brought by the German and eastern European immigrants who settled in this region of the United States in the nineteenth and early twentieth centuries. This recipe is fairly straightforward; the key is to use high-quality bratwurst and fresh, flaky buns. The honey provides a sweet counterpoint to the tangy sauerkraut and the hot mustard infuses each bite with zing.

HEAT THE OIL in a cast-iron skillet over medium-high heat. Add the onion and bratwurst and sauté until the onion is translucent and the bratwurst is brown on both sides, 6 to 8 minutes; it will not be fully cooked at this point. Transfer the bratwurst to a paper towel–lined plate to drain. Increase the heat to high and add the sauerkraut, honey, and beer to the onion in the pan. Season with salt and pepper and bring to a boil, then reduce the heat to medium. Return the bratwurst to the pan and cook, turning once, until they are cooked through, 15 to 20 minutes. At this stage, the liquid in the pan should have dissolved by about two-thirds and will be quite thick and flavorful.

SPREAD BOTH SIDES of the interior of each bun with mustard, add a bratwurst, and spoon some of the sauerkraut and its zesty liquid on top. Serve warm with a pint of icy beer, if desired.

SERVES: 4
PREPARATION TIME: 30 minutes

2 tablespoons vegetable oil
1 small yellow onion, coarsely chopped
4 uncooked bratwurst
2 cups sauerkraut, store-bought or homemade (page 51)
2 tablespoons honey
1 cup brown beer, such as porter or a stout, plus more for serving (optional)
Salt and freshly ground black pepper
4 flaky hot dog buns, toasted
Spicy brown mustard, for serving

Maple Syrup

Canada might be the most renowned place for maple syrup, but the monks at Saint John's Abbey hold their own when it comes to producing one of the monastery's most coveted items. Saint John's maple syrup is never sold and can only be received as a gift. The syrup also builds community. Throngs of volunteers arrive at the monastery in late March and early April when the syrup is ready to be harvested. In exchange for their services, they are typically given a precious bottle of syrup. Brother Walter Kieffer has been harvesting syrup at Saint John's since the 1960s, but it was manufactured at the monastery as early as 1942, when the resourceful monks tapped 150 trees for syrup as a way to counter wartime sugar rationing.

Maple syrup is derived from red, black, and sugar maple trees in colder climates throughout the United States and Canada. Minnesota yields about 13,000 gallons a year, accounting for only 1 percent of total American maple syrup supply, a far cry from the 2 million gallons processed in Vermont. Every drop of Saint John's syrup is cherished and savored, whether on pancakes, waffles, biscuits, ice cream, or oatmeal.

Maple syrup is made from xylem sap that collects in the tree's roots and trunk in warmer spring and summer months. Wintertime temperatures convert the starch to sugar, and the sap rises up through the tree trunk, which is tapped. The liquid is collected in a bucket or plastic jug; it's not technically syrup at this stage but more a runny liquid closer to tea. The sap is heated until only syrup remains, with each tree offering up 5 to 15 gallons of syrup each year.

Saint John's hosts an annual maple syrup festival in early April, a celebration of tradition and of the many volunteers, students, and monks who come together on an annual basis for the syrup harvest. Brother Walter tells me what he likes most about that time of year: "It's the period when the world is waking up again after a deep wintertime slumber. The birds are singing, the bees are buzzing, the trees and flowers are blooming again. It's a time of rebirth, it's time for Easter, it's time for life to begin once more."

Parsnip and Cream Cheese Pierogies with Maple Sour Cream

MAKES: about 36 pierogi
PREPARATION TIME: 1½ hours

FOR THE DOUGH:
5 cups all-purpose flour, plus more for dusting
1 teaspoon salt, plus more to taste
3 large eggs, room temperature
5 tablespoons unsalted butter, chilled and cut into ½-inch cubes

FOR THE FILLING:
6 large parsnips, peeled and cut into 1-inch pieces
3 tablespoons unsalted butter
1 medium yellow onion, finely chopped
3 garlic cloves, finely chopped
1 cup grated Parmesan
½ cup cream cheese
Leaves from 4 flat-leaf parsley sprigs, finely chopped, plus more for garnish
¼ teaspoon grated fresh nutmeg
½ teaspoon salt
¼ teaspoon freshly ground black pepper
1 tablespoon maple syrup
½ teaspoon dried sage
1 cup sour cream
Finely chopped fresh chives, for garnish

Hyacinth of Poland, a Polish monk who spent time in a monastery in Kyiv, is the patron saint of pierogies. Legend has it that the pierogi was introduced to Poland in the thirteenth century when Saint Hyacinth brought the recipe back home with him. Pierogi are beloved throughout Minnesota, where there is a large population of Polish immigrants. They are stuffed with everything from potatoes, butternut squash, and leeks to mushrooms, beef, and cheddar cheese, and for a dessert pierogi, cinnamon apples and cream cheese. The savory versions are most often served with plenty of sour cream sprinkled with scallions or chives. The dough can be used as a vehicle for any stuffing and can be made ahead and frozen for up to a month if wrapped tightly in plastic wrap to avoid freezer burn. This recipe includes parsnips, which add a sweet note to the pierogi, a version beloved by the monks at Saint John's, who typically enjoy them during their festive Friday night suppers. These riotous evenings are hosted about once a month. They offer the monks an opportunity to share time-tested family recipes with each other, experiment with new ingredients and recipes, listen to music or watch a new movie, and enjoy one another's company in a relaxed setting made even more merry with a glass (or two) of wine or a pint of local beer.

FOR THE DOUGH, combine the flour, salt, eggs, and butter in the bowl of a food processor and pulse until a dough forms. If the dough is too dry, add ice water, 1 tablespoon at a time, until a soft dough forms. Transfer to a bowl, cover with a damp cloth, and let rest for 30 minutes.

MEANWHILE, MAKE THE filling. Put the parsnips in a large, heavy-bottomed pot and pour in enough water to cover by 4 inches. Bring to a boil over high heat, reduce the heat to medium-high, and simmer until very tender when pierced with a fork, 20 to 25 minutes. Drain. Once the parsnips are cool enough to handle, pass them through a ricer or mash with a potato masher until mashed. Transfer to a large bowl.

WHILE THE PARSNIPS cool, melt 1 tablespoon butter in a sauté pan over medium-high heat. Add the onion and sauté until translucent, 5 to 7 minutes. Add the garlic and sauté until aromatic, about 1 more minute. Add the onion mixture to the parsnips, along with the Parmesan, cream cheese, parsley, nutmeg, salt, and pepper.

Recipe continues

IN A SMALL bowl, combine the maple syrup, sage, and sour cream. Stir together with a fork until incorporated, then cover and refrigerate until serving time.

TO ASSEMBLE, DIVIDE the dough into 4 equal portions and cover them with a towel so they don't dry out. Fill a small bowl with water. Lightly flour a work surface and roll the dough out to about ⅛ inch thick. Punch out circles using a 3-inch biscuit cutter. Spoon about 1½ tablespoons filling on one half of a circle, leaving about ½-inch border to enable sealing. Using your finger, moisten the edge of the circle with water and then fold the empty half of the circle over to form a half-moon shape. Using a fork, seal the edges. Repeat with the remaining dough and filling.

BRING A LARGE pot of salted water to a boil. Line a plate with a double layer of paper towels. Put about 6 pierogi at a time into the water and wait until they rise to the surface, 1 to 2 minutes, then use a slotted spoon to transfer them to the paper towels to drain. Repeat to cook the remaining pierogi.

ONCE ALL THE pierogi have been parboiled, line a second plate with a double layer of paper towels. Heat the remaining 2 tablespoons butter in a sauté pan over medium heat. Working in batches so as not to crowd the pan, cook the pierogi until golden brown on the bottom, about 2 minutes. Flip over gently using a fork or slotted spoon and cook until golden brown on the other side, about 2 minutes more. Transfer to the paper towels to drain. Serve hot, topped with the maple-sage sour cream and chives.

Cheesy Biscuits

These biscuits make an appearance at least once a week at the monks' dinner table at Saint John's, usually on the weekends because their rich, buttery flavor makes them feel festive. The key to achieving a fluffy biscuit texture is to avoid overkneading the dough. To really make these a treat, add a handful of crumbled crispy bacon, which pairs well with the sweet honey, earthy scallions, and assertive cheddar.

PREHEAT THE OVEN to 425°F. Line a rimmed baking sheet with parchment paper.

SIFT THE FLOUR, baking powder, garlic powder, and salt into a large bowl. Add the butter and, using your fingers, pinch the butter into the dry ingredients until it resembles coarse crumbs. It will be lumpy. Add the milk, scallions, and cheese and stir until incorporated.

DUST A CLEAN work surface with flour and knead until the dough just comes together, 10 to 12 rotations. Do not overwork it or the biscuits won't rise properly. Roll the dough out into a 1½-inch-thick rectangle. Using a 3-inch cutter, punch out circles and transfer to the prepared baking sheet. Gather up the scraps and continue rolling and punching until most of the dough has been used. Brush the top of each biscuit lightly with milk. Bake the biscuits until they have risen and are light golden brown, 18 to 22 minutes. Serve warm or at room temperature, drizzled with honey and sprinkled with crunchy sea salt, with softened butter for spreading. Leftover biscuits will keep in a covered container at room temperature for up to 3 days or in the freezer for up to 2 weeks.

MAKES: about 10 biscuits
PREPARATION TIME: 40 minutes

2½ cups all-purpose flour, plus more for dusting
2 teaspoons baking powder
1 teaspoon garlic powder
½ teaspoon salt
8 tablespoons (2 sticks) unsalted butter, chilled and cut into ½-inch cubes, plus softened butter for serving
1 cup whole milk, plus more for brushing
2 scallions, thinly sliced
1 cup grated sharp cheddar cheese
Honey, for serving
Crunchy sea salt, such as Maldon, for garnish

Swedish Meatballs with Cranberry Sauce

SERVES: 4
PREPARATION TIME: 45 minutes

3 slices whole wheat bread, torn into bite-size pieces
⅔ cup whole milk
5 tablespoons unsalted butter
1 small white onion, finely chopped

2 garlic cloves, finely chopped
12 ounces ground pork
12 ounces ground beef
2 large eggs
¼ teaspoon grated fresh nutmeg
¼ teaspoon ground cinnamon
¼ teaspoon ground allspice
Salt and freshly ground black pepper to taste

3 tablespoons all-purpose flour
2 cups beef stock
1 cup dry white wine
½ cup heavy cream
Finely chopped fresh flat-leaf parsley, for garnish
Cranberry Sauce (page 237), for serving

Swedish meatballs traveled a long way to reach Minnesota. They were introduced to the state by the many Swedish immigrants who call Minnesota home, but their origins date back centuries earlier in Turkey. It was Charles XII who, in the early eighteenth century, fell in love with the Middle Eastern dish kefta and carried the recipe back home to Sweden. Swedish meatballs are so iconic in Sweden that it's virtually blasphemous to mention their Turkish origin, but the monks at Saint John's don't mind. For them, it reflects the way that so many recipes, techniques, seeds, and ingredients that traveled for centuries from one monastery to another, carried by monks from one place to another.

The trick to these meatballs is to soak the bread in milk before adding it to the beef and pork. The result is a remarkably tender meatball—made even better if the bread crumbs are from homemade bread, but store-bought will also work. A savory gravy and tart cranberry sauce round out the dish. This recipe calls for cranberries because they are easier to source than the iconic Scandinavian lingonberry, but if you can get your hands on them, by all means feel free to substitute.

PREHEAT THE OVEN to 400°F.

PUT THE BREAD in a medium bowl and cover with the milk. Set aside at room temperature until the bread has absorbed nearly all of the liquid, about 10 minutes.

MEANWHILE, MELT 1 tablespoon butter over medium-high heat in a large sauté pan. Add the onion and sauté until translucent, 5 to 7 minutes. Add the garlic and sauté until aromatic, about 1 more minute. Transfer to the bowl of a food processor, along with the bread and milk, pork, beef, eggs, nutmeg, cinnamon, and allspice. Pulse until incorporated, then process until pureed but still slightly chunky, about 1 minute. Season with salt and pepper. Using your hands, roll the mixture into 1-inch balls and place on a plate.

WIPE OUT THE sauté pan and melt the remaining 4 tablespoons butter over medium-high heat. Add the meatballs in an even layer and sauté until golden brown, about 3 minutes. Using tongs, turn the meatballs over and sauté until golden brown on the other side, about 3 minutes more. Using a slotted spoon, transfer the meatballs to a casserole dish, cover, and bake until cooked through, 15 to 20 minutes.

WHILE THE MEATBALLS bake, reduce the stovetop temperature to medium, add the flour to the drippings in the sauté pan, and cook until golden brown, stirring constantly with a wooden spoon or a whisk to prevent scorching. Add the stock and wine and whisk until the sauce is thick enough to coat the whisk. Reduce the heat to low and add the cream. Whisk until the gravy is very thick but still loose enough to run easily from a spoon. If it thickens up too much, whisk in a little more stock to loosen it up. Season with salt and pepper.

POUR THE GRAVY over the meatballs. Garnish with parsley and serve with cranberry sauce. Leftover meatballs will keep in a covered container in the refrigerator for up to 4 days.

Cranberry Sauce

There are over one hundred varieties of cranberries throughout the world. The three that are most prominent in northern Minnesota are the northern mountain cranberry, small cranberry, and large cranberry. Cranberries flourish in the dense tamarack swamps, sphagnum bogs, and fern, leatherleaf, and cattail stands of the region. It's not one of the state's primary crops, but for foragers in the know, the cranberry harvest is an event that is looked forward to in late autumn. It is the perfect tart accompaniment to Swedish Meatballs (page 235) and also lovely as a sandwich spread. The flavor of this savory sauce is a tantalizing sweet and sour, with a flash of brightness and a hint of heat from the spices. Fresh cranberries are called for, but frozen will work just as well. This sauce is a must on the feast table at Saint John's every Thanksgiving.

IN A MEDIUM, heavy-bottomed saucepan, combine the sugar and 1 cup water and bring to a boil over high heat. Reduce the heat to medium and simmer until the sugar is dissolved, about 5 minutes. Add the cranberries, ginger, orange zest, cloves, cardamom, and star anise and simmer until the cranberries pop and then become syrupy, stirring occasionally to prevent scorching, about 15 minutes. Season with the salt and pepper. Cool to room temperature, then remove the cloves, cardamom, and star anise with tongs or a fork and serve. The sauce will keep in a covered container in the refrigerator for up to 1 week.

MAKES: about 1½ cups
PREPARATION TIME: 20 minutes

1 cup granulated sugar
3 cups fresh or frozen cranberries
1 (½-inch piece) ginger, finely chopped
1 teaspoon grated orange zest
6 whole cloves
4 green cardamom pods
1 star anise pod
½ teaspoon salt
¼ teaspoon freshly ground black pepper

Beekeeping

Beekeeping is a tradition that was lost for many years at Saint John's until Brothers Nick Kleespie and Lew Grobe discovered beekeeping equipment in one of the monastery's cavernous cellars. They decided to revive the tradition, and taught themselves the art of beekeeping through textbooks and classes. They have only two hives right now, but they plan to expand their operation and hope to entice other monks and university students to participate in their beekeeping practice. The bees serve as an indispensable pollinator at Saint John's, their honey infused with notes of the riot of flowers, fruits, and vegetables that thrive on the grounds, including apples, chives, lavender, sage, crocus, aster, hollyhock, fennel, tomato, thyme, sunflower, and heliotrope. Another benefit of keeping bees is that it reflects the robust work ethic that Benedictine monks embrace. Just as their bees work tirelessly to produce honey, the monks' ingenuity shines through the honey-based products they produce and sell, such as beeswax candles, honey butter, and glistening amber bottles of the coveted honey itself.

Christians see bees as a symbol of Jesus's sweet and empathetic character, and a bee's sting as a reminder of the way Jesus suffered on the cross. For Christians and many other religious followers, bees represent strength, wisdom, and hope. As Brother Lew says, "As Benedictine monks, we believe in hard work and in serving the community. I can't think of a better reminder of this than the bee. It's what I think about every time I visit my bees, appreciating their relentless intention to produce something positive, to protect one another, and to protect their queen from danger. It's a lesson for us all."

Beekeeping is certainly challenging, but through education or a mentorship with a veteran beekeeper, a beekeeper should be able to successfully keep bees and produce honey within four seasons. Here is the standard list of equipment that every beekeeper needs to begin their bee journey; most of these items can be ordered online:

- A beehive.
- Frames. They should either be stackable or line up vertically, side by side.
- An outer cover, typically wood or metal, to protect the frames and the hive.
- A screened bottom for ventilation. Bees generate so much energy buzzing in their hive to protect their queen and to produce honey that a healthy hive will typically maintain a temperature of around 92°F, even during the most bitterly cold Minnesota winter. The screen also prevents the buildup of varroa mites, a pest that can prove fatal for bees.
- A base to lift the hive from the ground. Something as simple as a double row of cinder blocks will work.
- A smoker. Smoke calms the bees down during a honey harvest. Pine needles work well as a nontoxic fuel.
- A hive tool: Bees produce a glue called propolis, which can make it difficult to separate the frame from the box to lift it out without a hive tool.
- A bee brush. This enables the beekeeper to scatter the bees during a harvest.
- A bee suit, veil, and gloves to protect the beekeeper from stings.

OPPOSITE
Honey production

Hot German Potato Salad

SERVES: 4
PREPARATION TIME: 45 minutes

4 large Idaho potatoes
4 bacon strips
1 small yellow onion, coarsely chopped
1 celery rib, thinly sliced
1 tablespoon all-purpose flour
2 teaspoons granulated sugar
¼ cup apple cider vinegar
Salt and freshly ground black pepper
   to taste
Coarsely chopped fresh flat-leaf parsley,
   to garnish

At Saint John's, German potato salad, with its tangy sweet-and-sour flavor notes, is a favorite of the monks—especially the older generation, as it reminds them of their parents and grandparents, many of whom were immigrants from Germany. A recipe brought with them across the ocean, it conjures a nostalgia for humble farmhouse dinners filled with warmth and the feeling of community. Saint John's hosts hundreds of visitors each year, drawn by a summer craft fair, hiking opportunities in the warmer months, skiing adventures in the winter, leaf peeping in the fall, classical orchestra concerts, and spirit-lifting walks through its arboretum. Many visitors also partake of the monastic dinner that is offered for a small fee. German potato salad makes at least a weekly appearance. Feel free to adjust the ratio of sugar and vinegar to achieve the perfect sweet-and-sour alchemy.

SCRUB THE POTATOES under cold running water to remove any debris. Put them in a large, heavy-bottomed pot and pour in enough water to cover by 4 inches. Bring the water to a boil over high heat. Reduce the heat to medium-high and simmer until the potatoes are fork-tender, about 20 minutes. Drain the potatoes in a colander and, when they are cool enough to handle but still warm, slip off the skins. Cut the potatoes into ¼-inch slices and put them in a large bowl; set aside.

WHILE THE POTATOES cool, line a plate with a double layer of paper towels. Cook the bacon in a skillet over medium heat until crispy and golden brown, 2 to 3 minutes per side. Transfer the bacon to the paper towels and reserve the fat in the pan. Once the bacon is cool enough to handle, break it into bite-size pieces.

ADD THE ONION and celery to the bacon fat in the pan and sauté over medium-high heat until the onion is translucent, 5 to 7 minutes. Spoon off all but 1 tablespoon bacon fat from the pan, add the flour and sugar, and sauté until the onion turns a light golden brown. Add the vinegar and 2 tablespoons water, scrape the flavorful browned bits from the bottom of the pan, and cook until thickened, stirring occasionally to prevent scorching, 2 to 3 minutes. Return the bacon to the pan and cook for 1 more minute.

POUR THE HOT bacon dressing over the potatoes and stir gently until the potatoes are glistening and well coated. Season with salt and pepper. Garnish with parsley and serve warm. Leftovers will keep in a covered container in the refrigerator for up to 2 days; after this time the potatoes become quite gummy.

Honey-Glazed Turkey Tinga

SERVES: 4
PREPARATION TIME: 2½ hours

2 pounds boneless, skinless turkey breasts, cut into six pieces
½ teaspoon salt, plus more to taste
½ teaspoon freshly ground black pepper, plus more to taste
4 tablespoons honey
2 tablespoons extra-virgin olive oil
1 large yellow onion, coarsely chopped
2 ribs celery, chopped

6 garlic cloves, finely chopped
Leaves from 5 oregano sprigs, coarsely chopped
Leaves from 5 thyme sprigs
1 teaspoon cocoa powder
2 teaspoons cumin seeds
½ teaspoon cayenne pepper
1 bay leaf
2 (7-ounce) cans chipotles in adobo, coarsely chopped
6 ounces adobo sauce

1 (14-ounce) can chopped tomatoes, undrained
2 tablespoons tomato paste
1 cup chicken stock

TO SERVE:
16 flour tortillas
Queso fresco, crumbled
Tomatillo Salsa (page 245)
Sour cream
Avocado chunks
Finely sliced scallions

Brother Pedro Alvarez, a monk in his mid-twenties from Mexico, introduced his favorite dish to the monks at Saint John's. Brother Pedro lived in a Russian Orthodox monastery in Mexico City before relocating to central Minnesota. But this isn't a recipe he learned at the monastery; he learned it from his grandmother.

As is the case with recipes that travel, this tinga reflects not only its Mexican origins but also its current home in Minnesota. Tinga is typically slow-cooked, shredded meat—anything from beef to pork to chicken—layered with the flavors of chiles, onions, garlic, and tomatoes. Brother Pedro replaced the chicken with wild turkey from central Minnesota. None of the monks hunt, but they do welcome the bounty donated to them from hunters in the area. The honey is the monastery's own and gives the dish a sweetness that provides the perfect counterpoint to the chiles. Tinga is comforting in the winter and fun for a summertime barbecue, too. Brother Pedro's advice is to "take it slowly, let the house fill with the smoky aroma. It will bring everyone to the table."

SEASON THE TURKEY all over with the salt and pepper and slather on 2 tablespoons honey. Place the turkey pieces in an even layer in a slow cooker.

HEAT THE OIL in a sauté pan over medium-high heat. Add the onion and celery and sauté until the onion is translucent, 5 to 7 minutes. Add the garlic, oregano, thyme, cocoa, cumin, cayenne, and bay leaf and sauté until aromatic, 2 to 3 minutes. Add the chipotles in adobo, adobo sauce, tomatoes with their juices, tomato paste, stock, and remaining 2 tablespoons honey and bring to a boil. Reduce the heat to medium-low and gently simmer for 8 minutes. Season with salt and pepper. Pour the sauce over the turkey, cover, and cook on low until the turkey is very tender, about 2 hours.

USING TONGS, TRANSFER the turkey to a plate. Discard the bay leaf. Once the turkey is cool enough to handle, shred it into bite-size pieces and stir it back into the sauce in the slow cooker until well incorporated.

TO SERVE, TOP each warm tortilla with a spoonful of the turkey and sauce, sprinkle with queso fresco, tomatillo salsa, sour cream, avocado, and scallions.

Recipe continues

Tomatillo Salsa

MAKES: about 1 quart
PREPARATION TIME: 45 minutes

7 large green chiles, such as Hatch,
   Anaheim, or poblano
3 small green chiles, such as serrano
   or jalapeño
1 tablespoon extra-virgin olive oil, plus more
   for brushing
½ teaspoon salt, plus more to taste
12 tomatillos
1 small white onion, coarsely chopped
2 garlic cloves, coarsely chopped
1 bunch cilantro, leaves and stems coarsely
   chopped
1½ cups chicken stock

Brother Aelred makes a large batch of this salsa each year when the tomatillos and chiles are in season in the monastic garden. Before arriving at Saint John's, he was a teacher in New Mexico, and this recipe is a nod to that region of America. He typically cans most of his salsa because it's a welcome reminder of summer during the unrelenting Minnesota winter. If you are canning, feel free to double, triple, or even quadruple the ingredient amounts. Brother Aelred's main tip is to be sure to char the chile skins until they're black and blistered because the smoky note in the salsa really makes it sing. Serve the salsa with Honey-Glazed Turkey Tinga (page 242) or enchiladas, stir it into stews and soups, or use it as a sandwich garnish or a dip for tortilla chips.

PREHEAT THE BROILER.

BRUSH THE CHILES all over with olive oil and season with salt. Arrange the chiles on a broiler-safe rimmed baking sheet and broil until they are blistered, about 4 minutes. Flip the chiles over and blister them on the other side, about 4 minutes more. Using tongs, transfer the chiles to a large bowl and cover tightly with plastic wrap. Once the chiles have cooled to room temperature, remove the charred skins using your fingers. They should slip right off; not all the skin has to be

removed, only as much as will come off easily. Using a paring knife, remove the stems and seeds and discard. Coarsely chop the chiles; set aside.

REMOVE AND DISCARD the papery husks from the tomatillos and rinse them under cold running water to remove the sticky residue. Transfer to a large, heavy-bottomed pot and pour in enough water to cover by 5 inches. Bring the water to a boil over high heat, reduce the heat to medium, and simmer until the tomatillos are tender and their bright green skin has turned slightly olive in color, 5 to 7 minutes. Drain, reserving about 1 cup of the cooking water.

COMBINE THE CHILES, tomatillos, onion, garlic, and cilantro in a blender or food processor, along with about ½ cup of the reserved cooking water, and blend on high speed until a chunky puree has formed, 2 to 3 minutes.

IN A LARGE pot, heat the oil over medium-high heat. Carefully add the salsa and stock and bring to a vigorous simmer. Reduce the heat to medium and simmer the salsa to your desired consistency. Season with the salt and cool to room temperature before serving. The salsa will keep in a covered container in the refrigerator for up to 1 week or in the freezer for up to 2 months.

Roasted Heirloom Tomato Tart

MAKES: 1 (12-inch) tart
PREPARATION TIME: 1½ hours, plus 1 hour to chill the dough

FOR THE CRUST:
2 cups all-purpose flour, plus more for dusting
½ teaspoon salt
1 cup grated Parmesan cheese
8 tablespoons (1 stick) unsalted butter, chilled and cut into ½-inch cubes
2 tablespoons ice water

FOR THE FILLING:
2 cups ricotta
1 cup grated Gruyère cheese
Leaves from 4 basil sprigs, torn into bite-size pieces, plus more to serve
Leaves from 2 oregano sprigs, coarsely chopped
1 teaspoon grated lemon zest
2 teaspoons freshly squeezed lemon juice
1 teaspoon garlic powder
1 teaspoon ground ginger
1 large egg
½ teaspoon red pepper flakes
Salt and freshly ground black pepper to taste
1½ tablespoons extra-virgin olive oil
1 tablespoon honey
1 pound heirloom tomatoes, cut into ⅛-inch slices
Crunchy sea salt, such as Maldon, to taste

Tomato season is a time to celebrate at Saint John's. The monastic garden bursts with vibrant red, orange, purple, and yellow tomatoes in late summer, and the monks harvest them for salsa, pasta sauce, pizza sauce, tomato sandwiches, salads, and this tomato tart, which Brother Aelred prepares on weekends during the summertime. Its riot of color is a cheerful reminder to relish the season because in Minnesota, it will inevitably be fleeting.

FIRST, MAKE THE crust. In a large bowl, sift together the flour and salt. Add the Parmesan and stir to incorporate. Add the butter and, using your fingers, pinch it into the dry ingredients until it resembles coarse sand. Add the ice water and knead until the dough just comes together. Do not overknead it or the crust will be tough. Dust a work surface with flour and roll the dough into a 14-inch round that is about ⅛ inch thick. Carefully place the crust over a 12-inch tart pan with the excess dough hanging over the edges. Gently press the dough into the pan. Roll a rolling pin over the pan to trim off the excess dough and remove it with your fingers. Prick the surface of the dough several times with a toothpick or a fork to prevent the crust from forming bubbles as it bakes. Cover with plastic wrap and refrigerate until chilled, at least 1 hour or up to 24 hours.

PREHEAT THE OVEN to 425°F.

GENTLY LINE THE tart dough with aluminum foil and fill with pie weights or dry beans. Bake until it is puffed and just golden brown, about 15 minutes. Remove from the oven and carefully lift the foil and weights from the pan. Put the crust back in the oven and bake until the surface is golden brown, 10 to 12 minutes. Remove from the oven and let it cool to room temperature; leave the oven on.

TO PREPARE THE filling, combine the ricotta, Gruyère, basil, oregano, lemon zest, 1 teaspoon lemon juice, garlic powder, ginger, egg, and red pepper flakes in the bowl of a food processor and pulse until everything is incorporated. Season with salt and pepper.

ONCE THE CRUST has cooled to room temperature, using a spatula, spread the ricotta filling in an even layer in the crust. In a small bowl, whisk together the oil, honey, and remaining 1 teaspoon lemon juice using a fork. Season with salt and pepper. Arrange the tomato slices in an attractive and even layer on top of the filling. Drizzle with the oil and honey mixture and bake until the filling is set and the tomatoes are wilted, 25 to 30 minutes. Cool to room temperature. Garnish with torn basil leaves and sprinkle with crunchy sea salt before serving. The tart is best enjoyed fresh, but it will keep in a covered container in the refrigerator for up to 3 days.

Sweet Potato and Corn Chowder

Minnesota is the fourth largest producer of corn in America. Seemingly endless, tawny fields of corn define the landscape of central Minnesota, and while the corn crop might not be as massive at Saint John's as it is at many of the surrounding farms, it plays an important part in the monastic harvest. It often finds its way into this corn chowder recipe that Brother Aelred serves at Friday night suppers throughout late summer and early autumn. He adds a sweet potato for additional flavor and a pop of color. This recipe calls for fresh corn kernels, but you can substitute frozen when fresh is out of season.

IN A LARGE saucepan, melt the butter over medium heat. Add the onion, celery, and bell pepper and cook until the onion is translucent, 5 to 7 minutes. Add the garlic and sauté until aromatic, about 1 more minute. Add the sweet potato cubes, 2½ cups corn, stock, thyme, red pepper flakes, and bay leaf and bring to a boil over medium-high heat. Reduce the heat to medium and simmer until the sweet potato is tender, 15 to 17 minutes.

COMBINE THE REMAINING 2 cups corn and cream in the bowl of a food processor and puree until smooth. Transfer to the saucepan with the sweet potato mixture and season with salt and pepper. Simmer until the soup thickens slightly, 7 to 10 minutes. Remove the bay leaf. Ladle into serving bowls, dollop with sour cream, and garnish with scallions. The chowder will keep in a covered container in the refrigerator for up to 4 days or in the freezer indefinitely.

SERVES: 4
PREPARATION TIME: 50 minutes

3 tablespoons unsalted butter
1 medium white onion, coarsely chopped
2 celery ribs, thinly sliced
1 red or orange bell pepper, seeded and coarsely chopped
3 garlic cloves, finely chopped
1 large sweet potato, peeled and cut into ½-inch cubes
4½ cups fresh corn kernels (from about 8 ears)
4 cups chicken stock
Leaves from 3 thyme sprigs
1 teaspoon red pepper flakes
1 bay leaf
2 cups heavy cream
Salt and freshly ground black pepper to taste
Sour cream, for serving
Sliced sausage, if desired, for serving
Homemade croutons, for serving
Thinly sliced scallions, for garnish

9.

Gurudwara Sri Bangla Sahib

SIKHISM
NEW DELHI, INDIA

"Truth is the highest virtue, but higher still is truthful living."
—*Guru Nanak, the first Sikh guru*

"From one light, the entire universe welled up," says Karanveer Singh, a spiritual guide at New Delhi's Sri Bangla Sahib, a Sikh temple also referred to as a gurudwara, which translates as "door of the Guru." Sri Bangla Sahib is one of the nine sacred Sikh shrines in New Delhi and arguably the most important and majestic. The expansive white marble building, with its imposing gold dome and towering Nishan Sahib flagpole, houses a holy pond for cleansing, an art gallery, a school, a museum, a library, and even a hospital.

The langar, or kitchen, is the most important feature of Sri Bangla Sahib, a shaded refuge of sustenance, kindness, and empathy for the thousands who gather there each day.

The langar at Sri Bangla Sahib is as big as a football field, and there are dozens of people busily working in it, stirring bubbling dishes in copper pots large enough to serve hundreds of people. There is a large chapati oven with an open flame so hot that it's burning blue. The chapatis move down the conveyor belt, puffing up into their signature shape as they pass slowly over the open flame. Hundreds of chapati drop each hour into massive baskets that two volunteer women wearing saris in vibrant shades of magenta and cobalt tend to for hours each day, running the baskets once they are filled to the volunteer servers in the dining hall.

Karanveer Singh stops by one of the chapati stations and invites me to sit alongside him to roll out a few chapatis. While we work, he explains, "Sikhism is one of the newest religions in the world. Its principles were laid down by our first Guru Nanak between the years of 1469 and 1539. Since Guru Nanak, there have been eight other gurus, each one adhering to the belief, much like Buddhists, that it is possible to achieve enlightenment in your current lifetime through jivanmukti, connecting to Akal, a genderless spirit that resides in everything. Like Buddhists too, Sikhs believe in reincarnation and in the concept of karma. It is why we serve free meals to anyone who needs one at our gurudwara; it is why you see so many volunteers giving selflessly today. It is a gift to give something of yourself, to help out your fellow human beings. Just imagine if everyone embraced this philosophy. Just imagine what a beautiful and compassionate world it would be."

The Gurudwara Sri Bangla Sahib, located near the bustling commercial center of Connaught Place in the heart of New Delhi, was built as a shrine by the Sikh General Baghel Singh in 1783 during the Mughal reign of the emperor Shah Alam II. It was constructed in honor of the eighth Sikh guru, Guru Har Krishan, who lived at the location in the mid-seventeenth century. During this time, smallpox and cholera were ravaging the population of New Delhi, and Guru Har Krishan offered those who were suffering water from his well. He eventually died from cholera himself, but his generosity was not forgotten. In the heart of the Gurudwara Sri Bangla Sahib today, the original well where Guru Har Krishna sourced his water is covered by a modern water tank and attracts visitors from all over the world.

Even though vegetarianism is not a requirement of Sikhs, many of the devout adhere to the Sikh code of purity known as the Akal Takht Sandesh. One of the edicts in the code instructs Sikhs to commit to a diet free from meat, fish, eggs, and other animal products. The one exception is milk and dairy products, which is why the Indian farmhouse cheese known as paneer is an acceptable dish in the Sikh culinary repertoire, although it must be made from nonanimal rennet. The Akal Takht Sandesh is the reason why

OPPOSITE
Chapati preparation

" It is a gift to give something of yourself,
to help out your fellow human beings.
Just imagine if everyone embraced
this philosophy. Just imagine what a
beautiful and compassionate world it
would be."

only lacto-vegetarian recipes are prepared and served at gurudwaras.

Besides the langar, every gurudwara has the same features. There are four entrance doors, one on each side of the room, to symbolize that all are welcome, regardless of occupation, religion, gender, status, wealth, or nationality. The divan hall is the main prayer room where everyone is welcome, regardless of which Waheguru, or God, they worship. The congregation of people who gather in the divan hall is referred to as the sangat. The manuscript that is most sacred to Sikhs, the *Guru Granth Sahib*, is on display in the divan hall but at night is transferred to a room known as sach khand, which means "realm of truth" in Hindi and represents an individual's union with God.

Many of the gurudwara's visitors are hungry Indians who rely upon the generosity of the volunteers at Sri Bangla Sahib to survive. Others are Sikhs making pilgrimages to this revered gurudwara from all corners of the world. There are curious tourists who seem mystified that in this space, meals are free, no questions asked, prepared and served by a volunteer army of cooks who embrace the belief that by engaging in this form of sewa, or selfless service to God, they will achieve nanak, their supreme purpose.

Karanveer Singh, much like many of the volunteers, is adorned with the symbols of Sikhism, referred to as "the five Ks." There is kesh, uncut hair, since hair is a symbol of strength and holiness; kara, a steel bracelet that symbolizes gentility and restraint; kachha, special undershorts that fall just below the knee, a symbol of chastity and a reminder of the garments worn by the Sikh warriors of the past; kanga, a wooden comb that symbolizes a clean body and mind; and kirpan, a ceremonial sword that is a metaphor for god, symbolizing the defense of the weak and the good, and the struggle against injustice.

The trademark Sikh turban worn by many Sikh men is a tool to protect their long hair but also serves to promote equality and to preserve the Sikh identity. "What is the meaning of the turquoise blue color of your turban?" I ask Karanveer Singh.

He grins for a moment before responding, "Fashion."

OPPOSITE
The sacred pool referred to as a Sarovar

RIGHT
Aromatics including dried rose petals, cardamom, cinnamon, and almonds

Gurudwara Sri Bangla Sahib   257

RIGHT
Chapati distribution

BELOW
The exterior of the gurudwara

OPPOSITE
Serving a meal at the gurudwara

Raita 3 Ways

Raitas are condiments made of yogurt that are eaten to help digestion. Yogurt is rich in probiotics and has been appreciated as a balancing ingredient in Indian cuisine for thousands of years. India's Ayurvedic cooking (see page 270) consists of food and beverages that promote optimal health. Raitas illustrate the alchemy that exists in recipes reflective of Ayurvedic principles; they not only serve as cooling agents for often fiery Indian dishes, they also benefit the body in that they aid in digestion and gut health.

There is always at least one variety of raita served at the langar of Sri Bangla Sahib. It's typically a simple cucumber raita, but on feast days beet, carrot, tomato, and pineapple raitas are also enjoyed. Raitas should be slightly runny, which means that Greek yogurt is not a good substitute for the whole-milk yogurt called for in these recipes because it is too thick. Raitas should be served with the meal in a small bowl alongside the other dishes or directly on individual plates.

BELOW
Beet raita (left), cucumber raita (middle), pineapple raita (right)

Cucumber Raita

MAKES: about 1 cup; serves 2
PREPARATION TIME: 10 minutes

1 cup plain whole-milk yogurt (not
   Greek-style)
1 teaspoon freshly squeezed lemon juice
Leaves from 1 mint sprig, finely chopped
1 scallion, thinly sliced
½ teaspoon ground cumin
½ teaspoon ground coriander
1 (6- to 7-inch cucumber), coarsely chopped
Pinch salt

IN A MEDIUM bowl, combine the yogurt, lemon juice, mint, scallion, cumin, and coriander. Stir vigorously, then fold in the cucumber and season with the salt. Raita will keep in a covered container in the refrigerator for up to 2 days.

Beet Raita

MAKES: about 1 cup; serves 2
PREPARATION TIME: 10 minutes

1 cup plain whole-milk yogurt
Leaves from 2 cilantro sprigs, finely
   chopped
½ small serrano chile, seeded and finely
   chopped
1 teaspoon granulated sugar
½ teaspoon ground cumin
1 large red beet, roasted (see page 145) and
   coarsely chopped
Salt to taste

IN A MEDIUM bowl, combine the yogurt, cilantro, chile, sugar, and cumin. Stir vigorously, then fold in the beet and season with salt. Raita will keep in a covered container in the refrigerator for up to 2 days.

Pineapple Raita

MAKES: about 1 cup; serves 2
PREPARATION TIME: 10 minutes

1 cup plain whole-milk yogurt
1 teaspoon freshly squeezed lemon juice
1 teaspoon granulated sugar
½ teaspoon ground cumin
Pinch cayenne pepper
1 cup coarsely chopped fresh or canned
   pineapple
Salt to taste

IN A MEDIUM bowl, combine the yogurt, lemon juice, sugar, cumin, and cayenne. Stir vigorously, then fold in the pineapple and season with salt. Raita will keep in a covered container in the refrigerator for up to 2 days.

Kala Chana

Kala ("black") chana ("chickpeas") is a warm and fortifying dish that is often served in the morning, but it can be enjoyed any time of day. Black chickpeas are slightly smaller than regular yellow chickpeas and have a slightly drier texture after they're cooked and a more robust flavor. If you have trouble sourcing them, yellow chickpeas can be substituted. Kala chana is frequently prepared at the gurudwara because it's an easy, one-pot vegetarian meal that is packed with protein and other nutrients. The mango adds a sweet note (although it's used only when in season), while the mint freshens it up. Amchur, dried mango powder, can be found at Indian markets. It infuses the kala chana with a hint of pungency.

IF USING DRIED chickpeas, rinse under cold running water for several minutes to remove any debris, then put them in a bowl and pour in enough water to cover by 2 inches. Soak for at least 5 hours, or overnight. Drain, then transfer to a small saucepan, cover with water, and boil until they are tender, 45 to 55 minutes. Drain. If using canned chickpeas, drain and rinse them.

IN A LARGE bowl, stir together the chickpeas, onion, tomato, green chile, cumin, amchur, and chili powder. Stir to combine, then add the mango, cilantro, mint, and lemon juice and stir gently. Season with the salt and serve immediately. Kala chana will keep in a covered container in the refrigerator for up to 3 days.

SERVES: 4
PREPARATION TIME: 1 hour, plus overnight to soak if using dried chickpeas

1 cup dried kala chana *or* 2 (15-ounce) cans chickpeas
1 small red onion, finely chopped
1 small tomato, coarsely chopped
1 green chile, seeded and finely chopped
½ teaspoon ground cumin
½ teaspoon amchur
¼ teaspoon chili powder
½ cup coarsely chopped mango
2 tablespoons finely chopped fresh cilantro leaves
1 tablespoon finely chopped fresh mint leaves
1 tablespoon freshly squeezed lemon juice
½ teaspoon salt

OPPOSITE
From top: caraway seeds, fennel seeds, black mustard seeds, black cumin seeds, ground turmeric, fenugreek seeds, ajwain seeds, whole ginger root

Chutney 2 Ways

Chutneys are sweet or savory condiments that are used to add balance and flavor to a meal. There are countless chutney varieties throughout India, and a chutney recipe is often reflective of the region where it was created. Chutneys can contain vegetables, fruit, nuts, seeds, herbs, spices, sugar or other sweeteners, and vinegar for health and preservation purposes (although citrus juice is sometimes substituted). Chutneys are highly seasonal and are an ideal way for Indians to preserve the flavor of ripe fruits and vegetables long after their growing period ends.

Cilantro-Mint Chutney

MAKES: approximately 1¼ cups
PREPARATION TIME: 10 minutes

Sikh meals are enlivened by this chutney, and while it's not a daily accompaniment to the recipes served at Sri Bangla Sahib, it's always welcome by diners when it is. It's made from the fresh mint and cilantro that is donated to the gurudwara by individuals and businesses each day. It's as ubiquitous on the Indian table as raita and rice. The combination of vivid green color and freshness from the mint and cilantro, plus the flash of heat from the chiles and brightness from the lime juice, enlivens countless Indian recipes. Indian green chiles—know as hari (green) mirch (chile) in Hindi—are thicker than Thai chiles and pack less of a fiery punch. They're longer and more slender than jalapeños and deliver a similar amount of heat. If you have trouble sourcing them, jalapeños or banana peppers are a good substitute. Green chiles are used in India in everything from chutneys and curries to pickles and soups. For those who prefer to ratchet up the heat during their meals, they're even consumed raw in between bites.

1 cup tightly packed fresh cilantro leaves
1 cup tightly packed fresh mint leaves
1 small ripe mango, peeled and pitted
5 Indian green chiles, jalapeños, or banana peppers, seeded
¼ cup freshly squeezed lime juice, plus more to taste
1½ teaspoons salt

COMBINE ALL THE ingredients in a food processor or blender and process or blend until smooth. Use water to achieve the desired consistency and adjust the seasoning with lime juice and salt. Cilantro-mint chutney will keep in a covered container in the refrigerator for up to 1 week, but it will lose its vibrant color as it ages.

Tamarind Chutney

MAKES: about 1½ cups
PREPARATION TIME: 30 minutes

Tamarind chutney is a required accompaniment for many of the recipes served at Sri Bangla Sahib. The lively flavor of homemade tamarind chutney is far superior to store-bought varieties. The wonders of tamarind, a fruit from a leguminous tree that thrives throughout tropical regions of Africa and Asia, cannot be overstated. Its seeds, pulp, roots, and bark are used in countless recipes to add a distinctive tanginess. It's also integral to traditional Indian medicine, where it's used for everything from fever and ulcer treatment to wound healing, lowering blood sugar, weight loss, and reversing fatty liver disease. Industrious Indian homemakers also use it to polish up their copper pans and bowls. Jaggery, an unrefined sweetener derived from cane or sometimes palm juice, is used in recipes throughout Asia and Africa. About 70 percent of the world's jaggery production comes from India, where it is considered a superfood because it's not spun during processing, which means that the nutritional molasses remains. (Dark brown sugar makes a good substitute.) Black salt is a kiln-fired, volcanic rock salt prized for its sulfides, which might smell like you're standing in the middle of Yellowstone National Park in its raw form, but once the aroma is cooked out, the salt adds distinctive pungency. It's loaded with magnesium and is available at any Indian market. Chaat masala is a popular Indian spice blend containing cumin, amchur (dried mango powder), asafoetida (see page 107), black pepper, and sanchal (black salt). It adds a pungent note to the chutney as a result of the black salt and asafoetida, two ingredients renowned for their umami properties.

1 tablespoon vegetable oil
1 teaspoon cumin seeds
1 teaspoon coriander seeds
1 teaspoon fennel seeds
1 teaspoon red pepper flakes
1 tablespoon minced fresh ginger
¼ cup golden raisins
¼ cup dried dates, coarsely chopped
1 (16-ounce) tamarind block, coarsely chopped
1 cup jaggery or dark brown sugar
1 teaspoon chaat masala
1 teaspoon ground ginger
½ teaspoon black salt
1 teaspoon salt

HEAT THE OIL in a sauté pan over medium heat. Add the cumin, coriander, fennel, and red pepper flakes and sauté until aromatic, about 2 minutes. Add the fresh ginger, raisins, dates, tamarind, and jaggery, increase the heat to medium-high, and bring to a boil. Reduce the heat to medium and cook until the sauce is thick and coats the back of a spoon, about 10 minutes. Stir with a wooden spoon throughout the cooking process to prevent scorching and to encourage the flavors to mingle. Once it is thick and aromatic, remove from the heat and stir in the chaat masala, ground ginger, and black salt. Transfer the mixture to a food processor or blender and process or blend until smooth. Season with the salt. Tamarind chutney can be stored in a covered container in the refrigerator for up to 2 weeks or in the freezer for up to 2 months. If you decide to make a larger batch of chutney, freeze individual portions in an ice cube tray, then pop out a cube and thaw before use.

Wild Mushroom Biryani

SERVES: 6

PREPARATION TIME: 1½ hours, plus 45 minutes to soak the rice

3 cups white basmati rice
1 tablespoon garlic-ginger paste
1 teaspoon cumin seeds
2 black cardamom pods
2 green cardamom pods
½ nutmeg seed
4 whole cloves
10 black peppercorns
1 cinnamon stick
2 bay leaves

1 teaspoon salt, plus more to taste
1 tablespoon vegetable oil
1 small yellow onion, thinly sliced
1 pound wild mushrooms, such as halved chanterelles, morels, creminis, or coarsely chopped portobellos
½ cup whole milk
1 tablespoon finely chopped fresh cilantro, plus more for garnish
1 tablespoon finely chopped fresh mint, plus more for garnish
4 tablespoons unsalted butter, cut into ½-inch pieces
Lemon wedges, for serving

We have the Persians to thank for introducing so many of India's most venerated recipes. This includes biryani, a universally beloved recipe deriving its name from the Persian word *birian,* which essentially means "to fry before cooking." The Mughal Empire controlled India from 1426 to 1857. During this time they introduced their recipes to the nation. Mughlai cuisine is notable for its heady blend of aromatic herbs and spices, sweetness from dried fruits, and nuanced sauces and gravies. Variations of biryani exist in nearly every state in India and often include chicken, but the biryani served at gurudwaras is a vegetarian version to comply with the Sikh code of purity. The mushrooms infuse the biryani with an unctuous earthiness.

It's important to use basmati rice for this recipe. This variety of aromatic, long-grain rice expands more than twice its length when cooked and can withstand the longer cooking time required without breaking down into a gummy mess like other rice varieties. Brown basmati rice is considered a whole grain because it includes all three layers of the kernel—germ, bran, and endosperm—which makes it a healthier alternative to the white variety.

RINSE THE RICE under cold running water for a few minutes to remove residual starch, then soak it in a bowl of lukewarm water at room temperature for 45 minutes. Drain, rinse, and drain again, then transfer to a large, heavy-bottomed pot and add 3 quarts water and the garlic-ginger paste. Cut a double layer of cheesecloth into a 6-inch square and place the cumin seeds, black and green cardamom, nutmeg, cloves,

peppercorns, cinnamon, and bay leaves in the center of it. Bundle it up and tie the top closed to make a pouch. Add the pouch to the rice pot and bring the water to a boil over high heat. Reduce the heat to medium, partially cover, and simmer for 20 minutes. The rice should be just tender but not fully cooked. Remove and discard the cheesecloth pouch, drain the rice, and season with the salt.

PREHEAT THE OVEN to 300°F.

LINE A PLATE with a double layer of paper towels. Heat the oil in a heavy-bottomed pot with a tight-fitting lid over medium-high heat. Add the onion and sauté until it is a deep golden brown, nearly crispy, and smells caramelized, 8 to 10 minutes. Transfer to the paper towels using a slotted spoon. Add half of the rice to the pot. Top it with half of the mushrooms, then add the remaining rice and, finally, the remaining mushrooms. Drizzle with the milk, then sprinkle with the fried onions, cilantro, and mint. Top with the butter, ensuring that it's evenly divided upon the surface. Cover the pot tightly and bake until the mushrooms are cooked through and the rice is a deep brown color, 35 to 45 minutes. Try not to peek too often because the steam that circulates within the pot results in perfectly cooked rice. Season with additional salt, if desired.

GARNISH THE BIRYANI with additional mint and cilantro and serve with lemon wedges. Leftover biryani can be stored in a covered container in the refrigerator, where it will continue to deepen in flavor for up to 5 days.

Cardamom-Pistachio Lassi

SERVES: 2
PREPARATION TIME: 10 minutes

2 cups plain whole-milk yogurt
1 cup milk
¾ cup brown sugar
½ teaspoon ground cardamom
2 tablespoons heavy cream
Finely chopped toasted pistachios,
    for garnish
Saffron threads, for garnish
Dried rose petals, for garnish (optional)

The Indian cows that gorge themselves on the nutrient-dense grass of northern India produce rich and flavorful milk that is transformed into lassi, a sweet or savory drink with a yogurt base that is churned until it is light and velvety. Lassi is traditionally served in a terra-cotta cup called a kulhar that keeps the lassi cool even on the most sweltering New Delhi day. Once the lassi is finished, the kulhar is usually discarded by dropping it on the ground, where it smashes into pieces. This might be disconcerting for a tourist, who admires the craftsmanship of the elegantly shaped cup. but for an Indian, it's the ultimate symbol of sustainability since the terra-cotta is made of nothing but earth and water baked beneath the Indian sun. It's an especially appropriate vessel at Gurudwara Sri Bangla Sahib, where single-use plastic has been banned since 2019.

Lassis are served often during the sweltering summer months, when they are appreciated for their cooling properties. The most significant day for lassis at the gurudwara (and for Sikhs throughout northern India) is on Chabeel Day. This annual June date of remembrance honors the martyrdom of the fifth Sikh guru, Arjan Dev Ji, executed in 1606 by the Mughal Emperor Jahangir, who feared the expansion of Sikhism throughout northern India. Arjan Dev Ji was renowned for his abiding message of eternal optimism even during times of duress. Chabeel, a Punjabi word that denotes a nonalcoholic, sweetened drink, is served on Chabeel Day at Bangla Sahib and throughout northern India as a lassi flavored with rose syrup to symbolize an escape from the burdens of life and to salute Arjan Dev Ji's courage and conviction that hope will triumph over adversity.

Lassis come in a variety of sweet and savory flavors. This recipe uses cardamom, pistachio, and saffron but the sky's the limit when it comes to lassi flavoring. Try:

- coarsely chopped walnuts or almonds
- mango, blood orange, pineapple, or watermelon juice
- rose water
- strawberries, blackberries, or peaches
- chai
- papaya and honey
- chocolate and toasted hazelnuts
- mint and cinnamon
- espresso

BLEND THE YOGURT and milk in a blender on high speed until it's smooth. Add the sugar and cardamom and continue to blend until the sugar has dissolved and a light foamy layer forms on the surface. Add the cream and stir it with a spoon until incorporated. Pour the lassis into 2 tall glasses filled with ice and garnish with pistachios, a few strands of saffron, or dried rose petals, if desired. Enjoy immediately.

Ayurvedic Cuisine

The word *Ayurveda* means "science of life." It's a set of holistic principles designed to strike a balance between the body and mind and encourage mental and physical wellness. Indians have incorporated Ayurvedic precepts into their culinary traditions for thousands of years. Devout adherents believe that the Hindu god of Ayurveda, Dhanvantari, passed his knowledge to the sages, who documented the health benefits of ingredients, cooking and farming techniques, exercise, and prayer. At gurudwaras around the world, including Sri Bangla Sahib, Ayurvedic doctors prescribe natural remedies for their patients, delving in to an ancient knowledge that seems so much more intuitive than a prescription drug.

The first principle of Ayurveda is that there are five key elements in the world—vayu (air), aakash (space), teja (fire), jala (water), and prithvi (earth)—and that each one fortifies in a different way, influenced by the three doshas or energy types. *Dosha* is a Sanskrit word that means a fault or a defect that causes problems. The three doshas that are believed to exist in the body are vata, kapha, and pitta. They are responsible for a person's physiological, emotional, and mental well-being, and each person has a unique ratio of all three doshas present in their constitution. Ensuring that a person's doshas are balanced and in harmony is said to be the key to attaining optimal health. Ayurvedic cooks also believe that there are six flavors: salty (derived from minerals, vitamins, and vegetables), sweet (derived from tubers, fruits, and whole grains), bitter (derived from leafy greens), pungent (derived from onions, ginger, and garlic), astringent (derived from beans and leafy greens), and sour (derived from citrus). Creating an alchemy of these flavors in a recipe or on the plate can assist in rebalancing a person's doshas in order to achieve a supreme level of well-being. Sikhs, like all Indians, embrace Ayurvedic principles because they know that there is immense power in food beyond its ability to bring us together to enjoy a meal. Food has the empowering ability to fortify us—mind, body, and spirit.

Brinjal Pickles

MAKES: 1 quart
PREPARATION TIME: 40 minutes

½ cup vegetable oil
2 teaspoons cumin seeds
2 teaspoons fenugreek seeds
1 teaspoon chili powder
8 garlic cloves, finely chopped
2 Indian green chiles (see page 265), finely
    chopped
12 dried curry leaves
1 tablespoon ground turmeric
1 tablespoon mustard seeds
3 medium Italian eggplants, cut into bite-
    size pieces (about 3 cups)
1 tablespoon finely chopped fresh ginger
1 cup distilled white vinegar
1 teaspoon granulated sugar
1 tablespoon salt

Achaar is the Hindi word for pickle, but make no mistake, these are not your Midwestern grandmother's sweet dill cucumber pickles. Indian pickles are often mouth-puckering affairs, typically made with a base of mustard oil in northern India and sesame oil in the south. Spices are added to achieve a fusion of pungent, tangy sweetness and fiery heat. Achaar is served as a condiment with virtually everything and, considering how flavorful it is, the tiniest drop on a spoonful of rice is enough to transform it from timid wallflower to liveliest guest at the Bollywood party. Indians pickle everything from eggplants, garlic, chiles, mangos, and carrots to hibiscus, coconut, mutton, shrimp, tomatoes, and gooseberries, and no gathering in India, whether celebratory or everyday, is complete without several jars of vibrantly colored achaar on the table. At Sri Bangla Sahib, pickles are a popular condiment, especially mango pickles, garlic pickles, red chile pickles, and eggplant pickles. They're stored in large terra-cotta vats. Each time one of the gursikhs opens up a vat, the pungent pickle aroma fills the air and tickles the nose. This recipe calls for dried curry leaves, which are stronger in flavor than the fresh variety. If you are able to source fresh curry leaves, use 14 to 16 of them instead of 12 dried leaves.

In northern India, pickled eggplant (brinjal) is a popular accompaniment for warming dals and rice dishes. The eggplants in India are much smaller than Italian or even Japanese eggplants, but because they can sometimes be tricky to source, this recipe calls for Italian eggplants.

COMBINE THE OIL, cumin, fenugreek, and chili powder in a large, heavy-bottomed pot over medium-high heat and bring the oil to a vigorous simmer. Reduce the heat to medium-low, add the garlic and green chiles, and sauté until the garlic is aromatic and the chiles have softened, about 3 minutes. Add the curry leaves, turmeric, and mustard seeds and sauté until the mustard seeds begin to pop. Add the eggplant, ginger, vinegar, ⅓ cup water, sugar, and salt and increase the heat to medium-high. Once the liquid begins to simmer, reduce the heat to medium and gently simmer until the eggplant begins to break down and the mixture has thickened, about 20 minutes. Remove from the heat and cool to room temperature. Spoon the eggplant mixture into a sterilized jar, seal, and refrigerate until chilled. The pickles will keep for up to 1 month in the refrigerator and will become slightly more pungent over time.

Dal Makhani

SERVES: 8
PREPARATION TIME: 3 hours, plus overnight to soak

1½ cups urad dal (black lentils)
1½ tablespoons garam masala
1½ teaspoons chili powder
½ cup drained canned kidney beans
3 tablespoons garlic-ginger paste
½ cup tomato paste
1 pound (4 sticks) butter, cut into
   1-inch pieces
½ teaspoon salt
Chapatis (page 275), for serving

Makhani is a Hindi word that means "with butter," and dal makhani is not playing around when it comes to the amount of butter added to bring its foundation of lentils and beans to a creamy and blissful finish. This dish has no patience for those who are shy around butter. It must be entered into with abandon or not at all. When you add butter to this beloved dish, the flavors meld in a way that is all at once a comfort and a delight. Dal makhani tastes even better the next day, after the flavors have had a little time to relax, so be sure to make enough for leftovers. At the gurudwara, dal makhani is spooned onto a tin plate and served with a stack of hot-off-the-griddle chapatis. It's a simple yet seductive combination.

RINSE THE DAL under cold running water for several minutes to remove any debris, then put them in a bowl and pour in enough water to cover by 2 inches. Soak overnight, then drain.

IN A LARGE heavy-bottomed pot, combine the dal, garam masala, chili powder, and 2 quarts water. Cook over medium-high heat until the dal is tender and has absorbed the water, about 30 minutes. Stir occasionally while the dal cooks and add more water if necessary to prevent scorching and to encourage the dal to soften and break down. Add the kidney beans and ginger-garlic paste, turn the heat down to low, and cook for 1 hour, stirring occasionally. Add more water if necessary to maintain a slightly thick consistency that does not turn pasty. Add the tomato paste and cook for 1 more hour, stirring occasionally.

ADD ABOUT ONE-THIRD of the butter cubes to the pot and stir over low heat until they have completely melted and been absorbed by the dal, about 4 minutes. Do the same with the next two batches. Season with the salt and serve hot with a side of warm chapatis to mop up all of the rich goodness. Dal makhani will keep in a covered container in the refrigerator for up to 1 week. To reheat, stir in 1 to 2 tablespoons water to reconstitute it and heat in a saucepan over medium-low heat until warmed through, adding more water if necessary to prevent scorching and to achieve your desired consistency.

Chapatis

MAKES: 10 to 12 chapatis
PREPARATION TIME: 1 hour, plus 30 minutes for the dough to rest

3 cups whole wheat flour, preferably Indian (see headnote)
1 teaspoon salt
1 tablespoon vegetable oil, plus more for greasing
¾ cup lukewarm water, plus more as needed
Butter or ghee, for serving

Chapati is a flatbread made with whole wheat flour that gives it a nubby texture and a warm brown color. Chapatis (or rotis, as they are called in the north) are enjoyed extensively all over India. Indian whole wheat flour, or atta, is typically made from durum wheat and is available at Indian markets. It's the foundation for several Indian flatbreads, including chapatis/rotis and puris, while naan is usually made with all-purpose flour. Unlike most whole wheat flour in the United States and Europe, atta is milled using a stone wheel, which results in a very fine powder. The pressure of the stone grinding also heats the atta slightly as it is ground, resulting in a slightly toasty flavor, a trademark of Indian wheat flatbreads. While American whole wheat flour will work in a pinch, for a truly authentic Indian experience, a trip to an Indian market to pick up a bag of atta is well worth the trek. All-purpose flour does not make a good substitute for either Indian or American whole wheat flour because the chapati will lose its signature nubby texture.

The best way to eat chapati is slathered in the richly flavored Indian clarified butter known as ghee if they're consumed alone or as a utensil to dip into dishes like Dal Makhani (page 272). Indians use a flat griddle called a tava, which is similar to the comal of Mexico and Central America. Tavas are made from iron, stainless steel, or aluminum. They are relatively inexpensive and available at most kitchen supply stores. If you don't have a tava or griddle, a cast-iron or stainless steel pan can be substituted. Be sure to serve chapatis hot off the griddle. No Indian worth their ghee would ever eat a lukewarm chapati.

PUT 2 CUPS flour on a clean work surface, sprinkle the salt on top, and then create a well in the center. Pour the oil and water into the well and begin to bring everything together using your hands. Once a loose dough has formed, knead it until it forms a smooth ball that bounces back just slightly when you poke your finger into it. This should take about 5 minutes. Put the dough in a bowl slicked with a thin layer of oil and cover with a damp cloth. Let sit at room temperature for 30 minutes.

PUT THE REMAINING 1 cup flour in another bowl. Form the dough into 10 to 12 balls and dip each ball into the dry flour, gently shaking it to remove any excess. Roll out each ball into a 6-inch circle about ⅛ inch thick.

HEAT A GRIDDLE over medium-high heat until it's hot. Test it by flicking a few drops of water onto it—if it sizzles, it's good to go.

IF YOU HAVE a gas stove, place the first chapati on the hot griddle and cook for 4 minutes. Remove the griddle from the flame and, using tongs, flip the chapati over and place it directly over the flame. This should cause it to puff up for a moment, which is what gives the chapati its light texture once it settles again. Cook it over the flame for another 30 seconds, then transfer to a plate. Repeat to cook the remaining chapatis.

IF YOU HAVE an electric stove, place the first chapati on the hot griddle and cook for 2 minutes. Wad up a paper towel and press gently and very carefully so you don't burn your fingers around the entire circumference of the chapati. Immediately flip it over using tongs and press it again in the same way using the paper towel. The step with the paper towel should cause the chapati to puff up on the griddle without the need for an open flame. Cook for another 2 minutes. Repeat to cook the remaining chapatis.

SPOON ABOUT 1 tablespoon butter or ghee over each chapati and serve.

Kichari

SERVES: 4
PREPARATION TIME: 1 hour

1¼ cups split yellow mung beans
¾ cup basmati rice
1½ teaspoons ground cumin
1 teaspoon ground coriander
1 teaspoon ground turmeric
1 teaspoon mustard seeds
½ teaspoon fennel seeds
½ teaspoon fenugreek seeds
Generous pinch cayenne pepper
½ cinnamon stick
6 cloves
2 garlic cloves, finely chopped
2 teaspoons finely chopped fresh ginger
2 bay leaves
Salt to taste
Finely chopped fresh cilantro, for garnish

Kichari is a fortifying, easily digestible dish made up of mung beans, rice, and a wide variety of nutritious spices. One of India's most ancient and venerated dishes, it was mentioned for the first time in the *Mahabharata*, an epic tale written in Sanskrit between the ninth and eighth centuries BCE and often referred to as the longest poem ever written. Kichari, sometimes spelled kitchari or khichdi, is also mentioned in ancient Indian texts as one of the dishes favored by Lord Krishna. Kichari holds an esteemed position in India's culinary history, but this does not negate its role in homes of everyday Indians; throughout the country, it's traditionally one of the first solid foods offered to Indian babies. Kichari is also a central dish of Ayurvedic cooking (see page 270) because of its ability to detoxify the body. It reflects the gurudwara cooks' philosophy that food should be consumed not only to quell hunger but also to contribute to optimal health. Kichari is especially comforting on a cool night when you're strapped for time but desire something nutritious and satisfying.

COMBINE THE MUNG beans and rice in a colander and rinse under cold running water until the water runs clear, 3 to 4 minutes.

IN A MEDIUM, heavy-bottomed pot, combine the cumin, coriander, turmeric, mustard seeds, fennel seeds, fenugreek, cayenne, cinnamon, and cloves and dry-roast over medium-high heat until aromatic, 3 to 4 minutes. Stir the spices occasionally with a wooden spoon to avoid scorching. Add the garlic and ginger and sauté for 2 more minutes. Add the mung beans and rice and stir until well coated with the spices. Increase the heat to high, add the bay leaves and 6 cups water, and bring to a boil over high heat. Reduce the heat to medium-high and simmer vigorously for 10 minutes. Reduce the heat to low, partially cover the pot, and cook until the rice absorbs all of the water and the mung beans are tender and begin to lose their shape, 30 to 40 minutes. The texture should be thick but still slightly runny, similar to split pea soup. Add more water, ¼ cup at a time, if the rice absorbs the water and the kichari becomes too thick before the mung beans are tender. Remove the cinnamon, cloves, and bay leaves and season with salt. Sprinkle with cilantro before serving. Kichari will keep in a covered container in the refrigerator for up to 3 days.

Gajar ka Halwa

SERVES: 4
PREPARATION TIME: 1½ hours

5 cups whole milk
2 pounds carrots, peeled and grated
4 cardamom pods
2 or 3 saffron threads
2 tablespoons granulated sugar
¼ cup ghee
½ cup paneer or Farmer's Cheese
    (page 304), preferably freshly made
1 (14-ounce) can sweetened condensed milk
2 tablespoons coarsely chopped cashews,
    toasted
2 tablespoons golden raisins, for garnish
    (optional)

This velvety carrot pudding thickened with sweetened condensed milk and paneer (an Indian cow's milk cheese similar to farmer's cheese) is subtly spiced with cardamom and garnished with pistachios. Thanks to carrots' availability during cooler months, gajar ka halwa is a staple at Sikh autumn and winter holidays, especially Diwali, the festival of lights that honors Lord Rama's return to Ayodhya with his beloved wife Sita after his defeat of Ravana, the mythical, multiheaded demon king of Hindu mythology who kidnapped Sita. Thousands of clay lamps, known as diyas, lit their pathway home. Each fall, the country is illuminated by millions of diyas in commemoration of Lord Rama's courage, the virtue of righteousness, and the triumph of love. It's a jubilant occasion, made all the more joyful when the gajar ka halwa is finally served. At Sri Bangla Sahib, gajar ka halwa is served only on Diwali, which makes this beloved dish especially coveted at the gurudwara. Traditionally made from red Punjabi carrots, any color carrot will give this dessert its vibrant color.

IN A LARGE saucepan, heat the whole milk over medium-high heat until warmed through, stirring occasionally with a wooden spoon, about 4 minutes. Do not let the milk come to a boil. Add the carrots, cardamom, saffron, and sugar and reduce the heat to medium. Cook until most of the milk has evaporated, the carrots are tender, and the pudding is beginning to thicken, stirring occasionally to prevent the carrots from burning and the milk from boiling over. This should take about 15 minutes. The color will diminish a bit as a result of the cooking process, but the carrots will maintain an impressively vivid hue.

ADD THE GHEE and paneer and cook for another 10 minutes, stirring occasionally. Add the condensed milk and reduce the heat to low. Cook for another 25 to 30 minutes, stirring often to prevent scorching, until the pudding is thick enough to hold up your spoon when it stands in the middle of it. Remove from the heat and gently stir in the cashews and raisins, if desired. Serve hot. Leftovers will keep in a covered container in the refrigerator for up to 3 days.

10

Abbaye de Saint-Benoît-du-Lac

BENEDICTINE CATHOLIC
QUEBEC, CANADA

"And all they that believed, were together, and had all things in common. And continuing daily with one accord in the temple, and breaking bread from house to house, they took their meal with gladness and simplicity of heart."

—*Acts 2:44–46*

Frère Pierre Loubier and Frère Clyde Gauthier stand together on an overlook eight stories above the surrounding pine forest in the cool Quebecois winter. A gusty wind blows their black habits behind them, like flags unfurling on their poles, but they are undeterred by the gray skies or temperatures so cold their breath appears before them in foggy bursts. They are inspecting the thickness of the ice layer on Lake Memphremagog in southeastern Quebec, where their monastery, Abbaye de Saint-Benoît-du-Lac, is located because they would like to snowshoe in the afternoon, once their work concludes for the day.

"I think it's a go," says Frère Pierre, a cheerful monk in his midthirties who wears a constant smile and often cocks his head when he walks, as if he finds the world to be a curiosity and is in perpetual awe at the wonder of it all.

"I think so too," responds Frère Clyde, who is around twenty years older than Frère Pierre yet has an energy level unrivaled by men half his age. "Let's finish up our projects and get out there. There's no time like the present."

Saint-Benoît du-Lac was established in the 1940s by the Benedictine monks of the Abbey of Saint-Wandrille in Normandy, France (see page 161), but its planning had been in the works for at least three decades prior. The monastic buildings rise like an inviting fairytale castle on the shores of the lake, home to thirty monks who adhere to the philosophy that their patron, Saint Benedict, asked of them nearly 1,500 years ago: accomplish your work with humility and obedience and devote yourself to your community and to service.

Their golden rule is on full display in every corner of the monastery, and the monks are committed to modernizing when they need to in order to remain self-sufficient and generate enough revenue to keep the monastic doors open. The monks at Saint-Benoît realize that in order to remain relevant, they must embrace the traditions from their past while at the same time discovering ways to update their production processes to make them more efficient and streamlined.

In 2017, an enormous state-of-the-art cheese-making facility opened at Saint-Benoît to pay homage to the monastery's cheesemaking history, which began in 1943. Frère Pierre dons a hairnet and blue cloth booties and asks his visitors to do the same. He proudly says, "The cheese made here is made entirely of milk from local dairy farms. Benedictines believe strongly in supporting the communities they live in and with our new production facility, it's satisfying to know that we are helping out our neighbors, too."

He offers a tour of the cavernous, industrial rooms where a dozen varieties of cheese are produced, including extra-old blue, smoked blue, Frère Jacques, Le Moine, Ermite, Mont Saint-Benoît and of course, cheese curds. Frère Pierre stops at a speed rack filled with hundreds of rounds of blue cheese, blooming healthily and filling the room, as big as it is, with a funky aroma. With gloved hands, he holds one of the rounds to his nose and inhales deeply, "Ah, glorious," he proclaims.

Saint-Benoît-du-Lac cheese is sold in the monastic gift shop and throughout Canada, but Frère Pierre also ensures that a small but steady supply finds its way to the cloistered kitchen of the monastery, too. "I can't imagine what I would do if I had to live a single day without cheese."

Deeper into the maze of corridors constituting the monastery itself, Frère Pierre steps into his weaving room, where looms are in various stages of production. "For many years, these looms were abandoned and weaving was not done at the monastery, but like any tradition that has once been lost, it can easily be revived should you

" I feel like a wizard up in my production
facility, like a magician coming up with
something new each day based upon
whatever has been harvested that week.
It's such a privilege to work here with my
brothers. It's such a joy to feel useful and
needed, to be a part of the community."

simply make an effort to do so. I love weaving. It's very meditative. I produce shawls that we sell in the gift shop."

"Do you pray while you're weaving?" I ask.

"No, I listen to hockey game," he laughs.

"Let me show you my production now," Frère Clyde says enthusiastically. We drive over to one of the monastery's outbuildings, where there are wooden crates and one-peck and half-peck baskets filled with the previous season's bounty—apples, squash, pumpkins, and cabbages—all waiting to be transformed into Frère Clyde's compotes, chutneys, jams, dressings, ketchups, and butters. "I feel like a wizard up in my production facility, like a magician coming up with something new each day based upon whatever has been harvested that week. It's such a privilege to work here with my brothers. It's such a joy to feel useful and needed, to be a part of the community."

The brothers walk side by side through the cloistered kitchen and into the massive dining hall where the monks meet for three meals a day in between vespers, work, Gregorian chanting, and Mass. Outside, the air is brisk but refreshing and an owl cries out in the distance. Frère Pierre and Frère Clyde strap on their snowshoes in preparation for their adventure.

"Are you allowed to talk during your meals or do you eat silently?"

"We eat in silence, but someone reads to us from a nook above the dining hall so there is entertainment."

"Is it the bible that they're reading?"

Frère Pierre looks up from strapping on his snowshoe and grins. "No, we read the bible all day long and sometimes we need a break. We read normal books during our meals. Right now it's *The Lord of the Rings.* My favorite."

OPPOSITE
The exterior of the abbey

RIGHT
An apple orchard during wintertime

OPPOSITE
The interior of the abbey

ABOVE
Frère Pierre Loubier weaving at
his loom

RIGHT
Apples harvested from the orchard
for cider production

Maple Bacon Beans

It might seem laborious to begin a dish 24 hours ahead of time, but this recipe requires less than 15 minutes active time. There's nothing like waking up to a home filled with the honeyed aroma of slow-cooked maple-glazed bacon and beans. Maple syrup is easily Canada's most famous food product, and even if you can't get your hands on genuine Canadian maple syrup, be sure to select a dark, high-quality syrup with no additives like sugar or corn syrup. And seek out a thick-cut smoked bacon in order to infuse the beans with smokiness. Quebecois winters are long and bitterly cold, and while the snow is initially a welcome feature on the landscape, after a few months of snowfall and icy conditions, the monks perk themselves up with this comforting dish. A few times per year, when the weather conditions begin to feel intolerable, they go all out with a full Quebecois breakfast that includes fried eggs, bacon, sausage, bread, jam, fried onions and tomatoes, sautéed mushrooms, and the star of the table, a pot of maple bacon beans.

IN THE MORNING, put the beans in a colander and rinse under cold running water to remove any excess debris. Transfer them to a large bowl and pour in enough water to cover by at least 3 inches. Soak the beans at room temperature for 12 hours.

JUST BEFORE BEDTIME, preheat the oven to 250°F. Drain the beans and transfer to a Dutch oven, along with the onion, garlic, mustard, red pepper flakes, maple syrup, bacon, and parsley. Season with salt and pepper and pour in enough water to cover by 2 inches. Cover and bake overnight. Wake up to the most comforting breakfast you've enjoyed in ages.

SERVES: 4

PREPARATION TIME: 15 minutes, plus 12 hours to soak the beans and 12 hours to cook

1 pound small navy beans
1 large white onion, coarsely chopped
2 garlic cloves, thinly sliced
1 teaspoon ground mustard
½ teaspoon red pepper flakes
⅔ cup maple syrup
6 thick-cut smoked bacon strips, cut into bite-size pieces
Leaves from 2 flat-leaf parsley sprigs, coarsely chopped
Salt and freshly ground black pepper to taste

Kale and Apple Salad
with Cider-Mustard Vinaigrette

SERVES: 4
PREPARATION TIME: 1 hour

FOR THE VINAIGRETTE:
¼ cup extra-virgin olive oil
2 tablespoons apple cider vinegar
1 tablespoon honey
1 teaspoon Dijon mustard
1 garlic clove, finely chopped
Pinch red pepper flakes
Salt and freshly ground black pepper to
   taste

FOR THE SALAD:
6 large eggs
6 cups loosely packed baby kale
2 tablespoons extra-virgin olive oil
1 teaspoon garlic powder
Salt to taste
1 small red onion, thinly sliced
2 tart apples, such as Granny Smith, cored
   and coarsely chopped
1 (6-inch) cucumber, coarsely chopped
Leaves from 3 flat-leaf parsley sprigs,
   coarsely chopped
⅔ cup coarsely chopped walnuts, toasted

FOR THE HERBED CROUTONS:
1 (8-ounce) loaf sourdough bread, torn into
   bite-size pieces
¼ cup grated Parmesan
1 tablespoon extra-virgin olive oil
1 teaspoon dried thyme
½ teaspoon garlic powder
¼ teaspoon red pepper flakes
Salt and freshly ground black pepper
   to taste

Like monks everywhere, the monks at Saint-Benoît make every effort to utilize the bounty around them and to cook seasonally using ingredients that enhance their health, both body and mind. Many of the elderly monks at Saint-Benoît have medical conditions, and there is always a focus on cooking for optimum well-being to keep the community physically healthy and mentally sharp. This recipe utilizes local resources and is packed with flavor and nutritional virtues. The many textures keep it interesting, as does the medley of vibrant colors and dance of aromas from the charred kale, caramelized onion, toasted walnuts, and herbed croutons.

FIRST, MAKE THE vinaigrette. In a medium bowl, whisk together the oil, vinegar, honey, mustard, garlic, and red pepper flakes. Season with salt and pepper and set aside until ready to serve.

TO START THE salad, put the eggs in a small saucepan and pour in enough water to cover by 3 inches. Bring to a boil over high heat, then remove from the heat, cover, and let rest for exactly 11 minutes—no more, no less. This is the magic moment for a perfect hard-boiled egg, free from the dreaded green sulfur ring. Prepare an ice bath, and when the 11 minutes are up, transfer the eggs to it using a slotted spoon, then let them chill until they are completely cool. Line a plate with paper towels and, using a slotted spoon, transfer the eggs to it to drain. Peel once they are dry and cut into ¼-inch slices. Set aside.

WHILE THE EGGS are cooling, make the croutons. Preheat the oven to 375°F.

IN A MEDIUM bowl, toss together the torn bread, Parmesan, olive oil, thyme, garlic powder, and red pepper flakes. Season with salt and pepper and transfer to a rimmed baking sheet. Bake until golden brown and toasted, 6 to 8 minutes; set aside. Leave the oven on.

TO COMPLETE THE salad, line a second baking sheet with parchment paper. In a large bowl, toss together half of the kale, 1 tablespoon olive oil, and the garlic powder. Season lightly with salt and spread out in an even layer on the prepared baking sheet. Bake until charred, about 10 minutes.

WHILE THE KALE chars, heat the remaining 1 tablespoon olive oil in a small sauté pan over medium heat. Add the onion and sauté until it is golden brown and caramelized, about 8 minutes.

IN A LARGE bowl, combine the charred and fresh kale, apples, cucumber, caramelized onion, croutons, and parsley. Add the vinaigrette and toss to coat. Transfer to serving bowls, arrange the hard-boiled egg slices on top, and garnish with the walnuts.

Hard Cider

Cider has a long and storied history in France, where it was first produced by the Celtic Gauls in the first century BCE. The Romans also enjoyed hard cider and produced it with gusto in the region from 100 to 300 CE. Charlemagne, the famed king of the Franks, Lombards, and Romans in the eighth and ninth centuries, ordered vast apple orchards to be planted throughout northern France to satisfy his hard cider cravings.

The monks who first arrived in Quebec from the Benedictine monastery of Saint-Wandrille in 1912 brought with them that region's illustrious cider-making tradition. They planted apple orchards in the mid-twentieth century that now flourish just beyond the monastic doors from which the apples for today's hard cider production are still sourced. Apples also find their way into the chutneys, jams, and dressings produced at the monastery, but Saint-Benoît's hard cider is by far their most beloved apple product.

Hard apple cider production hit its stride at Saint-Benoît in 1971 when the first bottles were sold to the public. The monastery now produces around 12,000 bottles of hard cider per year, bottling their liquid gold in emerald-green bottles that are offered as gifts to important visitors and sold in the monastic gift shop and throughout Quebec.

Like their counterparts in Normandy, the monks follow the méthode champenoise, a process invented at Hautvillers Abbey by French Benedictine monk Dom Pérignon in the seventeenth century. The method, whether used for champagne or cider, involves a first fermentation to achieve the desired alcohol level and a second fermentation to produce the trademark internal pressure. The result is a crisp and complex flavor that pairs well with all the recipes in this chapter.

Tourtière

MAKES: 1 (9-inch) pie
PREPARATION TIME: 2 hours, plus 30
minutes to cool

FOR THE CRUST:

3 cups all-purpose flour
1½ teaspoons ground mustard
1 teaspoon ground ginger
1 teaspoon kosher salt
1 teaspoon grated lemon zest
2 sticks unsalted butter, chilled and cut into
    ½-inch cubes
½ cup ice water
2 teaspoons freshly squeezed lemon juice

FOR THE FILLING:

Salt and freshly ground black pepper
    to taste
2 Idaho potatoes, peeled and cut into thirds
2 tablespoons unsalted butter
⅓ cup milk
2 tablespoons vegetable oil
1 pound ground pork
1 large yellow onion, finely chopped
2 celery ribs, thinly sliced
1 large carrot, peeled and finely chopped
5 garlic cloves, finely chopped
⅔ cup hard cider
1 teaspoon Dijon mustard
1 teaspoon celery seed
½ teaspoon ground cloves
½ teaspoon ground cinnamon
¼ teaspoon ground nutmeg
1 bay leaf

TO ASSEMBLE AND SERVE:

Butter, for greasing
All-purpose flour, for dusting
1 large egg, beaten
Rhubarb Jam (page 299) or Cranberry Sauce
    (page 236), for serving (optional)

The tourtiére, a double-crusted minced meat and vegetable pie, is beloved throughout the province of Quebec. A single slice of tourtière is a hefty meal, but don't let its substantive nature and flaky crust fool you into thinking it's a complicated affair to make. The earliest printed mention of the tourtière appeared in 1840's *La Cuisinière Canadienne*, Canada's first French cookbook, but this venerable pie recipe stretches back to the early seventeenth century, when réveillon, a festive Christmas feast fit for a king, first took hold in the province. It's a tradition the monks at Saint-Benoît embrace every holiday season. No Christmas party would be complete without a tourtière on the table. Traditional pork is sometimes substituted with wild game that the region's hunters sometimes gift to the abbey. To lighten up the pie and add a refreshing tart note, the monks typically enjoy their slice of tourtière with Father Clyde's rhubarb or blackberry jam.

FIRST, MAKE THE crust. In a large bowl, sift together the flour, mustard, ginger, and salt. Add the lemon zest and butter and, using your fingers, rub the mixture together until it resembles coarse grain. Add the ice water and lemon juice and knead until the dough just comes together. Transfer the dough to a clean work surface and knead it very gently until a ball forms. Do not overknead; at most it will require 4 to 6 rotations to bring the dough together. Divide the dough in half and shape each half into a disk about 1½ inches thick. Wrap each disk in plastic wrap and refrigerate for 1 hour.

Recipe continues

WHILE THE DOUGH chills, make the filling. Bring a large, heavy-bottomed pot of salted water to a boil. Add the potatoes and cook until fork-tender, 10 to 12 minutes. Drain and return the potatoes to the pot. Add the butter and milk and mash using a potato masher or fork; set aside.

HEAT THE OIL over medium-high heat in a large sauté pan. Add the pork, onion, celery, carrot, and garlic and sauté until the pork is golden brown, the onion is translucent, and the carrot is tender, about 20 minutes. Add the cider, mustard, celery seed, cloves, cinnamon, nutmeg, and bay leaf and simmer until the liquid has completely evaporated, about 6 minutes. Remove from the heat, remove the bay leaf, stir in the potatoes until incorporated, and season with salt and pepper. Cool to room temperature.

PREHEAT THE OVEN to 400°F. Lightly butter a 9-inch pie dish.

LIGHTLY FLOUR A clean work surface, unwrap one dough disk, and roll it into an 11-inch circle about ¼ inch thick. Carefully transfer it to the prepared pie dish, then spoon the filling in an even layer into it. Roll out the second dough disk into an 11-inch circle about ¼ inch thick and place it on top of the filling. Using a kitchen scissors, trim the dough, leaving about 1 inch excess all around. Pinch the edges together using your fingers, then roll the edge onto the rim of the pie dish and, using a fork, crimp it together. Using a pastry brush, brush the top of the pie with the beaten egg.

USING A PARING knife, cut 4 or 5 slits, about 1½ inches long, in a star shape in the center of the pie to allow steam to escape as it bakes. Place a rimmed baking sheet on the bottom rack of the oven to catch any drippings and place the pie on the center rack. Bake until the crust is a deep golden brown, about 1 hour. Allow to cool for at least 30 minutes before serving to give the filling juices time to settle. Slice and serve with rhubarb jam or cranberry sauce, if desired. Leftover tourtière will keep in a covered container in the refrigerator for up to 5 days.

Rhubarb Jam

MAKES: about 3 cups
PREPARATION TIME: 2 hours

Frère Clyde, a tall, energetic monk in his early fifties with a penchant for silly jokes and physical comedy to rival Charlie Chaplin, oversees an industrious fruit production facility housed on the second floor of one of the monastery's outbuildings. It is reached via a steep set of stairs that gives way to a large, light-filled room filled with modern canning machinery, conveyor belts, and labelers. It's a slick, contemporary operation, reflective of the way monasteries are embracing the food traditions of their past while also looking toward the future by identifying ways to make operations more efficient to drive revenue and remain a self-sustaining monastic community. Frère Clyde's production includes a dizzying amount of products, most of which are sourced throughout the grounds of the monastery. There's apple butter; apple cider vinegar; plum compote; apple chutney; peach chutney; strawberry, raspberry, and blueberry jam; fruit salad dressings; and even a blackberry compote sweetened with white chocolate. Many of his products are sweetened with the maple syrup that is produced at the monastery. This rhubarb jam is a summertime favorite. The monks often enjoy it on their morning toast but also as an accompaniment to meat dishes such as Tourtière (page 297). Frère Clyde's advice: "Be sure to enjoy it with friends."

1 lemon, cut into 4 wedges, juiced, and seeded (reserve the wedges, juice, and seeds separately)
4½ pounds rhubarb, trimmed and cut into ½-inch pieces
4½ cups granulated sugar

PREHEAT THE OVEN to 250°F.

WASH 6 PINT-SIZE canning jars and their lids with warm, soapy water and rinse well. Dry them with a kitchen towel, then put the jars and their lids in a warm oven to sterilize them and dry them completely, about 15 minutes. Carefully remove from the oven and cool to room temperature before using. (Alternatively, you could run them through a dishwasher.)

WHILE THE JARS sterilize, place a small plate in the freezer.

TIE UP THE lemon seeds in a small square of cheesecloth; they will help the jam develop pectin in order to solidify. In a large, heavy-bottomed pot, combine the rhubarb, sugar, lemon wedges, lemon juice, and lemon seed bundle. Set aside at room temperature for 1 hour.

ADD 1⅔ CUPS water to the pot and bring to a boil over high heat. Reduce the heat to medium and simmer for 15 minutes, stirring constantly and using a slotted spoon to remove any scum that accumulates on the surface. Reduce the heat to medium-low and continue to simmer, stirring frequently, for another 30 minutes. To test if the jam is set at this stage, spoon a small amount of jam onto the frozen plate. If the jam holds its shape, it's ready. If it's still jiggly, it needs more time. Continue this test every 5 minutes until it's ready.

WHILE THE JAM cooks, preheat the oven to 300°F. Fill a baking pan with 1 inch of water and heat it in the oven.

ONCE THE JAM is set, discard the lemon seed bundle and lemon wedges and carefully pour the jam into the sterilized jars. Wipe away any excess jam using a damp kitchen towel and tamp down each jar to remove air bubbles, then seal each jar with its lid and ring. Using tongs or an oven mitt, carefully transfer the jars to the water bath in the oven for 5 minutes. Carefully remove the jars using tongs or an oven mitt and let them cool to room temperature. Test to see that the lids have sealed properly by removing the rings and gently pulling up on the lid (not hard enough to pop it off but just enough to tell if there's a proper seal). If they've sealed properly, store the jam at room temperature in a cool, dry place for up to 6 months. Once a jar is open, it will keep in the refrigerator for up to 3 weeks.

Poutine

SERVES: 4
PREPARATION TIME: 30 minutes, plus
1 hour to chill the fries

FOR THE FRIES:
8 Idaho potatoes, peeled (optional) and cut
  into fries
3 tablespoons vegetable oil
Salt and freshly ground black pepper
  to taste

FOR THE GRAVY:
2 tablespoons cornstarch
3 tablespoons unsalted butter
⅓ cup all-purpose flour
4 cups chicken stock
½ teaspoon salt
¼ teaspoon freshly ground black pepper

TO SERVE:
8 ounces cheese curds (or more if you really
  like curds!)
Thinly sliced scallions

Poutine was most likely invented in the 1950s in Quebec, where it became a popular rural truck stop and snack shop offering. Its popularity soon spread throughout the province, and today gussied-up poutine recipes can be found even at the nation's most high-end dining establishments. The authentic version of poutine includes freshly cut potato fries, gravy, and cheese curds, which are chunks of fresh cheddar before it's been shaped and aged. They're beloved not only for their tanginess but also for their trademark squeak when you bite into one. The monks make their own cheese curds, but they're fairly easy to find at specialty cheese shops and some grocery stores.

Popular additions to poutine include green peas, shredded chicken, mushrooms, bacon, and, in Montreal, smoked meat. This is the unadulterated recipe, offered by Frère Pierre, who advises to make a double batch because "there can never be enough poutine." He says, "I enjoy poutine at least once a month with my friends who I grew up with. I miss them and sometimes miss the life I lived with them, so at least one Saturday a month, I invite them to the monastery and we enjoy some beer, a hockey game, and a lot of poutine. It connects me to my past and it's so tasty."

PUT THE FRIES in a large bowl, cover with a damp kitchen towel, and refrigerate for at least 1 hour or up to 3 hours. This step ensures crispier fries after they are baked.

PREHEAT THE OVEN to 400°F. Line a rimmed baking sheet with parchment paper.

PAT THE POTATOES dry and put them in a large bowl. Add the oil and toss to coat completely. Season with salt and pepper. Arrange in a single layer on the prepared baking sheet and bake until the potatoes are golden brown and crispy, 20 to 25 minutes, turning once using tongs for even browning.

WHILE THE FRIES are baking, prepare the gravy. In a small bowl, whisk together the cornstarch and 2 tablespoons water to form a slurry. Melt the butter in a large sauté pan over medium-high heat. Add the flour and cook, stirring constantly with a wooden spoon, until the flour turns a latte brown, 5 to 6 minutes. Slowly add the chicken stock in a steady stream, then add the cornstarch slurry while stirring constantly. Continue to stir until the sauce thickens into a gravy, 6 to 8 minutes. Remove from the heat and season with the salt and pepper.

TO ASSEMBLE, TRANSFER the fries to a serving platter, drizzle with the gravy, and garnish with the cheese curds, and scallions. Serve hot.

Flatbread with Pears, Blue Cheese, and Hazelnuts

MAKES: 4 flatbreads
PREPARATION TIME: 1 hour

FOR THE FLATBREAD:
1 cup whole wheat flour
⅓ cup all-purpose flour, plus more for
  dusting
1 tablespoon kosher salt
½ teaspoon baking powder
1 cup whole-milk yogurt (not Greek-style)
1 teaspoon garlic powder
1 teaspoon finely chopped fresh rosemary

FOR THE TOPPING:
1 tablespoon extra-virgin olive oil
1 medium red onion, thinly sliced
3 garlic cloves, finely chopped
1 tablespoon finely chopped fresh rosemary
1 tablespoon apple cider vinegar
1 tablespoon firmly packed dark brown
  sugar
2 Bosc pears, cored, halved, and thinly
  sliced lengthwise
Salt to taste
1½ cup crumbled blue cheese
⅔ cup coarsely chopped hazelnuts, toasted
Crunchy sea salt, such as Maldon, to taste

Frère Pierre likes to prepare flatbread on Friday evenings at the monastery when, after a week of hard work, there's a festive atmosphere in the air. He often includes a protein such as shredded smoked duck or smoked pork from a nearby smokery; feel free to add whatever you like to your flatbread for a more substantial meal. The flatbread contains yogurt, which the monks make on-site. It lends a hint of tanginess, mellowed out by the earthiness of the pears and rosemary. Blue cheese makes a frequent appearance at Saint-Benoît, fresh from Frère Pierre's fromagerie.

FOR THE FLATBREAD, sift the whole wheat flour, all-purpose flour, salt, and baking powder into a medium bowl. Stir in the yogurt, garlic powder, and rosemary. Transfer the dough to a clean work surface and knead until it's smooth, about 2 minutes. Dust the surface with a bit of flour if the dough is sticking to it. The result should be smooth and moist but not too wet and not too shaggy. Divide the dough into 4 equal pieces, shape into balls, and wrap each one with plastic wrap. Let rest at room temperature for 15 minutes.

PREHEAT THE OVEN to 500°F. Line 2 rimmed baking sheets with parchment paper.

WORKING WITH ONE at a time, roll out the dough balls on a lightly floured surface, sprinkling the dough with flour as needed to prevent sticking, until about ⅛ inch thick.

HEAT A MEDIUM cast-iron or other heavy-bottomed skillet over medium-high heat until very hot. Cook one flatbread until the underside is golden brown and puffy with a few charred spots, about 2 minutes. Turn with tongs and cook on the other side until golden brown, about 1 minute. Transfer to one of the prepared baking sheets, then repeat with the remaining 3 flatbreads, putting 2 on each sheet.

HEAT THE OIL in a large sauté pan over medium-high heat. Add the onion and sauté until translucent, 5 to 7 minutes. Add the garlic and rosemary and sauté until aromatic, about 1 minute. Add the vinegar and brown sugar and sauté until the sugar is dissolved and bubbling, about 2 minutes. Add the pears and gently stir until they just begin to soften, about 1 minute. Remove from the heat and season with salt.

SPOON THE PEAR mixture evenly over the flatbreads, then sprinkle with the blue cheese, hazelnuts, and crunchy sea salt. Bake until the cheese just begins to soften, about 5 minutes. Remove from the oven, cut into squares, and serve hot. Leftovers will keep in a covered container in the refrigerator for up to 1 day, but the crust will be a bit soggy.

Farmer's Cheese

MAKES: about 1 cup
PREPARATION TIME: 1 to 1½ hours

2 quarts whole milk
¼ cup freshly squeezed lemon juice
1 teaspoon kosher salt

The cheese production at Saint-Benoît might be a high-production, technical affair, but that doesn't mean you can't make your own cheese at home. Farmer's cheese is so easy to make and sounds so impressive to tell your guests that it's homemade that there's no reason not to give it a try. You only need a little milk, lemon juice (or distilled white vinegar for a more neutral flavor), and some patience to allow the curds to split from the whey in their own sweet lactic time. If you opt for a softer cheese, the result will be similar to ricotta, which makes an incredible lasagna stuffing, pizza spread, or dessert when drizzled with honey and sprinkled with toasted almonds or pine nuts. If you wait a little longer, the result will be a firmer, sliceable cheese that's irresistible on sandwiches.

Either way, don't discard the residual whey. It's an incredible meat tenderizer, making it an ideal marinade ingredient. It also adds brightness to grains such as barley and amaranth, when they're soaked in whey instead of water.

ATTACH A THERMOMETER to the side of a medium, heavy-bottomed saucepan. Add the milk and warm over medium heat. Stir almost constantly, but with a gentle hand, so as not to scorch the milk and prevent it from boiling. Once the temperature reaches 175°F, remove the milk from the heat and add the lemon juice, 1 tablespoon every few minutes; keep stirring gently until the separation of curds and whey begins to happen. It might not seem like anything is happening, but then it will start to separate all of a sudden—you can't miss it. At this point, pat yourself on the back and step away from the saucepan for 15 to 20 minutes to allow the full separation to work itself out on its own.

LINE A COLANDER with a triple layer of cheesecloth and pour in the cheese mixture. Let the curds drain at room temperature for at least 20 minutes or up to 1 hour, depending upon your desired consistency (see headnote). Gently stir in the salt.

IF YOU WOULD like your cheese to have a firmer consistency, gather up the edges of the cheesecloth, spin the cloth to bring it together at the top, and squeeze hard to remove the residual whey. Let it drain in the colander in the cloth and top with a plate weighed down with a few canned goods. Let the cheese firm up for a few hours, or less time depending upon your desired consistency. If you prefer softer cheese, skip the pressing step and use the drained curds as you would use ricotta. Farmer's cheese is best when freshly made, but it will keep in a covered container in the refrigerator for up to 1 week.

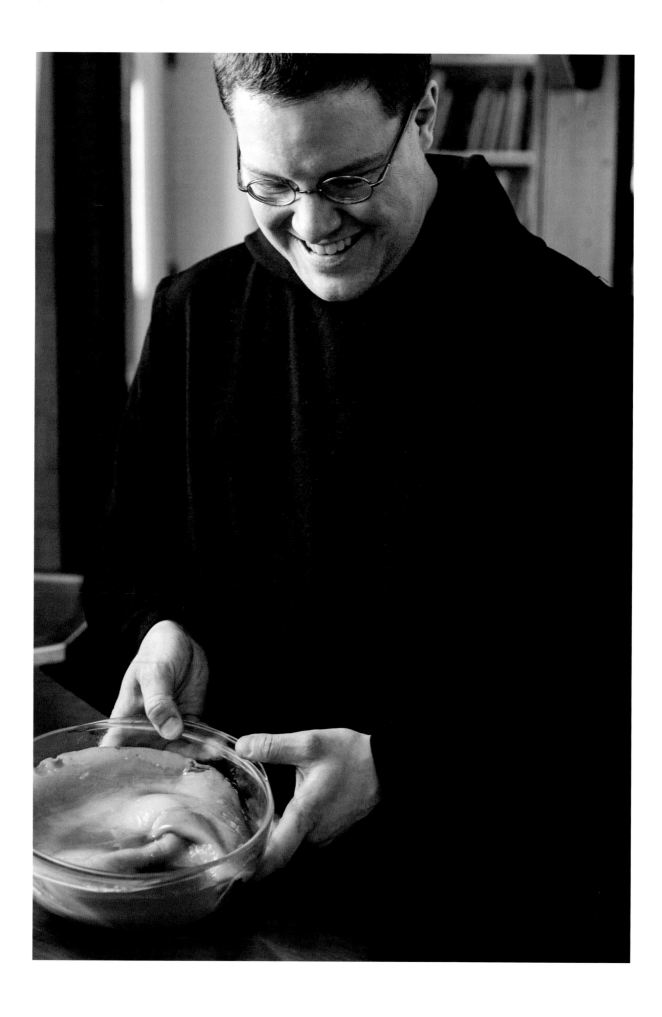

Kombucha

MAKES: about 1 quart
PREPARATION TIME: 1 to 2 weeks

1 cup granulated sugar
¼ cup distilled white vinegar
10 green or black tea bags *or* 3 tablespoons loose tea in a tea ball
2 cups prepared kombucha

Frère Pierre always has a batch of kombucha brewing in his pantry. The monks appreciate it for its probiotic attributes and its fizzy, sour-effervescent flavor. He uses whatever is in season to flavor it, including apples, blueberries, raspberries, blackberries, lemons, cranberries, honey, and maple syrup. It begins its life as a high-sugar tea fermented by a SCOBY (symbiotic culture of bacteria and yeast), and while it might not be attractive, it's a workhorse that continues to proliferate. You can make your own SCOBY or ask around your community for someone who has an extra, but they are easiest to obtain by ordering one online. It will arrive dehydrated and, while it initially looks like a piece of leather that has seen better days, once it's activated, it will deliver batch after batch of refreshing, tingly, healthful kombucha. Kombucha does contain a bit of alcohol due to the fermentation, but it's less than 1 percent.

In addition to the SCOBY, you will need a 1-gallon jar, a funnel, and several swing-top glass bottles. You'll also need to buy a bottle of kombucha at the grocery store, but after you make your first batch you can just use that each time! Once you've got the knack of it, feel free to experiment with flavors, too.

BRING 1 GALLON water to a boil in a large stockpot, then remove from the heat and stir in the sugar and vinegar until the sugar has dissolved. While the water is still hot, add the tea and allow it to steep until the liquid has cooled to room temperature, 2 to 3 hours.

REMOVE THE TEA and add the prepared kombucha. Pour the liquid into a 1-gallon jar and add the SCOBY. Be sure your hands are clean when handling the SCOBY so you don't contaminate it with unhealthy bacteria. Cover the jar with a clean, doubled-up linen or cotton napkin or kitchen towel and secure it using a rubber band.

SET THE JAR aside in a dark place at room temperature for 7 days. Your SCOBY might float to the surface or a piece could separate from it. This is a positive thing—it means the SCOBY is thriving and healthy. The SCOBY might also develop strings, sediment could develop at the bottom of the jar, or bubbles could form around the SCOBY. Don't fret. These are also positive signs that you have a healthy SCOBY fermenting your tea.

AFTER 7 DAYS, taste your kombucha. If it has that trademark kombucha tart-tangy-sweet flavor, it's ready. If not, keep fermenting for up to 4 more days, tasting each day. Once it's achieved the flavor you desire, transfer it to clean swing-top bottles with the help of a small funnel. Add any aromatics you'd like at this stage—ideas include ginger, hibiscus, citrus (lemon, lime, blood orange, or grapefruit), herbs (rosemary, basil, or mint), or whichever fruit or vegetables are in season. Gently transfer the SCOBY to a new pot of starter tea and begin the process all over again.

STORE THE BOTTLES at room temperature for 5 days to allow the kombucha to ferment. This is when it will develop its trademark effervescence. After that, store in the refrigerator for up to 2 months.

OPPOSITE
Maple syrup kombucha production

Split Pea Soup

Canadian split pea soup most likely has origins stretching back four hundred years to the first ships that arrived in Canada from France. The voyages these explorers made lasted for weeks, if not months, and ingredients with a long shelf life were required to sustain them through the journey. The tradition of split pea soup carried over into farmhouses, where bread ovens were commonplace, a slice of crusty bread a staple for a rich bowl of split pea soup. The split pea soup in Canada is typically made from split yellow peas, but feel free to substitute split green peas if they are easier to source. At Saint-Benoît, this is a popular recipe during the winter months, and it always includes a splash of apple cider vinegar made at the monastery along with the required loaf of bread, baked fresh each day in the monastic bread oven.

IN A LARGE, heavy-bottomed pot, melt the butter over medium-high heat. Add the onion, bell pepper, celery, and carrot and sauté until the onion is translucent and the carrot is tender, 8 to 10 minutes. Add the garlic and sauté until aromatic, about 1 minute. Add the split peas and stir for 2 minutes. Increase the heat to high and add the ham hock, stock, thyme, red pepper flakes, bay leaf, and 4 cups water. Bring to a boil, then partially cover the pot, reduce the heat to medium-low, and gently simmer until the liquid has reduced and the soup is quite thick, the peas are mushy, and the smoky flavor of the ham hock permeates the soup, 1 to 1½ hours.

DISCARD THE BAY LEAF and season with salt and pepper. Remove the ham hock from the soup and, once it is cool enough to handle, shred the meat and stir it back into the soup. Ladle the soup into bowls, dollop with sour cream, and garnish with blue cheese, if desired, and parsley. Serve with a large hunk of crusty bread. The soup will keep in a covered container in the refrigerator for up to 4 days or in the freezer indefinitely.

SERVES: 6
PREPARATION TIME: 2 hours 15 minutes

2 tablespoons unsalted butter
1 large yellow onion, coarsely chopped
1 yellow, orange, or red bell pepper, seeded and coarsely chopped
2 celery ribs, thinly sliced
1 large carrot, peeled and coarsely chopped
4 garlic cloves, finely chopped
2½ cups split yellow or green peas
1 (1-pound) smoked ham hock
4 cups chicken stock
2 teaspoons dried thyme
1 teaspoon red pepper flakes
1 bay leaf
Salt and freshly ground black pepper to taste

TO SERVE:
Sour cream
Crumbled blue cheese (optional)
Coarsely chopped fresh flat-leaf parsley
Crusty bread

Walnut Butter and Oatmeal Energy Bites

One of the cooks at the monastery, Frère Bernard Trembley, was concerned that the older monks were not receiving an adequate supply of nutrients. So, he invented this no-bake recipe for tasty, wholesome energy bars. While they're wonderful when chilled in the refrigerator, they're just as good when eaten frozen because the fat in the walnut butter prevents them from freezing solid and instead transforms them into a tempting ball of fudge. The walnuts are harvested on the grounds of the monastery, but feel free to swap both the walnut pieces and the butter for any nut desired, such as cashew, almond, or peanut.

IN A LARGE bowl, combine the oats, flax seeds, chia seeds, coconut, and chopped walnuts.

IN A MEDIUM bowl, combine the walnut butter, maple syrup, and vanilla and stir with a fork to incorporate. Add these ingredients to the larger bowl, along with the sea salt, and stir until a dough is formed.

USING YOUR HANDS, roll out 1-inch balls and store in a covered container in the refrigerator or freezer until chilled. They will keep in the refrigerator for up to 1 week or in the freezer for up to 1 month.

MAKES: about 24 (1-inch) balls
PREPARATION TIME: 15 minutes

1 cup steel-cut oats
⅓ cup flax seeds
1 tablespoon chia seeds
1 cup unsweetened shredded coconut
⅔ cup finely chopped walnuts
1 cup unsalted walnut butter
2 tablespoons maple syrup or honey
1 teaspoon vanilla extract
½ teaspoon crunchy sea salt, such as Maldon

11

Zawiya

SUFISM
FES, MOROCCO

"Seek the wisdom that will untie your knot. Seek the path
that demands your whole being."

—*Jalal ad-Din Muhammad Rumi*

Jonathan Friedmann, aka Hassan, is a long way from his original home in Montreal, where he used to run a restaurant called Rumi with his brother Todd Friedmann, aka Husayn. Hassan, a red-bearded man with an easy smile, grew up Jewish but was attracted to the teachings of Sufism and today considers himself both a Sufi and a Jew. He now lives in Fes, Morocco, where he is a pir, a spiritual leader of Sufism. He runs a khanqah, a spiritual center where Sufis from throughout the world are hosted and gather together for meals, spiritual sessions, prayer, meditation, and the performance of religious poetry and music. Sufis believe they are on a spiritual journey during their lifetimes toward the Divine. It is a mystic philosophy that embraces the spiritual discipline and dimension of the Islamic faith and is practiced by both Sunnis and Shiites.

Like all Muslims, Sufis consider the Prophet Muhammad as the ideal being who embodies God's morality. Through singing, whirling dancing, rhythmic chanting called dhikr, and a dense body of poetry and literature written as a guide for Sufi mystics who are on their spiritual journey, Sufis strive to experience love, to understand the mystery of the human soul, and to experience encounters with the Divine. Sufism is an apolitical and peaceful form of Islam. Hassan explains, "Sufis encourage interreligious dialogue in order to strive toward intercultural harmony in pluralist societies. Sufism is flexible and tolerant and disciples embrace nonviolence as a way to achieve peace within society and within ourselves."

In Morocco, Sufi brotherhoods known as tarikas are gatherings intended to allow the participants to experience mystical ecstasy by reaching a trance state through singing, playing musical instruments, and chanting. Sufis form different congregations and orders that come together around a grand master, and together they strive for perfection of worship in order to understand and internalize the science of purifying the heart. Sufis are ascetics who strictly observe Islamic law, but while all Muslims strive to become close to God in the afterlife, Sufis believe there is the potential to reach the deepest parts of the soul and to travel through the "narrow gate" here on Earth.

Hassan, a Grand Sufi Master, is hosting two Sufi travelers from London who are of Pakistani descent. They wear long white robes and have an easy rapport with Hassan, who welcomes them as old friends, because he says, "Sufism is not only the way to nourish ourselves, but it's also about nourishing those who are in need of physical and spiritual sustenance. These meetings are no accident. We might be strangers, but no one can find themselves together unless our souls are already entwined. We might have different origin stories, be from different countries, but we are all sharing the same thing and, inshallah, God willing, our deepest hope is that God will bless you, make you happy and feel more inspired. We will gather in prayer and song and chanting tonight and then we will eat together because food brightens our light and enables us to walk out into the world feeling better and more interconnected than we did when we first sat down together."

After dhikr concludes, Hassan and his visitors gather in a nook lined with plum velvet pillows where they enjoy a sumptuous spread of vegetarian dishes such as an artichoke and pea tajine, eggplant slow-simmered with tomatoes, and meskouta, a cheerful spiced orange cake. Steaming cups of cardamom-laced qahwa, Arabic coffee, fuels a boisterous conversation.

To Hassan, "Food is an essential tool. Sufism was spread through feeding people. It's an essential part of the way. Of course there is a physical

OPPOSITE
Hassan Friedman enjoying a glass of mint tea

" We will gather in prayer and song and chanting tonight and then we will eat together because food brightens our light and enables us to walk out into the world feeling better and more interconnected than we did when we first sat down together."

eloquence around food, it sustains us physically, but when food is prepared with a good intention and a spiritual light around it, when it is cooked in a state of love, it also has the ability to raise people up. When a chef is cooking in a spiritual state filled with brightness and optimism, free from anger and other negative emotions, it's reflected in the food, you can taste joy."

When the great Sufi master Rumi, who lived during the thirteenth century, would send his students studying Sufism to other parts of the world, the first thing he wanted them to do was to learn how to cook with the local people. Hassan continues, "He believed that through food you can shine a light. Feeding people will lighten the spirit. If food is prepared with love, if there is a blessing in what people are eating, it will awaken the hearts of those who are enjoying it."

After a long dinner filled with laughter and a few vulnerable tears, Hassan and his guests retire for the evening in Hassan's spacious riad. The next morning, after prayers, the men gather once more in their cozy nook for breakfast, which is served beneath a beam of sun streaming in from the ceiling window above. It illuminates the preserved lemons and tiny bowls of flaming red harissa.

"Rumi said there are three questions for every human being in order for life to have meaning,

regardless of where they are or what they believe in. First, where are we coming from? Second, why are we here? And third and most importantly, where are we going and what will we leave behind in this life? If you are asking yourself those questions, the inspiration will come to you, it will open you up for deeper understanding," Hassan says before taking a long, contemplative sip of qahwa.

After a long pause, filled with the clattering of silverware on plates, the din of the copper tea kettle hitting a cobalt blue glass, and the aroma of mint from the tea and garlic from the hummus, Hassan says, "I try to take it a step further each day. I ask myself, how do these beliefs translate into my daily life? When you're asking yourself those questions, when you're trying to translate them into ideas and exchanges, you will be able to go deeper into your soul, to awaken your heart, to illuminate your mind." He dips a torn pita wedge into his harira, takes a bite, and savors it with his eyes closed before concluding. "The best place to begin is in your kitchen. If your kitchen is filled with light, if you prepare your food in the spirit of generosity, you have tapped into the truest source of happiness, dove deep into the deepest well of love."

OPPOSITE
Enjoying a meal in the Zawiya

RIGHT
Artichokes

RIGHT
The marketplace near the Zawiya

BELOW
Wood-fired pita bread production

OPPOSITE
Sufis enjoying a meal together

Harissa

MAKES: about ½ cup
PREPARATION TIME: 1 hour

2 ounces dried chiles de arbol, stemmed
    and seeded
2 ounces dried guajillo chiles, stemmed and
    seeded
½ teaspoon cumin seeds
½ teaspoon caraway seeds
½ teaspoon coriander seeds
½ teaspoon smoked paprika
½ teaspoon salt
3 large garlic cloves, coarsely chopped
1½ tablespoons freshly squeezed
    lemon juice
2 teaspoons extra-virgin olive oil

The hot chile paste known as harissa is said to have origi-nated in Tunisia, but the condiment is popular throughout North Africa and beyond. Every family has its own recipe that is passed down from one generation to the next. It's ubiquitous on virtually every table regardless of the time of day or the meal being served. On special occasions, such as the eight-day-long Sufi Cultural Festival that takes place in Fes every April to honor the spirituality and music of Sufism, harissa containing rose petals is enjoyed. The name *harissa* is derived from the Arabic verb *harasa*, which means "to pound" or "to crush," since this is what needs to be done to release the ingredients' full flavor poten-tial. In the souks of Fes, vendors prepare their customers' harissa to order to ensure its freshness and flavor. A mortar and pestle is traditionally used to accomplish this, but a blender or spice grinder will also work.

Use red chiles such as chiles de árbol or guajillo chiles if you want more heat; for a more moderate heat level, use cascabel or seco del norte chiles. For a smoky flavor, use ancho or chipotle chiles. To avoid skin irritation, wear kitchen gloves when seeding the chiles.

PUT THE CHILES in a small bowl. Pour in enough boiling water to cover and let them soak and soften for 45 minutes.

WHILE THE CHILES are soaking, heat a small sauté pan over medium heat. Add the cumin seeds and swirl the pan over the heat to prevent the seeds from burning and to toast them evenly. Once they are aromatic, about 1 minute, transfer them to a dry plate. Repeat with the caraway and coriander seeds. Do not toast the spices together because each spice will have its own toasting time; even though it might vary by only 30 to 60 seconds, this difference can mean a burnt seed versus a perfectly toasted one. Once all of the spices are toasted, transfer them to a mini food processor or spice grinder and pulverize them into a fine powder (or use a mortar and pestle). Stir in the smoked paprika and salt.

ONCE THE CHILE peppers are tender, drain them and, using a paper towel or a kitchen towel, gently squeeze out any excess water. Add the chiles and garlic to the spice blend. Blend (or crush) until a chunky paste has formed. Transfer to a bowl and stir in the lemon juice and oil. Transfer to a glass jar, cover, and store in the refrigerator for up to 1 month. If you plan to store harissa for longer than a few days, top it off with a bit of olive oil to prevent it from drying out too much.

Preserved Lemons

MAKES: 1 pint
PREPARATION TIME: 1 month

6 Meyer lemons, plus more lemon juice
    as needed
¼ cup kosher salt
Boiled water, cooled to room temperature,
    as needed

Preserved lemons are a mainstay in the souks of Fes and are omnipresent on tables throughout North Africa, the Middle East, and in a few regions of India. Some claim that their plucky flavor can be replicated with fresh lemon juice, but there really is no substitute for the insistently bright and astringent taste of this pickled condiment. They make a frequent appearance in tajines and are served alongside lamb, beef, seafood, and chicken dishes. For Sufis who adhere to a vegetarian diet, preserved lemons are a guaranteed way to add flavor and nuance to even the most humble pulse or vegetable dish. It might seem counterintuitive to eat a lemon rind, but after it's soft and pickled, there's really nothing better to perk up the palate.

In Morocco, preserved lemons are traditionally made using boussera or doqq lemons, but Meyer lemons work well, too. Much like Smen (page 323), this recipe takes about a month to complete due to the long preservation time required, but also like smen, the distinctive flavor this recipe imparts makes it well worth the wait. The one thing to be sure of during the preservation process is that the lemons remain fully submerged in the salty lemon juice. A filmy grayish residue forms on the interior of the jar as the lemons ferment, but while it's not aesthetically pleasing, it's harmless.

TRIM THE NUBS off both ends of the lemons using a paring knife. Cut each lemon into quarters lengthwise but do not cut all the way through the bottom; the lemons should remain intact throughout the preservation process.

SPRINKLE THE BOTTOM of a sterilized jar with 1 teaspoon salt. Gently open up each lemon and salt its flesh with 1 teaspoon salt. After you salt each lemon, add it to the jar, cut-side down. Press each lemon addition hard to release as much juice as possible and to compress it in the jar. Add an additional 1 teaspoon salt to the top of each lemon. Once all of the lemons have been salted and added to the jar, half of the jar should be filled with lemon juice. If it's not, add enough additional freshly squeezed lemon juice to get to the halfway mark. Fill the rest of the jar with cooled boiled water until it reaches the top. Seal the jar with a sterilized lid and store it at room temperature for 3 days, shaking it vigorously at least once a day to redistribute the liquid. After 3 days have passed, refrigerate the jar for 3½ weeks. Use the lemons for cooking or serve them as a condiment, but either way, be sure to rinse them under cold running water to remove excess salt before using. Typically, only the rind is used and the pulp is cut away and discarded, but feel free to also use the pulp. Preserved lemons will keep in a covered container in the refrigerator for at least 3 months, if not longer.

Smen

MAKES: about 12 ounces
PREPARATION TIME: 1 hour, plus 1 month or more for fermentation

1 pound (4 sticks) unsalted butter
1 tablespoon kosher salt

Smen, a fermented clarified butter, imparts a unique funkiness to countless Moroccan dishes, including tajines and Harira (page 324). It's also enjoyed simply slathered on bread. Smen adds so much character to a dish that the long fermentation time required is totally worth it. Herbs and other aromatics are sometimes added to smen before it's tucked away in a dark, cool corner for its long period of rest, but the unadulterated version gives it more flexibility. The longer smen ferments, the stronger and, some would argue, the more appealing its pungent, earthy flavor.

You will need an abundance of cheesecloth to make smen because the clarification process requires several fresh layers. You will also need a clean ceramic crock with a tight-fitting lid that is similar to what sauerkraut is fermented in (see page 50). Feel free to double the recipe if you're ready to fully commit to smen, and use a high-quality butter.

MELT THE BUTTER over low heat in a heavy-bottomed saucepan. Simmer gently until the fat solids fall to the bottom of the pan and have turned a light amber color, 35 to 40 minutes. Keep a close eye on the butter during this phase to ensure it does not begin to simmer too vigorously, which could scorch the fat and impart an undesirable flavor to the smen. If it does begin to boil, turn the heat down to the lowest possible setting.

PLACE A DOUBLE layer of cheesecloth over a large bowl and slowly pour the clarified butter into the bowl. Try not to include the milk solids, since smen is solely composed of clarified butter. Discard the cheesecloth and any solids that have collected in it. Set a second double layer of cheesecloth over a second large bowl and pour the liquid into it. Repeat this process until all traces of the milk solids are gone and nothing but clear, golden clarified butter remains.

STIR THE SALT into the clarified butter using a clean stainless steel spoon, then pour the butter into a ceramic crock, cover, and store in a cool, dark place for at least 1 month. Although it might be tempting, do not check on it during the preservation stage because it will disturb the fermentation environment. Once you're ready to begin using your smen, store it in a covered container in the refrigerator. It will have a tawny yellow color and a similar texture to the Indian clarified butter ghee. It should keep indefinitely.

Harira

SERVES: 6

PREPARATION TIME: 1½ hours, plus overnight for soaking

1 cup dried yellow lentils
1 cup dried green lentils
1 cup dried chickpeas
1 tablespoon extra-virgin olive oil
1 large yellow onion, coarsely chopped
2 celery ribs, thinly sliced
1 large carrot, unpeeled and thinly sliced
4 garlic cloves, minced
2 teaspoons ground turmeric
1½ teaspoons ground ginger
1 teaspoon ground cumin

1 teaspoon ground cardamom
½ teaspoon cayenne pepper
1 (14-ounce) can crushed tomatoes
1 tablespoon tomato paste
2 tablespoons freshly squeezed lemon juice, plus lemon wedges for serving
8 cups vegetable stock
Leaves from 4 cilantro sprigs, finely chopped, plus more, to serve
Leaves from 5 flat-leaf parsley sprigs, finely chopped, plus more to serve
1 teaspoon salt
½ teaspoon freshly ground black pepper
Pita or crusty bread, for serving

Harira is enjoyed by Sufis throughout the year, but it is especially welcome as a comforting way to break fast during Ramadan, which takes place during the ninth month in the Islamic calendar. Ramadan embodies the Sufi's commitment to deep reflection, mindfulness, prayer, fasting, and fortifying and connecting with the community. Lamb is sometimes added to this warming chickpea, lentil, and tomato soup, but it's satisfying and substantial enough in its vegetarian incarnation. For a more substantial version of harira, add pasta, rice, or your favorite grain; simply time the addition of the grain to ensure that it is tender and has had time to absorb the soup's flavor. If you like, top each bowl with a spoonful of Smen (page 323) and Harissa (page 321) before serving. For more flavorful spices, toast them before using (see page 321).

RINSE THE LENTILS and chickpeas in a colander under cold running water for a few minutes to remove any residue. Transfer them to a large bowl and pour in enough cold water to cover by 2 inches. Soak the legumes overnight to soften. Drain in a colander and give them another rinse under cold running water to remove any scum that might have formed during the soaking process.

HEAT THE OIL in a Dutch oven over medium-high heat. Add the onion, celery, and carrot and sauté until the onion is translucent and the carrot is tender, about 7 minutes. Add the garlic, turmeric, ginger, cumin, cardamom, cinnamon, and cayenne and sauté until the garlic and spices are aromatic, about 3 minutes. Add the lentils and chickpeas, crushed tomatoes, tomato paste, and lemon juice and reduce the heat to medium-low. Simmer for 5 minutes. Increase the heat to medium-high, add the stock, cilantro, and parsley, and bring to a vigorous simmer. Reduce the heat to low, cover, and gently simmer until the lentils and chickpeas are tender, 45 to 50 minutes, stirring occasionally with a wooden spoon to prevent it from scorching the bottom of the pan. Keep an eye on the liquid during this step to ensure that the soup does not thicken too much.

THE HARIRA SHOULD be thick but still be easy to pour. Add water, a few tablespoons at a time, if it begins to thicken too much. Season with the salt and pepper. Ladle the harira into warmed bowls, garnish with cilantro and parsley, and serve with lemon wedges and pita or crusty bread. Harira can be stored in a covered container in the refrigerator for up to 5 days, its flavors intensifying as they mingle with one another. Or freeze it for up to 1 month. Stir in a few tablespoons of water to loosen it up while reheating.

Tajine

A tajine is a ceramic or clay vessel that is used to slow-cook recipes throughout North Africa. It's also the name of whatever is cooked inside of it. The tajine consists of a shallow, circular base topped with a cone-shaped lid that enables air to circulate throughout the tajine while it cooks. This creates an immersion environment that infuses the dish with refined flavor while tenderizing the meat and mellowing and mingling the spices and whatever else is added to it, such as nuts, dried fruit, and vegetables.

The origin of the tajine is up for debate, with some historians claiming it emerged during the late eighteenth century when the fifth Abbasid Caliph Harun al-Rashid controlled the Islamic Empire. Others believe the tajine goes back much farther. They claim the ancient Romans brought their ceramic cooking traditions with them to North Africa and introduced it to the region. This would align with the appearance of tajine-style recipes, which were first documented in the ninth-century Arabic language story collection *One Thousand and One Nights*. Either way, one thing is certain: the tajine is the centerpiece of many Moroccan kitchens, appreciated not only for the flavors it coaxes from whatever is cooked in it but also for the way its rustic beauty enhances the dining table.

If your new tajine is unglazed, the first thing it requires is a proper seasoning in order to remove any residual clay particles that could impart food with an off-taste. Preheat the oven to 250°F. Soak the tajine for 30 minutes in warm, soapy water, then rinse it well under warm running water and dry it completely. Rub the base and lid all over with olive oil. Place both components in the oven, keeping them apart to enable uniform heating and leave it for 2 hours. Carefully remove the tajine from the oven and let it cool to room temperature. Your tajine is ready for its first tajine.

For Hassan Friedmann, the tajine also reflects the fundamental tenets of Sufism: "The Sufi believes in the interconnectedness of all beings. That's why food is very important. Food is what brings all people together. We can all gather around the tajine, we can all gather around the table, regardless of what religion we are, we can meet here at the table, share a meal from a communal vessel. When you break bread with someone else, there is a contract signed by both of you that you are in fellowship with one another, that you are connected in this life.

The creator is guiding each person to their destination, and it is an honor to invite someone to share a meal at your table; their presence is a divine blessing. Communicate in the spirit of goodness when enjoying the tajine; try to be the most generous one. Don't bring your judgment to the table, bring only your heart and your hope that while this person is in your presence, they will find peace and joy in their heart. A slow-cooked meal like a tajine will bring delight through its flavors, which will encourage a feeling of togetherness. Be generous. Embody love. This is the spirit of Sufism."

Eggplant and Chickpea Tajine

SERVES: 4
PREPARATION TIME: 1 hour

2 tablespoons extra-virgin olive oil
1 large yellow onion, coarsely chopped
1 red bell pepper, seeded and coarsely
   chopped
1 tablespoon minced fresh ginger
3 large garlic cloves, minced
1 teaspoon ground cumin
½ teaspoon ground cinnamon
¼ teaspoon cayenne pepper
1 tablespoon honey
5 Roma tomatoes, coarsely chopped
3 cups vegetable stock
3 (6-ounce) eggplants, peeled and cut into
   ½-inch cubes

1 (14-ounce) can chickpeas, drained and
   rinsed
Leaves from 2 flat-leaf parsley sprigs, finely
   chopped, plus more for garnish
1 tablespoon freshly squeezed lemon juice
1 tablespoon chickpea flour or all-purpose
   flour
2 teaspoons dried mint
½ teaspoon salt
½ teaspoon freshly ground black pepper

TO SERVE:
Couscous (page 331)
Sour cream or Greek-style yogurt
Pita bread, cut into triangles and warmed
Lemon wedges

The Arabic word *fuqara* denotes people who must depend upon others in the community for the things they need to survive, such as food and shelter. This can include those who are elderly, those who were born into poverty or who find themselves in poverty due to unforeseen circumstances, and those who are ill or disabled. Sufis believe that preparing and sharing a meal with someone who needs it without asking for anything in return fortifies the bridge between the giver and the receiver—and also between the giver and their deepest spiritual self. It is the ultimate source of sustenance and nourishment. This fortifying stew is one of the dishes that the Sufi community in Fes offers to those who are in need. It is served alongside couscous in the spirit of generosity and togetherness. Select small eggplants because they have a milder flavor and are less likely to be bitter. Chickpea flour imparts a subtly nutty flavor; it can be found in Middle Eastern or Indian markets.

HEAT THE OIL in a large sauté pan over medium heat. Add the onion, bell pepper, and ginger and sauté until the onion is translucent, about 7 minutes. Add the garlic and sauté until the garlic is aromatic, about 2 minutes. Add the cumin, cinnamon, and cayenne and sauté until the spices are aromatic, about 2 minutes. Add the honey and sauté until the honey is incorporated. Add the tomatoes and vegetable stock and bring to a simmer. Cook for 5 minutes, stirring occasionally, then add the eggplants, chickpeas, parsley, and lemon juice. Return to a simmer, reduce the heat to low, partially cover, and gently simmer until the eggplants are tender and have begun to break down, about 20 minutes, stirring occasionally to prevent scorching.

IN A SMALL bowl, whisk together the chickpea flour and 1 tablespoon water to form a slurry. Add the slurry to the pan, along with the mint. Simmer until the liquid begins to thicken, about 3 minutes. Season with the salt and pepper. Transfer to a serving bowl, garnish with parsley and serve with couscous, sour cream, pita, and lemon wedges. Leftovers can be stored in a covered container in the refrigerator for up to 3 days.

Chicken, Green Olive, and Almond Tajine

SERVES: 6

PREPARATION TIME: 2 hours, plus 3 hours to marinate the chicken

1 teaspoon ground turmeric
1 teaspoon ground ginger
1 teaspoon freshly ground black pepper
½ teaspoon ground cumin
½ teaspoon paprika
¼ teaspoon cayenne pepper
1 cinnamon stick
2 whole cloves

4 large cloves garlic, minced
3 tablespoons extra-virgin olive oil
1 tablespoon freshly squeezed lemon juice
1 (3-pound chicken), cut into 8 pieces
1 teaspoon salt, plus more to season the chicken
2 medium onions, coarsely chopped
1 tablespoon honey
2 tablespoons whole raw almonds, skin-on
¼ cup cracked green olives, pitted and halved

Leaves from 2 cilantro sprigs, finely chopped, plus more for garnish
Leaves from 2 flat-leaf parsley sprigs, finely chopped, plus more for garnish
1 cup chicken stock

TO SERVE:
Couscous (page 331)
Lemon wedges
Pita bread
A fresh salad of lettuce, onions, and tomatoes, dressed simply with vinegar and olive oil (optional)

Hassan Friedmann adheres primarily to a vegetarian diet in accordance with the Sufi belief in the interconnectedness of all living beings, but on rare occasions he does enjoy a meat dish. This tajine is one of his favorites. He explains, "One of my friends who is a chef told me that when someone dies and finds themselves in paradise, they will eat a lot at first because the consumption of food is one of the things we most enjoy on Earth and God wants to build a bridge from Earth to paradise to make the journey a peaceful and joyful one. So in the beginning of our time in the afterlife, everything we knew on Earth will be there. Feasts will include meat dishes at first because it will make us feel comfortable since it's what we know here on Earth. Eventually our spirit will no longer require food, will no longer crave the taste of meat, but in the beginning, the three components that comprise who we are on this planet need to remain connected: the mind, the body and the soul."

This recipe uses a tajine (see page 327), but if you don't have one, you can use a roasting pan with a tight-fitting lid or a Dutch oven. Hassan sometimes adds dates to his recipe. If using, coarsely chop 6 to 8 of them and add them at the beginning of the roasting process. A few tablespoons of pine nuts sprinkled over the tajine just before serving also makes a nice addition. If you would like to coax more flavor from your spices, toast them before marinating the chicken (see page 321). Although you might be compelled to peek at your chicken during the cooking, try to avoid the temptation. The secret to a perfect tajine is to retain all of the flavors inside the vessel until it's ready for the final reveal at the table.

IN A SMALL bowl, stir together the turmeric, ginger, black pepper, cumin, paprika, cayenne, cinnamon stick, cloves, garlic, 2 tablespoons olive oil, and lemon juice until well mixed.

SEASON THE CHICKEN pieces with salt. Wearing kitchen gloves to avoid staining your hands with turmeric, rub the chicken pieces all over with the spice mix. Put the chicken in a container, cover, and refrigerate for 3 hours.

PREHEAT THE OVEN to 325°F.

HEAT THE REMAINING 1 tablespoon oil in a nonstick skillet over medium heat. Add the onions and honey and sauté until the onions are just tender, about 3 minutes. Remove from the heat and stir in the almonds, olives, cilantro, parsley, and stock. Season with the salt. Pour half of the sauce into the base of a tajine or Dutch oven, arrange the chicken pieces in an even layer on top, and pour in the remaining sauce. Cover and roast until the chicken is cooked through and most of the liquid has evaporated, about 1½ hours. Serve family style, revealing the tajine at the table for dramatic effect. Garnish with cilantro and parsley and serve with couscous, lemon wedges, and pita bread alongside. Serve with a fresh salad, if desired. Store leftovers in a covered container in the refrigerator for up to 3 days or in the freezer for up to 1 month.

Artichoke and Pea Tajine

SERVES: 4
PREPARATION TIME: 1½ hours

3 tablespoons freshly squeezed lemon juice
16 (4-ounce) artichokes
1 tablespoon extra-virgin olive oil
2 small yellow onions, coarsely chopped
5 Roma tomatoes, coarsely chopped
2 large garlic cloves, minced

Leaves from 2 flat-leaf parsley sprigs, finely
    chopped, plus more for garnish
1 cup vegetable stock
½ teaspoon ground cumin
½ teaspoon ground turmeric
½ teaspoon ground ginger
½ teaspoon salt
½ teaspoon freshly ground black pepper
¼ teaspoon cayenne pepper
1 cup fresh or frozen green peas
Toasted pine nuts, for garnish

TO SERVE:
Couscous (page 331)
Sour cream
Lemon wedges
Pita bread

Artichokes flourish in Morocco, nourished by hot, dry days beneath the Mediterranean sun. The market tables at the souks overflow with them in late summer through early winter. This recipe includes instructions for separating the hearts from raw artichokes, but if you have trouble sourcing fresh artichokes, substitute frozen hearts. The dish is prepared in a traditional Moroccan tajine (see page 326), but if you don't have one, use a roasting pan with a tight-fitting lid or a Dutch oven instead. For additional flavor, toast the spices before using (see page 327). Fresh green peas are preferable, but frozen will work if they're out of season. Lamb is often served with artichokes in Morocco, but this is a vegetarian alternative. If you would like to add lamb, sear 2-inch seasoned cubes over high heat, browning on all sides, then add to the tajine along with the artichokes. For a distinctive Moroccan flavor, add Preserved Lemons (page 322) and Smen (page 323) with the peas for the final stage of cooking.

PREHEAT THE OVEN to 350°F.

FILL A LARGE bowl with water and add 2 tablespoons lemon juice. Rinse the artichokes under cold running water to remove any debris, then pat them dry with a kitchen towel. Peel off any loose leaves from the stem of each artichoke. Snip the tips off of the leaves with a sharp kitchen knife. Do this carefully because the thorns can be quite sharp. (This recipe doesn't use the leaves, but they can be steamed and served with aioli for a delightful snack.) Using a serrated knife, cut about 1½ inches off the top of each artichoke, then remove about 1 inch from the stem. Peel the fibrous layer from the remaining stem using a vegetable peeler. Peel and completely remove the leaves from the artichoke until the tender pale ivory heart is revealed, after 5 to 6 leaf layers. Cut the crown from the heart at the line between the white heart and the pale green crown using a serrated knife. Using a melon baller or a teaspoon, scoop out the fuzzy choke of the heart. Put the hearts in the acidulated water to prevent them from browning.

HEAT THE OIL in a large sauté pan over medium heat. Add the onions and sauté until just tender, about 3 minutes. Remove from the heat and stir in the tomatoes, garlic, parsley, remaining 1 tablespoon lemon juice, stock, cumin, turmeric, ginger, salt, black pepper, and cayenne. Pour half of the sauce into the base of a tajine or Dutch oven. Drain the artichoke hearts and pat dry with a kitchen towel. Arrange the hearts in an even layer on top of the sauce in the tajine, then pour in the remaining sauce. Cover and roast until the artichoke hearts are tender and about two-thirds of the liquid has evaporated, about 55 minutes. Sprinkle the peas on top of the tajine, cover again, and roast for an additional 5 minutes. Garnish with parsley and toasted pine nuts. Serve with couscous, sour cream, lemon wedges, and pita bread. The tajine will keep in a covered container in the refrigerator for up to 3 days.

Couscous

MAKES: about 4 cups
PREPARATION TIME: 15 minutes

1 cup water or chicken or vegetable stock
1½ tablespoons extra-virgin olive oil
1 cup couscous
½ teaspoon salt

"You know what love is? It is all kindness,
generosity."

—Rumi

Couscous is omnipresent at mealtime throughout Morocco. This diminutive, pellet-shaped pasta dish is made from durum wheat semolina that is usually served with a flavorful stew called a tajine (see page 327) spooned over it. Hassan Friedmann says, "Couscous is not only delicious and nourishing, but its creation mirrors the Sufi's commitment to the fortification of community. Today, much of the couscous that is used throughout the world is made in a factory, but traditionally the preparation of couscous was something that was enjoyed by a multigenerational group of women who would prepare large amounts of couscous to be used throughout the week. The custom was about the couscous itself but also, and perhaps most importantly, it was about the connections that would be made between the women. It was about the wisdom that would be passed from one generation to the next, about the laughter, sometimes about the tears, about the stories that would be shared. Fortunately, there are still villages throughout Morocco that prepare couscous in the traditional way. It's such a beautiful way to strengthen the community, the fellowship between people."

Couscous is made from scratch by hand-rolling it. Hand-rolled couscous is fluffier than factory-made couscous. This is accomplished by first sprinkling semolina with just enough water to dampen it. The semolina is then rolled into tiny pellets that are dusted with more semolina flour to prevent them from sticking together. The pellets are transferred to large sieves that are vigorously shaken to remove the smaller pellets. The pellets that remain in the sieve are rolled once more into larger pellets, which are dusted once more with flour and run through a sieve. The process continues until all of the semolina has been formed into couscous. Fresh couscous is steamed for several minutes before being served.

BRING THE WATER and olive oil to a boil in a small saucepan. Add the couscous and salt, remove from the heat, stir once or twice to evenly moisten the couscous, and cover for 10 minutes. Fluff with a fork and serve.

Meskouta

MAKES: 1 cake; serves about 12
PREPARATION TIME: 1 hour

Nonstick cooking spray
2 cups all-purpose flour, plus more for
  dusting
1½ cups granulated sugar
4 large eggs
½ cup vegetable oil
2 teaspoons baking powder
½ teaspoon salt
1 teaspoon almond extract
¼ teaspoon ground cinnamon (optional)
2 teaspoons freshly grated orange zest
½ cup freshly squeezed orange juice
Confectioners' sugar, for dusting (optional)

This cheerful spiced orange cake is a lovely way to add a flourish to the end of a meal or to serve for an afternoon tea or with a robust cup of qahwa (see page 333). It's also enjoyed by the Sufi community during iftar, the meal enjoyed at sunset to conclude the fasting period during Ramadan. It's very moist and quite simple to prepare, and while this recipe is flavored with orange, other Moroccan variations include swapping out the orange for lemon and adding full-fat yogurt for a bit of a tangy finish. For more texture, add finely chopped almonds or walnuts during the step when the orange juice is added.

PREHEAT THE OVEN to 350°F.

SPRAY A BUNDT pan with nonstick cooking spray and lightly dust with flour. Turn it over and lightly tap the pan to shake out excess flour.

IN A LARGE bowl, whisk together the sugar and eggs (or use an electric mixer) until well mixed. Add the oil and blend until incorporated.

IN A SEPARATE bowl, sift together the flour, baking powder, and salt until incorporated. Fold in the wet mixture until thoroughly blended together. Add the almond extract, cinnamon (if using), orange zest, and juice and blend until incorporated. Pour into the prepared pan and bake until set and golden brown and a toothpick inserted into the center comes out clean, about 40 minutes.

LET THE MESKOUTA cool in the pan for 10 minutes. Carefully invert the pan over a wire rack, gently catching the meskouta to turn it upright on the rack, and let it cool to room temperature. Dust with confectioners' sugar just before serving, if you like. Leftovers will keep in a covered container at room temperature for up to 3 days.

Qahwa

SERVES: 2
PREPARATION TIME: 20 minutes

2 tablespoons freshly ground Arabica coffee
6 green cardamom pods, lightly crushed
3 whole cloves
6 saffron threads (optional)
1 teaspoon rose water (optional)

"Strange how the bitterness of coffee makes
  life sweet."

—Rumi

Arabic coffee, or qahwa, is traditionally made from coffee beans that have been roasted and then ground and boiled instead of filtered. It's usually served black without sugar and is quite robust and bitter. Aromatics such as cloves, rose water, saffron, and cardamom pods are often added, infusing it with a distinctive flavor that distinguishes it from its non-Arabic counterparts. Dates or dried apricots are often served with qahwa, along with almonds or walnuts.

The word *qahwa* initially was translated as "wine," which was used by Sufi mystics to focus concentration and for "spiritual intoxication" that was achieved by chanting the name of God during its consumption. Now the word means "coffee," and it became popular in Mecca as early as the fifteenth century and soon spread throughout the Middle East and Northern Africa. Along with mosques, the coffee shops that emerged around the consumption of qahwa were the epicenters of the community. They were institutions where Sufis gathered to play backgammon and chess, debate politics, discuss books and new ideas, and listen to poetry readings and live music. Qahwah and the coffee house tradition are as critical today as they were centuries ago. They foster the sense of belonging that is so critical to the endurance of the Sufi community.

IN A SMALL saucepan, bring 2½ cups water to a boil over high heat. Add the coffee, reduce the heat to low, partially cover, and simmer gently for 10 minutes. Add the cardamom and cloves and simmer for 5 more minutes. Remove from the heat, cover, and let the ground coffee settle to the bottom of the pan for 2 minutes. Do not stir or disturb the pan during this step because this is when the coffee is essentially being "filtered." Add the optional saffron and rose water after the coffee has rested, then strain it through a fine-mesh strainer into 2 mugs. Serve hot.

OPPOSITE
Fes

LEFT
Couscous production

BELOW
Sifting flour for couscous production

In Gratitude

The scope of this book is so vast that it would be impossible to thank all of the people who provided assistance, advice, connections, wisdom, and inspiration throughout the course of researching and writing it, but I will do my best. I am grateful to the spiritual leaders I met along the way who generously opened the doors to their monasteries, mosques, synagogues, and temples to share their wisdom, along with their favorite recipes. There would be no book without these incandescent lights.

There would be no book without the editor Maria Guarnaschelli, who acquired *Elysian Kitchens* just a few months before she passed away. Our conversations about the book were too few but I will never forget her solid advice not only about writing but about living too. I am grateful for my wise and patient editor, Melanie Tortoroli, and for my agent, Jonah Straus.

I would also like to thank Henrik, Niklas and Willow Anderson, Ultimate Wingman Mark Anderson, Theresa Anderson, Peter Bragelman, Patrice Eddy, Todd Eddy, Janine Ersfeld, Grace Ersfeld-O'Brien, Colleen Foster, Claire Handleman, Melissa Henderson, Mary-Frances Heck, Jeanna Christiansen, Michael Kress, Rita LaChapelle, Courtney Knapp, Jad Kossaify, Erin Jurek, Ana Sortun, Anne and Ron McBride, Anna Painter, Kamal Mouzawak, Shinobu Namae, the Rosene family, Brian Shekleton, Brother Aelred Senna, Cameron Stauch, Tara Stevens, Jean Stearns, Pat Bragelman Sweeney, Marty Travis, and Claudia Woloshin.

My mother died unexpectedly at nearly the exact moment I discovered I would be writing this book and my grandmother died after a long illness just as I finished up testing the last few recipes. I am grateful to my mom, Mary Eddy, for loving me so deeply and instilling in me a sense of curiosity and a lifelong love of fearless travel. I am grateful to my grandmother, Evelyn Bragelman, for providing me with a lifetime of affection, love, and home-cooked meals.

A Note on Photography: I am grateful for Kristin Teig, who photographed the breathtaking images in Elysian Kitchens and traveled with me to every location. Our behind-the-scenes escapades as we traversed the world could fill the pages of a second book, but that's a story for another day.

Index

B

Butternut Squash Potage with
  Toasted Walnuts and Crème
  Fraîche, *180*, 181

C

Cabbage. *See also* sauerkraut
  colcannon, 154, *155*
  creamy red cabbage slaw, 147
  Eihei-ji cabbage rolls, *210*, 211
  tangtse with roasted peanuts
      and cilantro-orange vinai-
      grette, 104
Calvados
  about, 171, 182
  in egg salad with potatoes and
      apples, 171
  in Saint-Wandrille tonic, 186
Camembert on Toast with Pears,
      Hazelnuts, and Salted Cara-
      mel, 175, *177*
Canada, 280–309
Caramel
  Camembert on toast with pears,
      hazelnuts, and salted cara-
      mel, 175, *177*
  salted caramel fudge brownies,
      158, *159*
Caramel Sauce, 175
Cardamom
  cardamom-pistachio lassi, 268,
      269
  in gajar ka halwa, *278*, 279
  in qahwa, 334
Carrots
  gajar ka halwa, *278*, 279
  in matzo ball soup, *56*, 57
  namasu, 198
  in nimono, 212, *213*
  in tzimmes, 53
Cashews
  in gajar ka halwa, *278*, 279
Chabeel Day, 268
Challah, about, 58
Chapatis, 275, *275*
  about, 255
Charred Artichokes with
      Caper-Bacon Dipping Sauce,
      75, *75*
Cheddar cheese
  cheesy biscuits, 237
  Irish cheddar and bacon soda
      bread, 157

Cheese
  about, 175
  in beef and mushroom wild rice
      casserole, *226*, 227
  buckwheat crêpes with spin-
      ach, fried eggs, bacon, and
      Neufchâtel, *172*, 173
  Camembert on toast with pears,
      hazelnuts, and salted cara-
      mel, 175, *177*
  cheesy biscuits, 237
  farmer's cheese, 304
  flatbread with pears, blue
      cheese, and hazelnuts, *302*,
      303
  Irish cheddar and bacon soda
      bread, 157
  manchego, ham, mushroom,
      and quince turnovers, 79
  parsnip and cream cheese piero-
      gies with maple sour cream,
      232, 233
  in poutine, 300, *301*
  in roasted heirloom tomato tart,
      246, *247*
  seaweed, beet, and barley salad
      with whipped goat cheese
      dressing and hazelnuts, 145
  smoked salmon, asparagus, and
      goat cheese frittata, 138, *139*
  spinach, ricotta, and barley
      momos with ginseng-yogurt
      dipping sauce, 105
  in stuffed cannelloni with bécha-
      mel sauce, 84
Cheese curds
  in poutine, 300, *301*
Cheesemaking, 285
Chicken
  chicken, green olive, and almond
      tajine, *328*, 329
  chicken Normandy, *184*, 185
  chicken with Catalan picada,
      87, *87*
  stock, 57
  in thukpa, *110*, 111
  in tingmo with shapta, 112, *113*
Chicken Normandy, *184*
Chicken schmaltz
  matzo ball soup, *56*, 57
Chicken with Catalan Picada, *87*
Chickpeas

about, 262
cooking, 21
eggplant and chickpea tajine,
    326
in harira, 324, *325*
hummus, 21
kala chana, 262, *263*
kibbeh bil sanieh, *26*, 27
kibbeh laktin, 24, *25*
Chile peppers
  about, 107, 265, 321
  in beet raita, *260*, 261
  in brinjal pickles, 271
  in cilantro-mint chutney, 265
  in harissa, 321, *325*
  in honey-glazed turkey tinga,
      242, *243*
  in kala chana, 262, *263*
  in sepen, 107
  in son labu, 116, *117*
  in tangtse with roasted peanuts
      and cilantro-orange vinai-
      grette, 104
  in thukpa, *110*, 111
  in tingmo with shapta, 112, *113*
  in tomatillo salsa, 245
Chipotles
  honey-glazed turkey tinga, 242,
      243
Chocolate
  in chicken with Catalan picada,
      87, *87*
  production in Ireland, 133, 158
  salted caramel fudge brownies,
      158, *159*
Chodak (in India), 99
Cholent, 46, *47*
Chopin, Philippe, 165, 167
Chorizo
  shrimp and chorizo paella, 70, 71
Chutneys, 264
Cider
  about, 171, 295
  kale and apple salad with cider-
      mustard vinaigrette, 292, *293*
Cider-Mustard Vinaigrette, 292
Cilantro
  cilantro-mint chutney, 265
  cilantro-orange vinaigrette, 104
  in rishta, 30
  in tomatillo salsa, 245
Cistercian Catholics, 60–91

PHOTO BY KRISTIN TEIG

JODY EDDY'S writing has been published in *Food & Wine*, *Travel + Leisure,* the *Wall Street Journal*, and elsewhere. She was the editor of *Art Culinaire*, has cooked at The Fat Duck and Jean-Georges, and lives in northern Spain.